T0110690

The Journeyman,
the Greybeard Sea and Kairos

Ron Dick

Trafford
PUBLISHING™

Order this book online at www.trafford.com
or email orders@trafford.com

Most Trafford titles are also available at major online book retailers.

© Copyright 2009 Ron Dick.

All rights reserved. No part of this publication may be reproduced, stored in a retrieval system, or
transmitted, in any form or by any means, electronic, mechanical, photocopying, recording, or
otherwise, without the written prior permission of the author.

Note for Librarians: A cataloguing record for this book is available from Library
and Archives Canada at www.collectionscanada.ca/amicus/index-e.html

Printed in Victoria, BC, Canada.

ISBN: 978-1-4251-8698-2 (sc)

*We at Trafford believe that it is the responsibility of us all, as both individuals
and corporations, to make choices that are environmentally and socially sound.
You, in turn, are supporting this responsible conduct each time you purchase a
Trafford book, or make use of our publishing services. To find out how you are
helping, please visit www.trafford.com/responsiblepublishing.html*

*Our mission is to efficiently provide the world's finest, most comprehensive
book publishing service, enabling every author to experience success.
To find out how to publish your book, your way, and have it available
worldwide, visit us online at www.trafford.com*

Trafford rev. 5/22/2009

www.trafford.com

North America & international
toll-free: 1 888 232 4444 (USA & Canada)
phone: 250 383 6864 ♦ fax: 250 383 6804
email: info@trafford.com

The United Kingdom & Europe
phone: +44 (0)1865 487 395 ♦ local rate: 0845 230 9601
facsimile: +44 (0)1865 481 507 ♦ email: info.uk@trafford.com

10 9 8 7 6 5 4 3 2 1

When I was young I had no sense I thought I'd go to sea,
I jumped aboard a Chinese ship and a China man
came to me, he buttered me all over and put me
on to boil and when the pot was boiling he
sang a Chinese song.

I bid adieu to Glasgow and the sooted slums of my childhood, and with my apprentice papers in my pocket boarded the S.S Georgic and took residence in Hamilton, Canada, then the pristine shores of Kootenay B.C. drew me and there I again settled and built my vessel, and the world lay awaiting me. Unknowingly, yet those poverty years in a Clyde side shipyard prepared me for what would come, for with rusted scissors and cardboard I cut insoles for my ever leaking shoes, and found out what a last was for, and with needle in hand discovered the art of darning my socks, and that needle, that had fitted so well in my young and artless fingers in fifty years would once again reside, in my now blue veined and gnarled hands.

The fifty years flew and eventually I was in Papua New Guinea, cleared by a corrupt customs agent and about to be thrown in jail, I quickly left, only to sail into the challenging monsoons as they vied for the supremacy of the sea, while I journeyed through them to the birth place of typhoons, which left me with tattered sails, a voyage of a 125 days, a lack of food that took fifty pounds of my body weight, and an experience I shall never regret, for with it came a light that brightened all and on tip toes entered that, that slowly manifested itself—Epiphany.

Table of content

Prologue

Aye, unknowingly, it had prepared me; those childhood years of mine when wide eyed and innocent I found myself learning to tear yesterdays newspaper into the appropriate strips and hang them on the rusty nail that lay hammered in the cracked plastered wall of the W.C.. Then all too soon, with canvas bag tightly grasped, I scrabbled over the soot ingrained blackened gravel bedded railway tracks, scrounging for spilled coal that came free for the picking. Then it was rusted scissors and cardboard and I cutting insoles for my ever leaking shoes, and finding out what a last was for. And before long, the shipyard, where I learnt to dry my snot saturated handkerchief over a charcoal fire and with needle in hand discovered the art of darning my socks, and that needle that had fitted so well in my young and artless fingers, in fifty years would once again reside, in my now blue veined and gnarled hands. Aye, the years flew—for all too quickly it was my fiftieth birthday and I lay in the port berth of my newly built and soon to be launched sea-going vessel. In my head a mixture of half dreamt adventures and alcohol fumes when through that welcome mist I heard the words of one of the party guests idly saying, 'he's living his dream.' My pondering ceased. Living my dream? I wasn't living a dream, I was living my life. In my innocent naiveté I had touched an energy source ... and I wasn't about to let it go.

Fourteen years after that wondrous launching I was still hitched to that wandering and spirited star and found myself somewhere between Australia and Micronesia. Aye, I had been long prepared, when I, ignorant and all too soon to be old, willingly set my wayward foot upon that wild and demanding sea. Ever searching, but what for. Alas, I never knew until after I had found it, out there, on the free and wild and incomparable Greybeard Sea.

Now aged, I write of that noble and outrageous time, attempting to make sense out of that soul defining period of my life. My need, to make it concise, intelligible, so I may understand all that had taken place during that most particular time, and most important, that I may never forget, for I wish desperately that all that had taken place be close to my hand so that I could reach out and touch it, and more importantly, have it touch me. For it was that last year, while my vessel with tattered sails voyaged through a raging sea, and I, lying in my chilled and sodden berth, my free and unshackled mind unwillingly traveled to the long locked shuttered doors of my past; arousing long forgotten memories and nurturing awakening thoughts that had long awaited such a—fertile— and cleansing time.

Aye, and now my fervent desire is to recapture that time, to have the wisdom to sift the grain from the chaff, the gold from the dross, brew it, distill it, and see it glitter, then bottle it and let it slumber. Then when the confusion of this world, the pettiness of people, the clamour of the city drowns me once again, reawakening those best forgotten memories of when all I wanted was to sever my ties to the emptiness that surrounded me, to tuck my body into some dark and silent cave and like an old bear, hibernate, but I didn't, nor was it likely that I would. So today, let a glass of that sea stormed vintage dwell comfortably in my hand, let me sip its nectar and like a confirmed drunk let the liquor bathe my mind with that fantastic and soul searching time that I spent, on that wild, energizing, and demanding ocean.

When I was young, nature in recognition of my youth supplied me with an over abundance of energy that of'times had overwhelmed me, and there I was in those later years simply expecting it to continue, what a fool. As for the future, it may have been veiled but those days were manifest and what was required from me was, commonsense, a quality not easily available in today's modern society. I was alone, except for my iron steed, my constant seaworthy companion that joyously carried me over those white capped spume laden wave tops. This vessel that I had shaped and formed, that I had welded and nurtured. Then at last the time is nigh and you take this being to sea and it becomes alive and is part of you, and carries you, when you once carried it. The masculine equivalent of giving birth. All quite silly isn't it, aye the giving birth, but also out on that outrageous sea. Yes, silly and magnificent where all there is, is the sea and sky and a howling gale—to mortify.

No I wasn't ignorant then, when the raging sea curdled the salted blood within me and the wind screeching in the rigging filled my ears with voices drawn from hell. Oh yes, there were times that I thought that I was in hell for I was in a realm that few alone had trespassed, yes, I think that is the right word. A path that only a fool would travel and how pleased I am that I have done so. For there I was, voyaging, there where the challenging monsoons sleep, or vie for the supremacy of the sea, while I traveled through them to the birth place of the typhoons. Yes, I knew the terrors that await fools such as I, ah, but should you survive the prize is indescribable. Though at that time I certainly never knew, for it's only afterwards when you are back, warm and well fed, dry, secure and thankful, you realize that you're not at all the man you once were. Yes it's true, for you will never again be the same.

Chapter 1

1943. Aye, I remember that day quite well, twelve years old I was, a naive and innocent child of the slums of Glasgow. It would be another two years before I'd be working full time, meanwhile, summer at last was here and there was I striding along in the chilled and pouring rain. I was going to where I lived, which is not the same as going home, and grasped in my arms was a wet canvas bag of coal that had been carelessly spilled on the railway tracks, and that I had painstakingly, rescued. I had just entered the close of our tenement building when I had a warm welcome from the neat old lady who lived on the ground floor. "Look you wee scunner, I've just whitewashed the flair and noo you've got your black dirty footsteps all over it."

She was dressed in a rather soiled floral apron that would have done well with whitewashing, one of the pockets in the apron held several packages of cigarettes, from the other pocket protruded the local racing form. Tears dribbled down her gray wrinkled cheeks, whether they were caused by my coal dust foot steps on her clean whitewashed flair, or whether they were caused by her undeniable gift of being able to smoke cigarettes and talk at the same time, well, I never did have the courage to ask. The hot ash fell from the tip of her cigarette and dropped into the enormous valley that lay in the opening in the front of her apron. She screamed what I thought was. "Duck in dell" and again something like "—it". Feeling that our friendly conversation was over, I nodded and smiling shyly at her, mounted the stairs that would take me to the top storey.

Oor hoose [no, they are no misspelling's] was on the left side of the landing on the third floor, the communal lavy was thoughtfully placed between oor hoose and the hoose on the other side. I entered oor front door, why it was called the front door I haven't the slightest idea, we only had one door. Fresh newspapers were spread on the floor. 'Ha' I thought, the floor has just been washed and we're expecting company, then just a minute I thought, I can't remember ever seeing the floor without newspapers. I bent down and picked up the corner of the newspapers, and of course I should have known what would be underneath, newspapers.

Just then a voice shouted. "Hey, is that you Ronnie." "Aye," I answered. My stepmother was standing by the coal and gas cook stove stirring a pot of potatoes and vegetables that she had been boiling for two days. In our neighbourhood it was a common belief that the good Lord had made a mistake by making cabbages green, carrots red, and potatoes a dirty white. It was thought that they were only fit for human consumption when they were boiled in huge amounts of water for an extended period of time, and until all had attained the same sickly gray colour. And, as at that time pre-pasted wallpaper had not yet been invented, and as wallpaper was required to hide the cracks in the ancient plaster, the left overs came in handy. My stepmother turned, took one look at me and burst into song; we were quite a musical family.

"Aye you must have been an ugly little bastard,
you must have been an ugly little child,
I can see the midwifes eyes,
as she cried out 'what a prize,'
and gave your mum a bigger pillow.
Aye you must have been an ugly little bastard,
'cause baby look at you now.

Chapter 2

1947. Yes, I wonder where it starts, those ideas that slyly inveigle themselves into our heads when we are young and ever after shape our lives and rule our destiny? Yes, slyly, without one ever being aware of what was happening, for inside my empty naive and yet willing brain one took root. I can assure you that those thoughts grew of their own accord for I was not lead in any fashion to that path that I so willingly followed. In truth I was not lead or guided in any manner, though since then I've often thought that a word placed in my young, waiting and willing ear would not have gone amiss, but that was then. From that you will gather that I make no excuses for who I am or whether you care for me or not. I, alone, am responsible for being the man that I am.

I was sixteen and had started my apprenticeship in Fairfields Ship Building and Engineering, I had a large box of flexible couplings to drill then afterwards drive locking pins into. I screwed up on two of them. I kicked them aside so that they sat close to where I had left my white bread lunch, and hoped the gaffer wouldn't notice. When the whistle blew for lunch, I, with them and my lunch in hand walked down to the very end of the docks. I remember noticing how quiet it was for the rivetters too had stopped and were sitting around their charcoal braziers with their blackened tea cans in their hands. Tea cans? Old bean cans with a hole punched in either side and a piece of wire wrapped around for a handle. A spoonful of tea leaves, a spoonful of sugar, and a match stick floating on top. Don't ask. I sat on a huge cast iron bollard and dug my teeth into my thick white bread sandwich, and acting casually, kicked my screw ups into the ebbing and oil streaked River Clyde.

It was the first time that I had taken notice of the river, how the free and variegated tide swirled around the tar coated pilings, how it swept all in its path out to the open and cleansing sea. Aye, my eyes too it carried—past ships being built and under repair, past giant cranes leaning hungrily over them like great praying mantises, to where I imagined myself— like Huckleberry Finn on an imaginary raft, drifting on that enduring tidal stream that lead to the great adventure and trials that the open sea would hold for me. Then the whistle blew.

1958. My two children and I were standing on the shore of Lake Ontario. My bride and I had emigrated six years earlier, as soon as my apprenticeship was finished. We had left Glasgow and voyaged from one smoky industrial city to another, Hamilton, Ontario, Canada. It was winter, a cold northern wind sweeping across the water sent white caps dancing on the chilled lake. I had got into the habit on those wintry Sunday afternoons to go down to the deserted shore and arrived with my toddlers in one hand, and in the other, a collection of thin sticks, pieces of cardboard and capped plastic Javex jugs. There was one great advantage in this selection of bric-a-brac that I carried, for except for the ballast that I had attached to the belly of the jugs, it was all incredibly light and could be carried in one hand, in any case my toddlers were in full use of the other. My simple preparations of the Javex jugs had been done at home, poking holes in the jug for a mast and scotch taping on the ballast. I had a thin stick for the mast and a selection of precut cardboard for the sail. I was assembling an inexpensive and rather tubby sailboat. Nearby my toddlers were having a great time sliding down the snow drifts that nature had conveniently placed there, while my attention was devoted elsewhere. My Javex jug fully rigged, her sail close hauled, I placed her rotund little belly into the ice cold water and—off she went.

The fool that I am. I was totally fascinated by those silly bloody jugs and their cardboard sails. I experimented with masts and shapes of sails but it didn't really matter, far more importantly was how the daft wee buggers just took off. It had naught at all to do with yacht design or rig, though I felt it had to do with balance. Something that we all need. I never did install a rudder of any kind, they never needed one, and in any case I never wanted them to come back. None ever capsized, at least if they did I never saw it. I put them in that white capped ice chilled lake and the silly little buggers leaned to windward and took off, as if they couldn't get away from me fast enough. Had they sank? Got dismasted? Perhaps they ran ashore 100 yards down the beach, but when I saw them last they were heading out, and did all of this matter? Well, to me it did, and perhaps to the residents that lived along the shore who would have wondered where in the hell were all those Javex jugs coming from.

The last of the Javex jugs were gone, but still I sat smiling as I gave thought to long ago advice. Do not sit on anything cold or damp, though in the winter in Glasgow, and most of the summer, everything was cold or damp. For you'll get chilblains, perhaps they meant hemorrhoids but no one knew how to spell hemorrhoids. In any case you got them from a chill. I ignored that advice as I have with so many others, and remained sitting on that frozen snow bank. My body heat causing puddles to form around my dreaming body, my chilblains unquestionably wallowing in this unexpected pleasure. But my eyes were on those little tubby farcical forms as they faced what must have seemed to them, momentous seas, yet, still they struggled through, up and down, battling their way through that bloody cold white water. Would I, could I, have that courage?

Chapter 3

1979. The construction took place facing the unblemished waters of Kootenay lake B.C., in the pleasant little town of Kaslo. I was building in steel, a forty two foot schooner that would take me off on those grand adventures and trials that I somehow needed. A sailing vessel that would shelter me from storms and let me tread the paths of the trade winds. As for making decisions, I've never had a problem with that, providing they didn't have to be quick. So there was I, with plans in hand teaching myself how to lay out the hull lines. Teaching myself to weld, to gaze on the white hot tip of the welding rod and see how the steel melted and wedded the vessel's plates together. Drilling holes and running a tap through them and they were threaded. Install the engine blocks, lower the engine, line it up and start it, and it runs. Erect the masts hoist the sails untie the lines, it sails. Teaching myself to read the heavens, how to hold a sextant and let the Sun kiss the horizon, to plot my position, and surprisingly, you realize you can navigate. All magic. Aye, to be out there on that bloody great ocean, with a plastic sextant, a book of tables and a fifteen dollar Taiwanese watch, and to actually know where you are. Aye, that was the greatest Magic of all.

But first there was the beginning. I ordered the steel, and from the local Sears Catalogue office, a welding machine. The steel arrived and I dragged the inch and a quarter plate that was the bottom of the keel and started welding. I wasn't a welder by trade, I was an engine fitter, and some times a plate fitter, but I could tell a poor weld from a bad. Learning can be such a gratifying experience. She grew, like a child in its mother's womb and with affection I tended to this creature's growth. We owned the Laundromat and my good wife would say, 'there's a washing machine that's not spinning.' I groaned, dragged myself down there and fixed it, and was back again caring for this creatures birth, silly I may have been and yet I felt that nothing was more important than this fulfillment of what I had long awaited. The construction went well, of course there were those odd little problems that one has to deal with.

Such as. The sandblasting of the built in water tanks. Plan 'A' was really quite simple. My good wife Marlene was in charge of the sandblaster, and I, dressed in coveralls now spotted with little brown welding spatter burns, work boots, welding gloves and with the sandblasting helmet tucked under my arm, stood ready. My instructions to her were remarkably simple, when I was in position over the tanks I would take the gun and bang it against the side of the hull, she would then start the sandblaster, when I wanted her to stop I would again bang the gun against the hull, nothing could be—simpler. I am a great believer in simplicity. I climbed down the companionway stairs, turned and accidentally banged the gun against the hull. The sandblasting engine roared, the hose began to vibrate, then the bloody sand came blasting out. Frantically I grabbed the helmet and jammed it on my head, only to realize that I had put the bastard on backwards. I couldn't see a damn thing. I dropped the gun, found the ladder and clambered back on deck, and looking in the wrong direction, struggled to get the bloody helmet off, and with the other hand waved furiously. Marlene eventually gathered that something wasn't quite right, and shut off the engine.

Plan 'B'. My instructions this time, two bangs on the hull to start and two bangs to shut it off. Simple. I descended the stairs and seated myself by the port water tank, overhead my work lamp, dangling happily on a bent welding rod lit my work area. I placed my helmet on, took the gun and banged it twice against the side of the hull. The sandblasting engine roared, the hose vibrated, and as sand came blasting out of the nozzle of the gun my overhead lamp fell, and there in mid air, directly in front of my astonished eyes the sand hit the bulb and blew the bloody thing to smithereens. The fact that I closed my eyes made little difference. I was in total darkness.

I banged, and banged, paused, and banged and banged—dropped the gun and holding my breath clambered back up the companion way stairs. This time looking in the right direction, I took my helmet off and gave Marlene a friendly wave. She shut the engine off then sweetly asked, "Why didn't you bang the hull?" "Bang the hull, I damn near punched a hole through it." "Over the noise of the engine I never heard anything." I desperately tried to smile. We started again.

Plan 'C'. This time Marlene would wear a watch, and after I had banged the hull twice she would run the blaster for three minutes then she would shut it off. All started well, until I realized that all too soon that I couldn't see, I was surrounded by a dust storm visibility zero. I left the gun thrashing in the water tank and once more went up on deck, took the helmet off and smiled weakly at Marlene. She shut the engine off and came over to hear about Plan 'D,' which was a minute and a half, then there was Plan 'E,' which was forty-five seconds. Finished at last, thank God.

Such as. Spraying the interior with an insulating foam. I had bought this foam kit in Vancouver, it consisted of two steel compressed cylinders that held the foam, and came with a hose, a gun shaped applier and several replacement tips for the gun. The salesman told me how easy it was to apply. I believed him. He did however warn me that every time I stopped using the gun I had to replace the tip, and as usual if you warn me about anything, I'm liable to go overboard—wrong word. His advice on the tips was well meant, however, he never mentioned that initially the pressure coming out of the gun was like Vesuvius erupting, and then all too quickly became a dribble, similar to what I receive when I am strangling the last drop out of my all too soon empty bottle of Scotch. Nor, did he say that it will stick to everything, including electrical tools, welding cables, coveralls, eye glasses, and hair. I had hair at that time. So there I was, already becoming suspicious of this weapon that I was fearful to shut off.

Ever concerned and having no intention of driving back to Vancouver for more tips, I persevered. Until I realized that I saw—vaguely. I stumbled through, spraying all that lay before my mist laden eyes. Until I tripped over my welding cables, the gun went flying and left me lying on my arse hoping desperately, that my bottle of Scotch wasn't empty. With my hand searching for a handhold I struggled to stand, eventually I realized that if I took my glasses off I could see. I did. I closed my eyes. I was in a cave where the stalactites and stalagmites were attempting to hold hands. At my feet lay the spray gun, dribbling toothpaste. Beam me up Scotty.

I peeled off my coveralls then realized that I had lost my glasses, and after tripping over numerous unidentifiable pieces of equipment found them, and the ladder. I clambered up. It was late fall and snowflakes swirled in the chilled air that now seemed so incredibly fresh and clean. Aye, Scotty had indeed beamed me up. Directly to my right was our dwelling, the 1896 Building, the front door that boasts ball bearing hinges opened easily to my touch. I climbed the stairs to our upper suite but before I ever reached the door, which doesn't have ball bearings, my ears were pleasured by the musical ability of my good and charming wife who was letting her fingers tips dance over the keys of her piano. Mozart. I strode in, past the six inch spikes though bent, held the upper door hinges, past the fire engine red kitchen shelves that the previous owner must have bought—at a fire sale, totally ignored the ceiling tastelessly covered with wood shakes, paused briefly to drool over something in a pot simmering on the stove, then innocently realized, that not only did I not smell anything but that I could hardly breathe. I lifted my hands to my nose and noticed that my hands were covered with blobs of well congealed foam. Quickly I reached to my mouth and removed pieces of foam with, 'Ouch,' hair attached. There are times when a mustache and beard are not a good idea.

I could now breathe and that tantalizing aroma of beef, onions, garlic, but that other smell, was that a touch of perfume? The sound of Mozart's something became louder. I slowly made my way to the piano while removing pieces of foam from what was far too soon to be, my balding pate. Our old pot bellied Quebec stove was throwing out that dry warmth that only wood heat can give, before me lay the view from our living room window, the waters of the northern reaches of Kootenay Lake lay still and black, the sky a lovely dark rich blue. 'Twas now dark enough that you could clearly see the autumn stars and the peaks on either side were beginning to lose that pristine alpine glow. That once light touch of perfume in the air was getting stronger, I turned to port, and I can assure you one or two would have gone down well, and there she was, my beautiful elegant female companion clad in something black and tight and low cut. She paused in her playing and turned and looked at me. My eyes pleasured themselves on her and I found myself humming, "When you came in sight I got that old feeling". She took one look at me, and with her musical fingers on the piano tiptoeing on the keys, burst into song.

"Aye, you must have been an ugly little bastard,
you must have been an ugly little child,
I can see the midwifes eyes,
as she cried out 'what a prize,'
and gave your mum a bigger pillow.
Aye, you must have been an ugly little bastard,
cause baby look at you now."

One gets older, one gets more verbose, but something's never change.

But back to. Such as. Painting the hull. On buying paint I discovered that there are those folk that are obviously, when it comes to choices of colour, far fussier than I. They had cans of excellent epoxy paint with 75% off, ordered by people who had changed their minds on their colour choice. With my final colour already chosen I bought several cans of those unwanted colours. I remember that orange and purple were quite predominant, and now haphazardly they covered the hull. At that time the hippy culture was flourishing in Kaslo, and my random choices thrilled them. I was hearing comments such as, 'far-out man,' 'way-to-go,' 'awesome', 'cool.' However, not all in town were enthused by my rainbow covered hull. The mayor, an older gentleman, had been quite interested in the building of Broom and what my plans were, was not only in a state of shock, but also tongue tied. I had finished for the day and was knocking the lids on the cans when I turned. He was leaning on his walking stick, his eyes traveling the length of Broom, he turned slowly, looked at me, and struggling for words, managed to say. "Are you going to sea in those colours?" I smiled and answered, "Well it doesn't look that good right now but when I get the flowers painted on, it will look so much better."

I was quite surprised at the number of children that were interested in what I was up to. On my way to lunch one day a little boy approached me and shyly said. "Can I see inside your boat?" "Sure," then I noticed behind him a group of children, standing silently, I smiled, "and I suppose you all want to see inside?" They beamed, and I, about to say "well your going to have to ask your mothers—," noticed the two teachers standing in the background, smiling. The whole bloody kindergarten class was there.

I placed a ladder on either side of Broom and explained that they would go up one ladder, and after they had seen inside, cross the deck and go down the other. With a teacher at the bottom of either ladder I led them to the port ladder. The little boy that had spoken to me was right beside me, the rest lined up behind. They stood there in military formation, their young faces alight with great anticipation of what may lie inside. I led them one by one up the ladder onto the deck, down the main cabin stairs, through the main salon, the galley, and the fo'c'sle then we turned and went aft. We were coming to the part that really tickled the boys. Broom has no cockpit, however it has something much better, an engine room. And though I can't stand erect in there they had no problem, with eyes wide open they entered the door to the engine room. Above their heads were glass prisms in the deck so that the engine room was a flood with light, there were lockers on either side of the engine that they could comfortably sit on. I told them to carry through and open the door on the other end of the engine room, in there, there is, and I emphasized, the 'Captains Quarters.' Then from there go up the stairs and cross the deck and go down the ladder on the other side. Aye, 'tis a child at heart I am, for I just adored looking at them, to be so young and so willing to show all on your face, but what was it they thought that might be inside this, steel thing? There was one little girl that expressed it so beautifully. She came down the stairs into the main saloon, with ribbons tied snugly in her hair and looking all the world like Alice in Wonderland, paused, looked around, her eyes agape and innocent, and with an astonished look, said. "I didn't know there was a house down here."

Chapter 4

1981. I had reached 50 years of age, it was my birthday and I was aboard and comfortably placed in the port pilot berth. I had a glass in my hand. Though Broom was not quite out of the womb the worst of my labours were over. Marlene had thrown a birthday party for me and there were people, some that I had only met once or twice pouring down the companionway steps. All wishing me a happy birthday. Meaning no disrespect to their good wishes, however, I do think that they came down those stairs as the kindergarten class had, with curiosity in mind.

And as I lay there they kept topping up my glass with their wine, and my mind as it always does with a glass or two, wandered. Yes, I was quite content to be silent and let my mind stray and as far as I know they had a great time. But every now and then their voices intruded into my thoughts, what was that they were saying? 'Oh, how lucky I was—and—I was living my dream.' I lay there, my mind already giving thought to my next task, now mused on this business of. 'Oh, how lucky I was'—'this living a dream.' What are they talking about? This building of Broom wasn't a dream, this was something that I had to do, what I felt was no casual and romantic fantasy it was as if I had no choice in the matter, nor did I wish to. I had touched an energy source and it was taking me along with it. Perhaps nature was unfolding for me as it should, but what ever it was I wasn't about to let it go. I wasn't living my dream or anyone's else's dream—I was living my life. I was doing something that was so incredibly natural for me to do that I couldn't consider doing anything else.

I have no doubt that I over indulged that night for the voices of the well-wishers began to fade and thoughts of my father entered my head.—'My Father—and the Iron Horse.' That he should enter my head that night was not too surprising for he was only 52 years old when he died. Yet, the Iron Horse, why would the Iron Horse enter my head? Was it this iron steed that I was building that would allow me to—I needed to slow down. Thoughts were tumbling through my mislaid mind, with my empty glass in hand I held it out, laughter rang out as someone filled it, and as I raised the glass to my lips all sight and sound faded before me, and all I saw was the iron grated stairs of the Iron Horse.

I was in the fourth year of my apprenticeship, and that morning I was in great need of the Iron Horse. I climbed the aged weathered stairs, before me lay a rusted steel door wedged open and beyond it ran a seven foot wide passage way. To my immediate right was a rusty ten foot high steel wall that ran the full length of the Horse. It was capped by a foot high grating that allowed the badly needed air, to flow in, and the fouled air, out. Overhead a curved steel roof encased the Horse. To my immediate left was a well bruised desk, behind it sat a beetle-browed surly guardian, his gnarled right hand firmly grasping a pencil, its end well chewed. By his left shoulder was a three foot wide bare steel wall, on it a large round clock happily ticked the minutes away, that wall separated him from the interior. On the other side of that wall a large metal trough ran the full length of the Horse, and on its stained surface water constantly trickled. They were cubicles, but no doors, and no toilet paper, in those days you equipped yourself with yesterdays newspaper. I approached the guardian. Slowly he raised his head and with soulless eyes stared blankly into mine. I said '1544' my badge number, he glanced at the clock, wrote down the time and my number and went back to ignoring me.

When I left he would again write down the time and my badge number. Fairfield Shipbuilding and Engineering obviously had a great need to know the length of time that their shipyard employees took for a bowel movement.

Innocent as always, I, on my first visit, took the first opening and quickly saw cigarette butts, cigarette packages, racing forms and numerous indigestible items sneak past my virgin buttocks. But it was the Turd Warden that troubled me as he sat scowling over his ledger, his pencil grasped firmly in his hand, while overhead that cheerful clock ticked the minutes away. Yet, my innocent eyes shied from his. Could it be possible that in fifty years it could be me sitting there, listening to the clock ticking my life away, while I timed how long it took someone to have a bowel movement? And all the while, loathingly, reluctantly, listening to the sounds of their bowels emptying while my nostrils became besieged by the stench of their excrement, and the nauseating odour of the rancid tobacco smoke that filled the air. No wonder the cleansing sea attracted me, no wonder I heard its beckoning call and with my all, embraced it.

1982. The roar of the boat movers engine and the screech of its brakes echoed in the morning air. Marlene ran down the stairs, opened the front door, looked out then turned to me and with a look of apprehension on her fine features, said. "Their going to haul a twelve ton boat to the coast on that." There are times when I am totally uncommitted, the truck looked fine to me, the painted naked woman on the truck's engine hood could have done with a touch of make up, but the engine rattled happily, as diesels do. The driver hopped out of the cab and approached me with hand outstretched. He was young, tall, and gangly, he wore an old, torn and oil stained coverall, that even my father would have thrown away. He smiled, a cigarette dangled from his lips, he badly needed a shave. I took a liking to him. Marlene, with a questioning look in her eyes turned to him and said. "You're alone." He smiled, and answered. "The highway code requires only one driver, that's me." I reckoned he had heard remarks like that before. I understood what Marlene thought, after all my labour, not to mention the money, couldn't they have sent at least three non-smoking men, clean shaven and wearing gold watches, and with their name sewn in gold braid on their sparkling white coveralls, but I came from a different world, this was quite acceptable to me.

He jumped back in to his great big truck and with that bloody great trailer behind it, twirled it around and with no directions from any one backed it up dead centre under the bow of Broomielaw. Then he climbed out off the truck and told me to knock the supports out from under the hull. I picked up my sledge hammer and cringed. He eyed me then strode over, took the sledge from my hands and knocked out a support on either side, then hopped back in to the truck and backed up to the next supports. Three clean shaven non-smoking men, dressed in crisp white coveralls with their names sewn in gold braid and wearing gold watches couldn't have done any better. Which reminds me of Toby, but that's much later. We launched Broom in Port Moody and spent the night at the dock until the next morning. And that morning the engine started like a charm, we cast off our mooring lines and headed for a spot that we had reserved on the marina wharf. I was in the highest of spirits, and need I add, with no assistance from alcohol.

Oh, I don't mind telling you, I felt great, wheeling the Broom around the harbour like that, coming neatly into dock with all those liveaboards waiting, all well aware that we had just launched, aye, it's true I was quite impressed [by myself] I had convinced myself that I knew what I was doing, until I tried to put the engine into reverse. The lever was stuck ahead I couldn't budge the bloody thing, and there was that nine foot widow maker heading right for those innocent smiling bystanders, aye, and there they were, waiting for this knowledgeable seaman to throw the engine hard astern,

Oh God, my imagination raced. Quickly I shut the engine off and leapt onto the wharf, grasped the mooring line that I had draped on the handrail and wrapped it around the nearest cleat. Broom carried on and the line grew as tight as a well-tuned guitar string, the dew that had settled on it overnight flew off in a vigorous spray, the wharf squealed in protest, then casually my good friends Ken and Eric hopped off to secure the forward lines. As Eric passed me I gave him one of those nauseating smiles than one saves for a good friend that mean's well. Moored, then afterwards I went down into the engine room. Eric had snugged up all on the engine that he thought it needed, which also happened to be, the reverse gear lever. I loosened and readjusted it.

Kissed by the salt chuck at Port Moody marina, where willing hands hauled on lines and raised her masts, and I was happy. With the engine spinning, with all sails hauled high and not a breath of air to fill them, we cruised under Lions Gate bridge out onto the open Strait, where my son in law cries. "Where now skipper?" I answer, " you see that condominium, that looks like it might be a ferry, follow it." On Desolation Sound we cruised and I had last tasted ... what I ever desired.

Chapter 5

1983. Late spring, the time of year to head for Alaska. I had bought the British Columbia Sailing Directions and devoured them, that was when to leave, when the last of the winter's south Easterlies slowly diminish you catch the winter's dying breath and let its last gasp take you north. Aye, I liked that. We left in early May, and motored practically all the time, for the wind blew not from the waning south but from the aspiring north, apparently the wind hadn't read the Sailing Directions. Cruising up those rugged fjords, finding a peaceful anchorage every night, giving thought to lowering the dinghy and walking the beach, that is, until we noticed the black bears, and somehow changing our mind. Indeed it was pleasure. Ever an early riser, I would awake and have the coffee brewing while the tardy sun lingered behind the snow capped peaks and the silent mist slept on the quiet waters, and my happy eyes pleasured themselves on the serenity that had wound itself around me.

But the weather had not been pleasant so when it changed it was, what else can I say, bloody great, we had just turned south and at last, a sunny day. We spied this little bay that was packed with the locals, their runabouts lay dragged up on the sandy beach. Men wearing yachting caps and baggy shorts stood around emptying cans of beer while their smoky barbecues cancerated meat. Women were gathered talking away to each other, all at the same time, meanwhile, doing their best to get a suntan. Children were splashing happily in that ice cold water [I shuddered at the thought]—bless them. On seeing them enjoying themselves I steered Broom into that little bay and quickly dropped the hook. When the locals had left, Loons visited us and while we dined we were entertained by their lonely haunting songs. Afterwards, when I could barely keep my eyes open the full moon rose over the distant white capped peaks, then as I succumbed to the weight of my weary eyelids, Marlene said, "Listen." In the quiet still of the night the only sound to be heard was the howl of wolves as they sung their nightly chorus to the young and resplendent rising moon. I slept that peaceful night away and awoke at dawn, lit the stove and put the coffee pot on, then went on deck. The first thing I noticed was our anchor, it was twelve feet forward of our bowsprit and almost as high, our anchor chain lay piled around it. During the night the tide having ebbed had left us smack dab in the middle of a—little duck pond, and though we were afloat, our anchor was most definitely aground. Crabs scuttled, dining on whatever the anchor had disturbed as it had settled itself in to the soft ground. We were totally surrounded by sand dunes. I went below and poured myself another cup. Marlene was still in bed, I handed her a cup, "it's a beautiful morning" I said, " you should see where we are." Luckily for us there hadn't been a breath of wind all night, nor was there all that day, or the next. The time spent in that little bay was the finest on that whole trip, for there in that pond with Broom barely afloat the day slowly wore on and birds landed around us. Mergansers first appeared, then came Murrelets and the Guillemots, later in the afternoon the Loons again returned with their haunting lonely air, and as the sun sank behind those eastern mountains and the dark stillness once again came upon us, the moon rose, and we heard again the gray wolves howling out their nightly welcome.

Dawn broke, and as we drank our morning coffee the early rays of the morning's sun caressed the sand dunes and what was once a brown shadowy embankment became a sun swept golden shore. Aye, to while the morning hours away, and eye the tide as it slowly sneaks in, so slowly as if it thinks you're not watching and you're not, you're dreaming, then with astonishment you realize that the golden sand bar had gone and in its place water sparkled with the days morning light. What beautiful days they were, more than that, exceptional days. Somewhere in my old log book the location of that bay is written, but I really don't want to go back there. I can't believe it would be the same as it was then. Silly isn't it, that certain days have an essence about them, that separates them from other days, almost as if a day—could have a soul.

After the quietness of Alaska it seemed so busy in Prince Rupert. We squeezed Broom into a spot at the end of the public wharf. I quickly lowered our crab pot, over loaded with the heads of fish, I wasted no time in doing so but simply lowered it down with all the line that I had on it. It was only when we were leaving that I realized how deep it was at the wharf, for the crab pot had dangled teasingly above the bottom. No sooner had we moored when I noticed three men fishing at the end of the wharf, and they certainly knew how to catch fish, however, there was one thing about them that bothered me. Every second fish they caught they threw back in, well, that won't do I thought, so I went over and had a few words with them. They were very particular about the kind of fish that they would eat, we however, were far less fastidious, soon we had more ling cod than we knew what to do with. The fishermen were very respectful, if I wasn't there they would not give Marlene the fish, but would wait till I appeared. I don't think as Marlene did that the fact that I gave them a shot of something now and then had anything to do with it. In the late afternoon and knowing full well what we would be having for supper we decided to wander off, along the way I picked up the local newspaper and on finding a pub we strolled in for a glass.

It was Friday, the pub was packed but as we entered two men got up and left, we quickly occupied their seats. We were seated at the edge of a stage, to my immediate right was the runway. I ordered a mug of beer and a glass for Marlene, then spreading the newspaper, read a few words then my mug of beer appeared, read a few more words, then I heard music, and quite innocently, realized that we were in a strippers bar. Not wishing to appear impolite I put the newspaper aside and quickly changed my reading glasses for my semi-distant pair.

Aye, in the quiet still of that Alaskan night while I struggled to keep my eyelids open, the only sound to be heard was the howl of wolves as they sung their nightly chorus to the young and resplendent rising moon.

It was Friday, and all the yahoos, working or not, were there. She came out wearing a fur stole that was wrapped around her neck, it must have been the only part of her body that had felt cold, then she started to do things with it, and then they started howling. I think it's known as wolf howling, but I had already heard proper wolf howling. Then as much as I tried to ignore the yahoos one of them eventually got to me, that was one with the bigger mouth than his peers, but with obviously less sense. He mouthed certain words to the stripper, and she, well my heart went out to her, for her repartee was sublime. If I had been him I would have crawled under the table and hid. I think he did for we heard nothing more from him, but she being a real trooper carried on, she neared us and squatting down close enough so that I knew undoubtedly that she was female, and looking directly at Marlene she said. "Honey—you've got a lot of guts sitting there."

Prince Rupert was far too busy so soon we left and headed for the Queen Charlottes. I had the sailing directions and it suggested mooring overnight at Larsen Harbour near the NW. end of Banks Island before crossing Hecate Strait. What made Larsen Harbour attractive was that it had six public mooring buoys. There was however, one unattractive comment that they made about that harbour, and that was, that it was only suitable for small craft and also that local knowledge was a necessity. Naturally, I ignored that comment. We entered the bay in the late afternoon on a rising tide, jagged rocks dotted the bay with tidal waters swirling around their unpleasant scabrous heads. It was not the kind of bay that you would enter on a dark and windy night. We had the harbour to ourselves. I moored to a buoy and quickly loaded and lowered the crab pot, we dined again on fish. Before I climbed into my berth I checked the tide tables, it would be low tide at dawn. I awoke with the first of the morning's light attempting to enter through our misty portlights, rubbed sleep from my eyes and glanced at my watch, it should be low tide. I rose, lit the stove and put the coffee pot on, then went on deck.

Daylight strived to emerge through the dew soaken fog meanwhile the sea was willingly offering its moisture laden breath to the awakened, but yet unseen sun. Light filtered through the damp mist and as it grew stronger, shapes appeared, reluctantly, ever defining themselves as the sun rose higher in the morning sky. An odour of kelp and coffee teased my nostrils. The fog hovered three feet above the sea and I saw what surrounded us. We were moored in a valley of cragged rocks strewn with bio-valves that squirted their excess liquid to the sky, while crabs and oyster catchers bustled back and forth reaping their harvest. The reluctant fog slowly dispersing shed tears that ran in dribbles on the rugged shaped rocks, their black gleaming edges hidden under the sharp shelled crusted barnacle.

We too reaped a harvest that morning, for after I had poured myself another mug of coffee I struggled to haul the crab pot up, thinking that its weight was caused by a sunfish who drape their ugly body over the pot and with their tenacious tentacles reach inside, and devour. But there was no sunfish responsible for the weight, for the pot was not only filled with crabs, for there were also those on top of the pot who couldn't get in, but had no intention of letting go. And so I also scurried, as the crustaceans and the birds had, finding buckets to put tonight's supper and tomorrow's lunch, and tomorrow's supper, into. As I bustled I remembered part of my childhood in Northern Scotland, in the fishing village of Wick. My step grandmother was cooking crabs, the live crabs were put in the pot, the lid was tied down, the stove was lit and the water brought to boil. I shall never forget how the claws of the crabs banged and rattled the pot, and how I sat wide eyed and innocent, wondering why they had to do that to the crabs. Those crabs that we had caught came to a quick death, as I hope that I shall, before they dine on me. We sailed south on the Hecate Strait and at the bottom of the Queen Charlottes, hung a right, and before me lay the magnitude of the open ocean. I had been long anticipating that immense vastness, my eyes ever waiting to dwell on what I felt would soon become, my mistress. My good wife, happy enough in the inland waters of B.C., had no interest in voyaging on the open ocean, whereas I was totally captivated by the prospect. It drew me, and no it wasn't the thought of foreign lands, but much more that there was a need that I had, that only the open ocean could offer. I wasn't about to let it go.

Chapter 6

1985. I was off again, yes, again. First let me say this. I'm a responsible man, going offshore alone without previous experience was not at all sensible, but I had, and awoke at 2: a.m. just south of Cape Flattery. I was hove to in a South East gale, surrounded by bright lights, dead centre in the middle of the shipping lane. I changed my mind. That was then. This time I had a young man who was buying my grub and his. A circumstance, I was quite willing to take advantage of, though I found out quite quickly that I was far more content to be alone—with my mistress. With a head wind and a flood tide we had anchored in Port San Juan, but before the mornings light had raised its head above those snow capped eastern mounts, a breeze from the land and an ebb tide had found me, unhesitating, with the anchor raised and the sails hauled bound for the open ocean. We cleared Cape Flattery in a rolling swell with dolphins happily frolicking around our bow, gulls clamouring overhead and my young companion hunched over the rail leaving his breakfast behind. I'm sorry to say that it didn't take me long before I wished that I had left him behind, for it was not until we reached the calmer seas south of San Diego that my young crew member was fit enough to keep watch, by that time I realized that I would be much happier without him. Until then I spoon fed him and listened to his complaints. One of them being, that he did not like how I had finished the interior of the main cabin, which only shows how much time he spent in his bunk.

We are becalmed. I have noticed that the lazy jack sheetlets that contained the bulk of the 485 square feet mainsail as it came down had got tangled in the radar reflector. There were no steps on the mast which meant that in order to free them, I would have to haul myself up the mast in the bosun's chair. There was no use sending my crew up as he was quite capable of being seasick on deck. I'd hate to see how he would be up there. I needed all the slack on the line that I could get so I asked him to hold on to the end of the line and not under any circumstances to let it go. He nodded his head and smiled. He had a very pleasant smile. I climbed into the chair then stopped, and climbed back out. Went back over to him and looking at him very intently repeated what I had already said. "Now whatever you do, do not let go the line." "Yes," he replied, and looking at me rather disdainfully added, "I understand."

If you have jumped to the conclusion that I never trusted him, you're quite correct. I climbed back on to the bosuns chair and hauled myself up the mast, reached the radar reflector and began to untangle the line. Then, 'whoosh,' the end of the line that he was supposedly holding onto whipped past my face, flew up to the top of the mast, through the block at the top and the sheetlets and all the line that held, fell, and came tumbling down around my shoulders. What could I say. I should have known better. I mean I was already suspicious wasn't I, I could have tied an extra line onto the end, no wonder it is known as .... the bitter end.

Could you conceive of how a fully battened junk sail of close to 500 square feet would lower without being controlled by those sheetlets? Why it would come down like a bloody great circus tent, now that we were becalmed would be bad enough, can you imagine how it would be trying to do it when the wind starts to howl. I had to reinstall that line, with the sheetlet line in hand I would have to haul myself up to the top of the mast, you don't really think I would let him do it do you? He would be liable to forget what he was doing and instead, decide to scratch his balls, if he could find them. Hauling yourself up the mast at a dock is one thing, at sea everything changes, as you desperately try to stop the violent swinging that you are subjected to as your body spins back and forth and around and around the mast. I did it, and came down with my body from my calves to chest, from wrists to arm pits covered in bruises, and amazingly for me, I never said a word.

Now don't get me wrong, this young man was far better educated than I. He was quite knowledgeable about many things, such as, humming birds. One day he pointed them out to me and said. "Look, humming birds." I admit to knowing little about humming birds. "Humming birds," I said with a questioning look, "600 miles off shore?" He looked at me with that look that knowledgeable people save for the likes of me. "Humming birds can fly 600 miles," said he. "Well, maybe your right, but do they usually drown themselves after doing it?" "Yes, that is strange them diving into the sea like that," he said.

"Well," I answered dryly, "perhaps that's because those humming birds think they're flying fish."

Log: July 8. Stuck in the Doldrums, where the hell are those South East trades? I'm sick of this stupid weather. Average days run for the last seven days, 60 mile and we wouldn't have done that if it wasn't for the engine. Meanwhile, all we are doing is bouncing up and down, with the booms swinging back and forth, clatter—bang clatter—bang. Next day I awoke and realized the clatter—bang had stopped. I lay in my berth hearing the sea as it gently murmured alongside the hull, if I was younger I would have sprang out of bed and rushed up on deck, but instead I slowly got out off my berth, lit the stove and put my coffee pot on. Then hesitantly looked up through the skylight. The foresail with the sunlight full and bright upon her white skin was gently curved like a young brides innocent and as yet unpregnant tummy. I sighed quietly, admiring the mornings air, but hopefully not loud enough to wake my exhausted interior decorator companion. Then with my mug of fresh brewed coffee in hand ventured forth on deck to face, what I hoped was the onset of the South East trades.

And there I sat in the grandest of spirits for life was again wonderful. I sat admiring all that surrounded me, enjoying the clear blue sky and that gentle breeze that had brought beauty into the cheeks of those now pregnant sails. Gosh, I was so happy. Then my eye caught a movement under the bowsprit and alongside the hull. That was when my gifted and unnecessary companion came on deck, and I, foolish as ever, who had never given thought to how bad his night may have been, blurted out. "Look," I said, "look at the size of that bloody big turtle." We were moving along at about four knots, the turtle now sliding along the side of the hull.

"A what?" He said. I answered, not taking my eyes from the turtle.

"A bloody big turtle." Then I raised my eyes and found him looking up at the top of the mast. God knows what he was looking up there for, he answered. "A tuttle?"

"No," I said, "A turtle, a, T-U-R-T-L-E ." I slowly and loudly spelt it out.

"Oh a turtle," he said, taking his eyes from the top of the mast and looking at me rather consolingly, said, "where?"

Turning and pointing astern I answered, slowly,—-"Away—to—fuck—back—there."

Log: July 18. 8.23 a.m. Land Ho! After 41 days at sea I sight land, an island in the Marquesas. According to my navigation it should be Ua Huka, still I questioned? At 10.30 a.m. another island appeared to the west of us, Nuka Hiva, we are where we should be. My crew all to anxious to get ashore suggested motoring all the way, a proposition that I found rather distasteful for even if we had it would be nightfall by the time we reached Taiohae Bay, no, I was not interested in entering and anchoring in darkness. We lay ahull for the night and at 5.00 a.m. hauled sail. By 12.30 p.m. we were anchored in Taiohae Bay, Nuka Hiva. Looking back how ridiculous it was, for I, foolishly, got quite upset for no one seemed to care whether we cleared customs or not. I even visited the police station, they just shrugged. Yes, fool that I was, I didn't know how lucky I was, but I quickly found out when I reached Tahiti.

Inwardly that morning I celebrated, I can navigate, my initial awkward and inept efforts have borne fruit. I must now look kindly on my young companion, for he believed in me when others wouldn't. How shallow and insincere I was for my kind thoughts on my companion quickly evaporated that evening in a bar run by a Canadian couple. The owner complained all the time about the French bureaucracy, meanwhile his wife was terrified that I may stand on a Gekko, for they ate certain crawly creatures that she was not too fond of. This was a dream that they always had cherished, but like many such dreams it had turned sour. In the bar we met this couple off an American yacht from Hawaii. He was a young charming lad from Norway? Sweden? She not as young, from Hawaii. I learned so much more from him later that evening but within that time I spent in that bar I quickly learned that she had to get off the American yacht that she was on. However, the skipper wouldn't let her go for he needed a full crew to sail his vessel. That was when those kind thoughts that I had turned to vapour, and I began to conceive, cunning exchanges.

There were festivities taking place in town, the locals were celebrating Bastille Day. Yes, it did remind me of Neah Bay for when I had anchored there the North American Indian was celebrating a week in advance, and here they were celebrating Bastille Day, that was four days ago. But my eye lids have grown so much heavier as I have grown older and I was all too willing to go back on Broom to dine and sleep. I was quite surprised that my young companion was willing to do likewise, I gave it little thought. Dined, then just as I was about to jump into my berth a great splashing took place alongside the hull. My mind given to flutter like a butterfly with the first breeze, recalled the Bounty and those native bare breasted women with flashing white teeth and darker nether parts who happily climbed aboard ship, and took advantage of those poor Christian sailors. Quickly I was on deck and right behind me was my young male crew member, who as far as I knew spent his life half asleep. Perhaps he had the same thoughts as I had, if so he was not going to miss anything for he had the ships heavy duty flash light in hand. Whatever may have entered my foolish head, I wasn't totally wrong. The couple that we had met at the bar were alongside, they had joined the local festivities, which was quite apparent for they were totally plastered. The dinghy that they were on for some strange reason had capsized, they had managed to right it, but then they couldn't find the drain plug to let the water out, and with that remark they burst into fits of laughter, which I welcomely joined in. At that time I felt that I better have another glass for I could see that it was going to be a strange evening. He, though not in full use of his senses had not lost his clothes, she however through whatever circumstances that had taken place was nude from the waist up.

My young crew member who was now by my side appeared to be in a state of shock, his eyes popping out of his head and the ray of the flashlight that he held focused directly on the woman's mammary glands. Their shape and size conveyed to me that nature played no part whatsoever in their manufacture or design. I turned, and discreetly put my hand on the flashlight and lowered it so that its ray shone on the deck, then went below and returned and handed each of them a towel and a robe for the woman. They dried themselves then came below. Being the generous host that I am I offered them a glass, which they took, although they were not at all in any need. The young Scandinavian who was probably in his late thirties must have saw me as a kindred soul with a willing ear for he started to tell me all his personal history, part of it being.

"Do you know that I am penniless? Yet I can travel anywhere I wish and buy almost anything." He paused as if waiting for me to speak, I sat silent. "Do you want to know how I do it?"

"No," I answered. "Not really."

"I'll tell you," he said.

"You don't have to" I replied. He ignored me.

"I have a little plastic card and with that piece of plastic I don't need money, I can borrow almost unlimited funds, do you want to know why?" By this time I was just wishing that the pair of them would bugger off so that I could go to bed. He was not the least bit dissuaded.

"No" I answered, "I'm not the least bit interested." I should have saved my breath.

"I'll tell you" he said.

"I thought you would," I answered.

"My family owns the original Gutenberg Bible," he paused, emptied his glass then continued. "None of us have ever seen it, it is kept under lock and key in a Swiss Bank, it is worth millions and every year it becomes more valuable, what do you think of that?" I never answered, I had fallen asleep.

There were certain formalities to be looked after in this exchange of crew, a circumstance that I thought rather silly in regard to how relaxed the officials seemed to be. The skipper of the yacht that Jackie, my soon to be new crew member was off took it all quite seriously. He was about the same age as myself and having sailed a few times from Hawaii to those Islands knew more about the official bureaucracy than I. He was right. His yacht was not old, but built in the classic design that I find so appealing to the eye, and with somehow an added artistic touch. However he was not happy with it, though from how he spoke I gathered that he had a hand in its design. He said it didn't sail worth a damn. I also had the distinct feeling that he was sizing me up as he offered me a glass, weighing me, as if deciding whether I was a fool or just an idiot. If he had but asked I would have told him. I could be wrong of course, but perhaps he saw everybody as within two classes. Later that night as I rowed back to Broom I wondered why would anyone want to sail with him. Then I remembered that his crew had their own private cabins, and the comments that were made about the freezer that was filled with roast beef and steaks, and something about a cooler overflowing with wine. I also heard that night that Jackie, my about to be new crew member, was the cook, and having heard the comments on the meat supply doubted very much what she may be able to do with a can of corned beef and a bag of rolled oats, but that really didn't matter to me. No, what mattered to me was when we neared the low coral islands of the Tuamotu Archipelago, for then I would want an opened eye when mine were all too willing to be closed.

Folks off yachts strolled the byways of the village, far too different from the locals to be regarded as such. We, off yachts were all quite willing to be sociable. Even I, the unsociable one, who with thoughtful intent had most conveniently misplaced my companion. I was invited aboard a yacht that was being sailed by a rather odd couple who had a one or two year old boy. I had first met them while walking in the village when I foolishly was concerned that no one cared whether I cleared customs or not. The mother of the little boy was French, her male companion was a white South African. She was a very pleasant woman and perhaps it is unfair of me saying that she was odd, though he, definitely was. During our conversation she mentioned that her little boy had spent all his life aboard and had learned to walk on a surface that was constantly moving. I gave little thought to that, until later. I boarded then realized there was another couple there, I had met them earlier, a rather straitlaced pair, the kind you meet on your doorstep on a Sunday morning with brief cases filled with religious tracts that you don't want. They were dressed as I, in shorts and tee shirt, however the South African was clad rather simply in a Tarzan style loin cloth, that he had made himself, out of an old welding jacket. It hung down somewhat like a square sporran protecting the family jewels. No sooner was I aboard when the cheerless couple got up and left. The sporran wearer then offered me a glass of his home made brew, I sipped it and being rather curious I asked him what he had made it from. "Oh" he said, "anything that I can get my hands on." From the taste I believed him.

All the time I had been in their company she had carried the child, but now she wanted to go below and put a meal on the stove. They asked me to come below, I followed them. She put the child down on the cabin floor and with his knees bent almost to a right angle, his back crouched, he crossed the floor dragging his finger tips along the wooden surface as if at any moment he might fall, all the world like a hairless baby gorilla, my heart went out to the poor wee bugger. Now I knew what she meant. He went to the other side of the cabin, and there, mounted on the yacht's side was a bilge pump. With his legs still partly bent he stood as tall as he could and reaching up with arms that seemed so incredibly long, grasped the handle of the bilge pump and worked the handle with a ferocity, that seemed so incredible coming from a little tyke like him.

Yes, that wee lad bothered me, there was something weird and uncanny about him, and the fact that my lips were becoming numb from my drink didn't help. With my eyes still on the wee lad his father, if that is who he was, walked past me, it was then I realized that he had shed his sporran and the family jewels were now on display. I pretended not to notice. He came over to where I sat and before I could say, no, topped up my glass, which thankfully, required little. "How are you enjoying that quality wine of mine" he asked. "Why" I stammered, quite understandably, at least under the circumstances I thought so, "it's really rather interesting, I doubt that I have ever tasted a brew such as this." I was being quite honest. He beamed, then opening a closet he drew out a jug. He placed it before me and said. "Have this." I reached up and grabbed the jug, firmly. I'm not at all sure why, except it looked solid and secure, whereas the situation that I now had found myself in, felt—flaky. I've never been too sure what that word meant, but somehow it felt right. Then standing by my shoulder he said. "Wouldn't you be far more comfortable with your clothes off?"

"No," I answered.

"Come now you're being silly, of course you will be more comfortable." His wife was by the stove engrossed in stirring a pot of something.

"No," I replied, "I'm really quite comfortable with my clothes on."

"Come now," he said "what are you ashamed off?" I was quickly becoming uncomfortable and taking my clothes off would certainly not have improved matters. I answered.

"Nothing that I am aware of," and attempting to be, what is described in today's vernacular, as cool, I added, "and if I was ashamed of something I doubt very much that I would tell you." Not waiting for him to answer I rose. "I'd better be going now" I said. Hearing my words she turned from the stove and I smiling to her, added, "it was kind of you to ask me aboard, thanks for the drink and thanks for the jug." She smiled. I headed up the companion way stairs, he was right behind me, he wasn't finished with me yet. Out off her hearing he put his hand on my shoulder and quietly said. "She's a fine woman."

"Yes, you're probably right."

"She likes you, you could make each other quite happy." Oh I'm sure that he never heard, but there in my insides I groaned. I, who had so easily smirked at the couple who had ran off with their imaginary brief cases between their knees. Who I now felt had more insight than I, but I had had enough of what ever game was going on and I was not at all willing to play it.

I often think of myself saying that, 'I'd better be going now'. As if I had a doctors appointment, or I have to go to the dentist and have a root canal, whatever that was. Aye, but simply, it was that I couldn't get away fast enough. What would you have done? And what would he have done, as he stands in the background, leering. No thank you.

Log: July 24. Weigh anchor for Papeete. We sailed past the yacht that had the French lady aboard, and there she was on deck with her weeks washing piled before her, hanging clothes up to dry. With a clothes pin between her teeth she smiled and returned my wave, the clothes pin fell from her mouth when she noticed the blond headed woman hauling up my mainsail. Log: July 29. We are now having squalls and unpleasant weather, the worst since the Washington coast. This in an area that I would rather the weather was clear for we are close to the Tuamotus, those low-lying coral islands that are also known as the Dangerous Archipelago. July 30. Sighted the tops of the palm trees on Matavia, the outer most island of the group. Now clear sailing to Tahiti. Day later anchored in Papeete harbour.

Ahead of me in the customs office was a heavily built American yachtsman, cordial, as most of them are. In front of him a French official and behind him and overhead was hung a painting. It was of a charter vessel and the crew on it were hauling aboard this large fish. Our friendly American being sociable, or so he thought, commented on the painting and asked the official what kind of fish that would be. The official raised his head and scowling at the American answered, "Why don't you people learn to speak French?" Needless to say the American was at a loss for words. When it was my turn I had the greatest temptation to click my heels, raise my right arm and say, "Viva La France" but my accent would have been all wrong. Yes, Tahiti may have been paradise once, but for me, I had no sooner got there than I was quite ready to leave.

I dropped Jackie off in Papeete, she said that she was unable to buy her own food. I received a free lunch by the natives in Nuka Hiva, and that, I had amply repaid with Jackie, but I was not about to continue with it. Ten years later we were moored in Honolulu, Marlene and I were on deck, we heard a shout from the wharf. "Ahoy, Broomielaw." And there she was standing on the wharf, waving. I was so glad that I had the wit to tell my good wife about her.

Chapter 7

Log: Aug.19. Aye, and there, displayed before me was another beautiful trade wind sailing day, the kind that I had long dreamt of where your sails are set and the vessel cruises freely with none at the wheel, while I happily lazed my hours away on those sublime warm sunlit days. Aye, the kind of sailing that so easily gets into your blood, that gives you a sense of being, of belonging to this planet and all that surrounds us. For there on the wide open sea you notice where the sun rises and where it sets, and the moon, the planets, and the stars as they all slowly change their nightly position, and the trade winds that blew me along this trackless path seemed to be telling me that I too am part of this cycle. Yet as that day aged I felt that there was something wrong and I couldn't figure out what it was. No, it did not sit well with me.

I had reckoned that Beveridge Reef should be ahead, 20 miles due west, and 7 miles south. I took two more sights, worked it out and everything seemed O.K. Yet, there was that feeling of discomfort. Confirmation is what I badly needed, due west was my course but was Beveridge Reef, seven miles south? I couldn't be sure that it was—and if it wasn't where it should be, where was it? Went below and lit the stove and placed on it a pot of water, it had almost started boiling when I leaned over and turned the stove off. I went back on deck, looked around but heard and saw nothing. Went below and relit the stove, stood there watching the water again come to boil then added macaroni, then decided that I would cook it, but not eat supper until after 10: p.m.. By that time I'd drop sails and just say to hell with Beveridge Reef and keep going. My supper cooked I opened the hatch.

The horizon was slowly fading, all too soon it would be unseen as it blended with the darkness of the sky, about to go below when I thought I heard something, perhaps it was just the sound of the wind as it left the mainsail, I wasn't sure. Went forward and sat just aft of the bowsprit on the anchor winch, listening, listening. What was it, my imagination? Was I actually hearing something? If I was, it was just the faintest sound, purse your lips and blow ever so gently, that was the sound that I thought I was hearing. Yes, there was a sound, and it was slowly, ever so slowly, getting stronger, a jet? My eyes searched the clouded heavens, but all was dark, then in that quickly graying dimness that appeared as if one was looking at an old school blackboard, there emerged slowly, as slowly as the sound had risen, a faint horizontal chalk line. I sat fascinated, gazing on that line, it was gradually gaining in length and losing its faintness, becoming more bold and distinct, and that sound that I was hearing, becoming louder. Slowly I began to realize that what I was hearing was the surf breaking, and what I was seeing, was Beveridge Reef. I quickly steered due north and never left the wheel until that sound had faded and the chalk line had vanished. It was 10:30 p.m. I ate and slept.

Log: Aug. 23. Nuku-alofa in Tonga was dead ahead, I reckoned we were 100 miles to the east of it, but that afternoon the barometer dropped and the wind came up. Soon it was blowing over 30 knots from the east, and the seas, 15-20 feet. Unless the conditions changed I was not about to wend my way through those islands, for one of the few things that I need no assistance with, is sleeping. I left my small jib up and steered south to clear Eau Island. That wind kept up and I gave up thought of going into Tonga, then it died leaving in its wake the discomfort of the battling seas.

My eyes, captivated by the loving sun as it gently kissed the warm horizon.

And those are times when one can comprehend the pleasures of home, when you suffer the restlessness of the sea and your vessel suffers the slam, the crash, the batter, the jostles, the ups, the downs, while your hand ever seeks for a handhold, and wonders, on which side? Ah, the pleasures of home, a warm dry and incredibly stable bed to slumber all night in, no need to raise your head from those soft warm pillows to see if a storm is headed your way, let the wind rattle your window panes, let the rain send torrents upon your roof, what care you, just turn onto your other side and go back to sleep. Fresh water showers of various temperatures, fresh vegetables that are not produced in a can. Alcoholic drinks that are actually cold, what am I saying, I'll settle for alcohol, with a shot of Lolo. No, Lolo is not one of those full lipped dusky brown maids with deep flashing flirting eyes that if you're not careful may lead you astray.

'Please, please, lead me astray' and so I cry as I lie alone, packaged firmly in my berth in those rolling seas while overhead the southern night sky is lit with stars that I, with my northern eyes have never seen, and my imagination easily filled with the thought of brown affectionate maids with gorgeous full ruby lips and I with my straying hands caressing their ... However, it is true that they dwell on your mind when you sail alone in those waters, when the weather is pleasant and your energy level is high.

Of course, it's also true, that is, if I was home. I wouldn't see the sun rise, couldn't think of getting myself out of bed to watch it rise over shingled roofed chimney tops. Or for that matter being interested in seeing it sink, not into the wild and uncontrollable sea, but hiding, as if embarrassed to be seen as it went to bed behind a facade of slated roofs and uninterested eyes. Aye, I wondered about that in the sense of where I stood, yes I mean that literally, for it's true for those last nights had not been comfortable, and the ability to stand without your innards being exchanged for your outards was a wish much to be desired. It was best just to lie down and dream as you tried not to rock and roll in your berth. Cushions on either side were a great help. By dawn the wind had died but the seas were still doing their squabbling act, then the warm rays of the sun aroused a light breeze. Off my starboard bow was an island, I headed for it. It wasn't something that I would customarily do, but I was fed up, why else would I be thinking about shingled roofs. The trouble is when you get fed up, trouble happens, which solves your problem for you forget about being fed up. I ignored that but took a sight and took a chance.

I had an interesting collection of charts aboard, some I had bought, others were discards from the University of Victoria, the rest I had scavenged. Spread out on my chart table was one of the latter. It showed a small group of islands south of Tonga, the chart was not in the best of condition but at least the dangers that lay around the islands were few. I took a chance. It seemed that the previous owner must have been as fond of red wine as I am, for he had managed to spill a glass over the name of the island, it was barely decipherable. On its northern coast it had a small cove, it was just what I needed. I steered for it, sailed around a point in a dying breeze and dropped the hook. It was idyllic, palm trees lined the golden shore and the water in that sheltered bay, protected from the squabbling sea was peacefully calm. I lowered the anchor in to the sand and multicoloured fish disturbed by my intrusion fled, then came back to see what tasty morsels my anchor had aroused. Bloody great it was, an excellent holding ground, yes, it suited me fine. I cleaned up the mess that the weather had created, then thoroughly enjoying the calm sea, cooked pancakes for lunch. In my search for pancake syrup I surprised myself by coming across that jug of homemade brew from the South African sporran wearer. I eyed it rather suspiciously.

Aye, and I know why I did. First, it had been a while since I had last drank, that is alcohol, and, secondly, I remembered the effect, still I took a swig and there it was my lips once again going numb. I ignored my lips. Had my pancakes then spread a canopy over my hammock that hung on the aft deck, laid my tired body down and sipped the brew. I enjoyed my hammock. I recalled the time that I had hauled it out off the dumpster at fisherman's wharf in Victoria. It had stunk something fierce, you would too if you had pieces of rotten fish sticking to your ribs, but I in my positivity had saw past all that. Now the seas, the sun and the pelting rain had washed it clean, and I happily lay on it with my numb lips sipping this sporran wearer's brew, and the more I drank the better it tasted.

It was strange what happened, yet, did it? For I slept, it was daylight and yet I slept, and did I tell you that I can't sleep during the day, but that is how it was, or how it seemed. As always I awoke with the first glimmer of light in the eastern sky and found myself naked, had I climbed into the hammock like that. I must have. I sat up, the skin on my back ached, and no doubt was covered with the criss cross weals from the harshness of the netting. As always my eyes slithered open to welcome a new day, then I noticed the sporran brewer's empty bottle lying beside the hammock. Had I drank all of it? The sun had not yet fully risen and traces of water that lay on the deck looked like prints from bare feet. Had I went for a swim? No I couldn't have, for the safety line that I have on the guard rail was still attached, and I'm getting too old to climb over that. But, just a minute my bucket with a line tied to it, I could have hauled a bucketful up and drenched myself, had I? Then slowly, as if opening a door to a long forgotten room, I remembered last evening.

The sun, all too ready to leave the heavens and bless others with its light, was shyly lowering its head behind the gentle palms. Night was falling. I had lay gazing on it as it modestly sank behind the tall and regal palm fronds, and that was when I heard the splashing and the sound of voices. Drowsily I pulled myself erect then saw two figures swimming towards Broom, they cried words that had no meaning to me, but I saw their arms waving. I was in no fit stage to help them aboard, nor was I willing. Yes, the effect of the brew was still brewing, inside me, had it created a still in my innards. I wasn't quite sure what to call what I must have drunk, or, more importantly was I drunk?

They came upon the western side and clambered aboard, stopped, and stood looking at me, wondering if they would be welcome. Their forms, silhouetted as the final light of the sun outlined their slim arms and shoulders, the warm curve of their waists and hips. I was just to pleased to realize that I had feminine company, at last. I smiled and waved them aboard. With enthusiasm they swung their legs over the rail and came towards me. As they came near me, they stopped, and looking at each other burst into fits of laughter. I smiled, I was only too willing to laugh, though I would like to know what it was that I was laughing at.

Then slowly through that brew laden fog that swirled in my head a light flashed. I was nude, was that what it was? Had they not seen a naked white man before. I lowered my eyes and surveyed myself. I was heavily tanned, except, then I too started to laugh for around what was is known as one's private parts was a narrow band of white. I looked like an old model car from the fifties, two tone, the idea made me laugh all the more. I couldn't resist it. I climbed out of the hammock and turning around leaned over, and showed them my snow white arse. Which only made them scream all the more. I turned to them and my foolish eyes feasted on them.

Their gleaming black hair glistening from their swim hung over their shoulders. Their earth toned eyes sang joyously with merriment, their laughing smiles framed their full ruby lips and white shining teeth. Their full and naked breasts trembling, teasing me with feminine frivolity. Was it my eyes, for their nipples seemed to stand out like red coated peanuts in the shell, had the water been that cold? The curve of their waists was amplified with the seductive and maternal swell of their hips. Draped loosely from their waists and clinging to their lithe brown thighs were colourful sarongs. Aye, females they were, the kind one dreams of in those southern tropical waters.

Was I dreaming? Was it real? What could I do? I had no problem answering that, I managed to walk over to them and opened my arms wide, and laughingly they entered. I hugged them, and as my hands clung to the moist and supple skin on their backs, my finger tips caressed the warmth that lay there, then soon my lips were on theirs and their breasts were pressed close to my chest. Aye, it was heavenly. But there it was? Had it happened? Was it the effect of the sporran wearer's brew and my over active imagination, and my wishful thinking. Aye, it was grand, but what troubles me is that I don't remember all that took place, just parts, that's what makes me think that, perhaps it was all a dream.

Like my hands slowly running down their backs and my tactile finger tips caressing their skin, then when I sensed the lower curve of their spine, my hands no longer mine, joyfully traveled over the alluring curve of their entrancing hips and slyly, slipped under the loose sarong. Then as if wishing never to forget, climbed over the alluring swell of their shapely and muscular young buttocks, and paused. It all being as if I had to interpret, to have it linger and become embedded in my mind. Then my hand would glide from one buttock and down into the valley that lay between, and again climb up the other. Yes, as if my hands were trying to remember, acknowledge and capture all that lay in that remarkable embrace.

Did those young maids know how much pleasure they gave me, did my eyes swell with joyous tears, they could have for they had been watching my eyes as theirs, uncontrollably, danced over mine. If they were reading my thoughts, and I am the kind of man who wears his heart on his sleeve, yes, it was quite possible. They smiled that wonderful smile that only the Polynesians can do, then they undid the knot that held their sarong and it fell to their feet, and my eyes followed it. I buried my head, did I weep or groan, aye, it's possible for I know how I am. I let my head sink between their breasts, and joyously with my tongue, tasted … the red coated pea nuts in the shell.

I stood there in the early dawn, yet I never saw it. For all I ever saw was their sarong as it slid from their firm brown hips and their shapely formed thighs, and I remembered how my uncontrollable eyes dropped and settled on—their black rich pubic hair, and what ever the man I am, turned to jelly, except for one part. Yet, I remember more, for we had danced, had that brew created music in my head, for it had played a tango. And there was I one who loves the romantic beat of the music, one who does know one foot from the other, doing the best that I can to teach those that have no knowledge of it. But stop, had we danced? Had I showed them how to lean back and stretch out one arm, and how to bend one leg and stretch the other, how to twist their head and look arrogant. Bless them they had a hard time with that.

Then suddenly I remembered and ran down into the main cabin and looked at the tape player. I pushed the eject button and read the sticker on the tape. Tango's. The music was not just in my head, it had been playing. But, had that been last night, or was it some other time that I had played it. My God why hadn't I thought of it sooner, the footprints, were they mine or were they those of a smaller foot. I rushed back on deck. Except for traces of water that lay in the shaded areas, the sun had dried all that had lain on the deck. I went quickly into the aft cabin and closed the hatch, it was cool there but it was the darkness that I badly needed.

I sat with my head completely in a daze, yet, feeling incredibly happy. Sitting there with a foolish smile on my face, trying so hard to remember all that had happened. In any case why did I feel so happy? Then I recalled the chart and leaned over to the chart table, but it wasn't there. Nor was it on the floor, had I taken it up on deck with me? Could I have done that? I went back up on deck and looked under the hammock and around the deck, but it was no where to be seen. And what was the name of the island? I could recall that some of the name was incomprehensible, but what was it? I returned to the aft cabin and with my eyes tightly closed bowed my head and held it in my hands. Then fragments of scenes appeared before me, slowly they coalesced, then I saw what may … have taken place.

I was laughing, gasping for air, aye, their young lungs were far fitter that mine. I had prostrated myself on the hammock, legs out stretched and arms splayed, laughing joyously. It was the sort of fun that I badly needed. Lolo or was it Lilo approached me, so I had named them but in whatever state I was in I could never quite remember who was who. They had also named me, now what was it? but as I lay there I quite forgot. Shall I call her Lolo, she that first approached me and lifting my legs placed them together, then smiling straddled my waiting hips. Then Lilo came from behind and brought my arms together and leaned over so that her breasts were now touching my face, she swung them to and fro, gently caressing me. Lolo slowly squatted down. Lilo raised herself so that her breasts were no longer dallying on my face, she moved forward and lowered her legs. Salt laden pubic hair brushed my nose and moist lips and hovered temptingly, over my mouth. The vague name of the island, yes, I think I know what it was, and what they called me … if they did.

Chapter 8

Log: Aug. 30. I awoke, went on deck and there crossing the bow of Broom was the 'Love Boat,' or one of that variety. The early risers among the passengers were standing at the rail looking intently at Broom, when they saw me appear they started waving. I raised my arms and waved back, then realizing that I was naked, I waved back with one hand. I heard laughter. This 'Love Boat' situation did not bother me at all, for if they had ran me down I hadn't the slightest doubt that I would have been well cared for. If I had lived. 'The Love Boat' cleared my bow and ahead lay the jagged pinnacles of the rocks that sat north of Kanduva. I had a most pleasant sail in to Suva and while trailing a line over the side, I caught a large dorado, but for me there was something much better than that, the harbour is protected by a reef. However, on Suva's reef there is a wreck of a large fishing vessel, showing exactly where the reef is, later I found out that there was also a wreck on Beveridge Reef, which I am glad to say that I never got close enough to see. On entering the harbour I anchored in the pratique clearing area and hauled up the pratique, a plain yellow flag that I had sewn up from one of Marlene's old negligees. I seldom buy anything that I can make, which means, I seldom eat out. I was soon boarded by their health vessel. It was so pleasant dealing with them after suffering the rudeness of the French officials.

After clearing pratique I anchored closer to the yacht club, had a badly needed fresh warm shower, a drink at the bar, then went back aboard for supper and bed. Marlene, and a good friend of mine Charles, were going to join me there. Two days later I was downtown Suva. I crossed the street, and there crossing from the opposite direction was Marlene, it was a wonderful surprise for both of us. Marlene's first words were. "I checked with the customs office and they told me that there had not been a yacht named Broomielaw that had cleared in." My eyes once again glazed over, I had completely forgotten to clear customs. We walked hand in hand to the customs office, at least she knew where it was. We spoke to a young customs officer who told me that I would be thrown in jail for failing to go through customs, there was only one consolation in this, and that was that the prison was directly across from the yacht club. He was the first customs officer to mention prison to me—but not the last. He led us in to see the head man, who would have been as old as myself. I apologized profusely, told him that it simply had slipped my mind and that I was an old fool, he smiled, nodded his head and agreed with me. I had the feeling that the young customs officer was rather disappointed.

Aye, I well remember that early evening in Suva, Broom well anchored and there I was, with my feet up, a position I find most comfortable and holding a glass of the local vintage in my hand, I was quite willing to let the sun knock off for the day. Strauss waltzes were resounding from our tape deck, meanwhile delectable odours were wafting from the galley as my good wife did wonders with what we had bought at the market. It was then that I noticed a yacht come sailing in and anchoring in the pratique area. Part of me recognized the yacht, and yet another part thought, no, for the mast was far too short. I went below got my binoculars, and realized, yes, it was the 'Fukatutu,' well, it's hardly a name you would forget is it?

It was a typical racing yacht sailed alone by a Japanese sailor, it been anchored not too far from mine in Papeete. Jackie had considered sailing with him, and she wanted me to size him up so she had brought him aboard. I must have been in one of my generous moods for I recall giving him a Scotch and orange. Jackie, who had already been aboard the Japanese yacht told me how Spartan it was, he, on the other hand was only too willing to tell me how fast it was. If I had known in advance that he was going to brag, he wouldn't have got the Scotch and orange. Somewhere in the vicinity of Tonga, that same night when the wind howled in anger, and I lost all interest in entering, there too was that Japanese yachtsman. He had attempted entry and got dismasted, however he had been fortunate in finding a mast of a wrecked yacht. Would it be presumptuous of me to think that while I was within those islands, I had a far better time than he. A few days later my friend Charles appeared and he managed, though I'm not at all too sure why, to round up two Canadian backpackers to join us on our passage to my next Port of Call, Bay of Islands, New Zealand. Marlene would fly and join us there, but first we cruised the islands bearing gifts of Kava to the local chieftains, who made it quite obvious that they would far prefer a package of cigarettes. And the lads and lassies visited us aboard and I tasted Kava, I smiled, recalling that numbing effect.

I believe I rather charmed the crew with my navigational skills for we held one tack all the way from offshore Suva into the Bay of Islands. We moored at the dock in Upoa and cleared customs. Charles, ever responsible was checking the mooring lines, I was off, trying to find a yacht club. Marlene was somewhere in New Zealand, but where? Meanwhile a voice on the wharf shouted. "Ahoy, Broomielaw." Charles answered— "Marlene?" "Charles, where's that old fart Ron?" she asked. "Where do you think—at the local yacht club bar." I was, at the yacht club bar, and counting the bar tender there were four of us. I had been there four minutes. It was close to empty, the bar and my glass. I had nothing to say, surprisingly neither had my companions. I was becoming bored, it was time to leave. Then the swinging doors swung and someone shouted, "How you doing you old fart." Gosh, she says the nicest things to me. Hugging in public is quite permissible in New Zealand.

In the yacht club bar in Suva we had met an older Kiwi who had insisted that Marlene call his wife when she arrived in New Zealand. When Marlene called she was about to move for the summer into a house in Upoa, she invited Marlene to join her. The house sat across the bay and overlooked the wharf, Marlene recognized the masts of Broom as she sailed past their living room window. She ran down to the wharf and got the first ferry across to where Broom was moored. Aye, another easy and happy reunion. From there we sailed down the coast to Auckland and moored at Marsden wharf, where the Rainbow Warrior had been dynamited. It was Marlene's birthday, and, as on any celebratory day aboard Broom, the Scottish Rampant lion joins the Maple Leaf in being prominently displayed. The Scots in Auckland came pouring out of the woodwork, some of them knowing the location of Broomielaw in Glasgow.

Among those that we befriended was a deck officer of a freighter that was just about to leave harbour, it was a custom aboard that ship to throw a party when leaving for offshore. He being an officer invited us to the party and asked us to bring friends, we had quickly made friends who were only to pleased to join us. We boarded the ship, met Warren who took us to the officers state room, where we were introduced to the Captain and his fellow officers, immaculate in their white uniforms. I for some strange reason must have been aware of this because for a change I was smartly dressed with my long white neatly pressed trousers [grand place Dunedin for picking up used cricketers clothing] hiding my well tanned knobby knees, and a long sleeved white shirt. It was all extremely posh, and our Kiwi friends were considerably embarrassed for they had dressed simply in tee shirts and shorts, they sat on a couch close together hoping that no one would notice them. Warren had told me to go to the bar and order drinks, however our friends were not going to budge from that couch, so there was

I returning with a tray of drinks for them. Only one tray was required for once they had knocked back that drink they forgot entirely how they were dressed, and were soon leaning on the bar chatting away to the bartender and anyone who would listen.

It was Kava we brought them, but their parents preferred tobacco.

The female companions of the officers were all quite attractive, a fact that Marlene could not help but comment on. When she said. "How come all their wives are so attractive?" I smiled, then Warren came over and said, "I'll be gone for a little while, I'm off for a naughty," winks, then was gone. I had a most pleasant evening which I paid for the following day, early in the morning there was a bang on the hull, then a voice shouted. "Hey Ronnie, we're just about to leave and I've brought you a bottle of champagne, a bag of sausages and bacon, and bum nuts." I might have known what a naughty was, but even the sound of bum nuts, whatever they were, made my stomach turn, I did not at all feel well. Such was his sense of humour that when I answered his kind words with a loud moan, it only put him into a fit of hysterics. Marlene took charge of the champagne, the sausages, the bacon and the bum nuts, while I buried my head under the bed sheet and complained bitterly about the quality of the Kiwi drinking water.

I liked Warren, he was an Aussie, full of quips and puns, those things that I'm also fond of, also there was a certain vulnerability about him. When we had boarded there was a few minutes when he had mentioned that he had thought that the party would be quite informal, and had entered the officers state room only to find out that his fellow officers were neatly dressed in white uniforms. Quickly he had left and changed. Yes, I could understand why he would have sympathized with the embarrassment of the Kiwi's in their shorts, and noticed how I went over to the bar and returned with drinks for them. I have no doubt that he was as big a fool as I am, perhaps that's why I liked him.

We were photographed under full sail as we cruised past the Hen and Chickens Islands, or was it the Whangarei Heads, no matter, though I could think of a far better name. With Broom on the hard and with backpacks over our shoulders we explored New Zealand, and I spent another memorable birthday in Dunedin. The name taken in part from the cities of Dundee and Edinburgh. While there Dunedin took part in inheriting some of the vilest weather that those fine cities can produce, it rained and rained and then it rained. That afternoon of my birthday we aimlessly wandered around Dunedin, it was raining but I was determined to enjoy myself. I was especially interested in seeing the town square where the statue of Rabbie Burns stood with his back to the kirk and faced the pub. The pub was gone, and not only the pub, all accommodation, the only place that we could lodge for the night was in the local Y.M.C.A.. Not only that, but all the restaurants and eating places were closed. On a certain day in Dunedin summer ends, and regardless how cold it may be cental heating is shut off, until the calendar says, it's winter. The room was freezing.

The ceilings were ten feet high and the windows were wide open. I attempted to move a chair in order to stand on it to close the windows, then realized that the chairs were bolted to the floor. As for food, all was not lost for we had bread and cheese in our backpacks and earlier in the day I had the foresight to purchase a bottle of rum. I had not the foresight to buy a mixer. Nonetheless, we were determined to enjoy ourselves, with a rum and water in hand I proceeded to make the two single beds into one. Except, the beds were also bolted to the floor, what could we do. Marlene sat on one bed while I sat by her side on the floor, we dined on our bread and cheese and drank our rum and water. I can assure you we had no need for ice cubes.

How innocent we were, though it was mainly my fault for I do try to avoid listening to the news, but that one night in Dunedin was enough. The following morning with our packs on our backs we headed down to the railway station to take the first train north, but except for a bored clerk behind his desk there wasn't a soul there, the station did seem very quiet. However, Marlene, smiling confidently approached the ticket desk.

"Two singles to Auckland please."

"Oh," the ticket seller says, "is that what you'd like."

"Yes," suspiciously Marlene answers.

"Oh would you now, have you noticed that it's been raining?"

"Yes," we answer.

"And have you also noticed how quiet it is around here?"

"Yes," we said.

"And you haven't been listening to the news have you now?"

"No" we answer.

"Well" he says, "the reason that I am the only silly bugger here, except for yourselves that is, is that the rail lines have been washed out, it will be days before all is working again, I suggest flying and for tonight going back to your room." With his last remark I bowed my head and loudly groaned, for some odd reason he thought it was all quite funny. I dragged myself back to the Y.M.C.A. having no doubt that the room would be vacant. After two nights in that cold and damp room we got the quickest flight we could get and flew back to the warmth of Auckland.

Chapter 9

I was off once more. Marlene was flying back to Canada and I with crew was heading for Bundaberg, Australia. We got hauled out in Half Moon bay, beside us was another steel sailboat and we became friends with the owners. They had a friend who was quite serious on going offshore, a grandmother, she, her nephew and a young woman became my crew. It was quite a simple agreement I had, they came aboard on a passage from one port to the next, as they all did, buying there food and mine, they could get off any time they liked. I also could ask them to leave any time I liked. We took quite easily to Janice, the grandmother who ended staying aboard with me until I eventually returned to Victoria.

On the morning of our leaving my crew had a going away party at Marsden Wharf. All their relatives and friends were there, and those friends that I too had made were there to see us off. Janice's father came, his blue veined hand grasped firmly on to his walking stick, Janice's arm around his old bony shoulder as she helped him along. I'm not very fond of the word, cute, but I cannot think of a better word to describe how I saw it. That old bugger, well, after all his daughter was a grandmother, had came, as Janet had warned me, to check me out. I'm afraid that I was a bit overwhelmed by it all, though I must have behaved rather well, something I don't always do, for he took my hand and shook it warmly. The young Kiwi lassie's father was there, with tears streaming from his eyes, he knew he would never see his daughter alive again. I really don't know if he did, but she was alive and well when she left Broom.

I left them teary eyed and walked down to the customs office, never recalling tears when I left. I entered the customs office. He sat there with the daily newspaper spread out in front of him, he obviously was very busy. I hated coughing to get his attention for I knew, that he knew, that I was there. It would have been most pleasant to have had an attack of flatulence just then. Eventually he deigned to raise his head. I presented him with the crew list and passports of all aboard and told him that "Broomielaw was leaving for offshore." His reply to that was "Why?" I'm not sure why he said, why. "Didn't anyone tell you that you have to make an appointment to leave." Silly me I thought that they would be quite happy to get rid of me, then he added, "we just can't be everywhere you know." Christ, we were right downtown Auckland. I replied.

"No, I was never told, in any case they're all Kiwis, their having a party right now, their mothers and fathers are there, shedding tears, they think they might never see them again, they're leaving with this mad Scotsman [so I had been told] they're working people, you want them to take another morning off, unpaid, to say good bye, right now there saying good bye." Painfully his eyes fell upon me, then slowly he rose and folded the newspaper that lay displayed in front of him. I sneaked a quick look, no it wasn't job ads, it was cricket scores, he placed it carefully in a drawer of his desk. I did wonder what the other drawers contained. He struggled out of his chair and mournfully walked all the way to where Broom was moored, a good half block, without saying a word.

That first night we left we anchored in Mansion House Bay, in Kawau, where we saw Haley's comet cross the heavens, leaving in its passage a trail of stardust. We too had an easy crossing to Australia, but all we left to mark our passage was that photo that a fellow sailor took of us with Hen Island [?] in the background.

My goodness the crocodiles are big in Australia.

Log: May 3. We found the entrance through the reef then anchored in Burnell River waiting for the tide to change. 2.30 p.m. Moored to Bundaberg Town Tourist Wharf waiting for customs clearance. Cleared customs then on mooring, stumbled and stubbed my toe. Aye, the disasters that await fools like I that venture forth to the deep sea. I lay on the deck feeling so sorry for myself, my poor toe held in my hand, then I stretched my leg hoping that the farther away my toe was the less that I would feel it. Then Janice came along, offshore Janice is great crew, out there we are a unit, she sleeps in the bow and I sleep in the stern, our purpose being to get this boat from here to there, safely. On land all changes, she goes her way and I go mine. But we weren't at sea were we, considerate as ever she came over to see what troubled me and in doing so managed to kick her foot, against my toe. Then said most sincerely. "Are you all right skipper?" I was beyond speech, I simply moaned.

Log: May 14. Today we entertained the members of the yacht club at Boat Harbour in Bowen. While entering the harbour we had ran aground between the markers, which consisted of pilings where the yachts, bow and stern were moored to, similar as to how it had been in Bundaberg. While in Bundaberg I most wisely had stocked up on their fine Bundaberg rum, which for some unexplainable reason unknown to me, I had not yet uncorked a bottle. On our port side stood the Boat Harbour Yacht Club bar, it was Friday evening and as we became stuck, from the yacht club bar came great guffaws, screams of laughter, and in general, idiotic behavior. I do so like to see people enjoying themselves. However, being the over sensitive gentle and soft spoken timid soul that I am, it's possible that I over reacted for I do believe that what I shouted to my Kiwi crew was. "Look, you bastards, I've got two poles we are going to push ourselves off this fucking sandbar and if we get off I'm opening a bottle of that over proof rum."

It is absolutely amazing what a few well chosen words can do. As we freed ourselves and entered the confines of the harbour, the wharfinger, at least that's who we presumed he was, came staggering down to us from the Yacht Club. He gave us a series of instructions, well, we thought that was what he was doing for none could understand a word he said. He had a great deal of trouble standing for he was constantly losing his footing, he must have spent a great deal of time at sea. He pointed past us. I turned and saw an empty spot between two pilings and gathered from his signaling that was where he wanted us to go. He stood there swaying and blinking as if he was trying to remember something, then he pulled up the sleeve of the nonexistent shirt he was wearing, looked at his wrist, blinked his eyes, then said. "Ish my quitting time I'msh now offsh duty." I was now beginning to understand his manner of speech. "Ifsh you should need me I'll be in ths bar—club—burp." Once more he stood there swaying, his eyes blinking as if again trying to remember, then he staggered up a rather circuitous path back to the pub. It is probably quite unfair of me to say this, but the condition that he was in implied to me that he had been offsh duty for quite a while, and for him seeming as if trying to remember, is it possible that he heard me cry? "Over proof rum."

Next morning. I have had my two cups of coffee, and no sooner had I downed them than nature called. I jumped into the dinghy and rowed to the yacht club to enjoy the sublime pleasure of a flush toilet. I remember it all quite well. Moored the dinghy to the wharf, sauntered into the immaculate empty washroom, entered a toilet stall, closed the door, dropped my shorts and sat on the toilet. Finished what nature had strongly suggested that I should do, cleansed my exterior, then stood up and threw my well used toilet paper into the bowl and flushed. Perhaps there's a habit that we all do as we throw our used toilet paper in to the toilet bowl, we give the toilet paper a casual glance to ensure that we are clean enough, then we dispose of it into the bowl, flush. No problem. Except, except, what was that, that caught my eye as I threw the paper into the bowl and flushed. Thinking that it was all in my imagination, I zipped up my fly and while doing so gave another glance in to the toilet bowl, as I once again flushed.

Funny thing about us humans, the things we believe in, the last few years angels have become quite trendy. Humans they were once, now they're only part human with wings sticking out of their shoulder blades. As far as I have read they are at least nine different classes of them, they come in all shapes and sizes. The seraphim are six winged but the cherubim have only got four, but they have four faces and not only that millions of angels can sit on a pinhead, but all that is far too much for my limited mind to handle. Some people even believe that they have their own special angel, that will protect them from all sorts of nasty unpleasant things, like running aground on a Friday night in front of a yacht club. I on the other hand being a fool can not for the life of me, or death for that matter, believe in angels, not only that but I also was having a hard time believing what my eyes were telling me.

For there was I kneeling, with my head almost in the toilet bowl, my senses null, my mind unbelieving, my eyes wide open, attempting to absorb what lay before my sight as I, flushed. I am quite sure that it is quite possible that I may have used up the Boat harbour yacht club supply of fresh water that morning of May 15, 1986. Had a native been watching me, it would have been quite reasonable for them to reach certain conclusions, and that what I was doing while I knelt so seriously before the toilet bowl was that I was paying homage to the toad, that had made a home under the upper lip of the toilet bowl. Who with every flush of the toilet popped out and like greased lightning jumped back up, to his clean and cozy dwelling under the lip. Could you imagine the response of a sophisticated woman, when they realized that under that lip of the toilet bowl, within inches of her defenseless buttocks, lived a great big horny toad, with warts. Needless to say, I could not wait to get back aboard Broom and tell all aboard of my amazing discovery.

Came back aboard and there was Greg, Janice's nephew, fine handsome lad he was, he reminded me so much of Cary Grant. Though he was I'm sure, too young to have any knowledge of, or been remotely interested in Cary Grant. However, his mother would have. He had this mannerism of slightly turning his head, and leaning back and saying something with that Kiwi accent that he had that came across your ears as English. Words that sounded deeply profound, but weren't. I'm quite sure he had already broken a few young female hearts. He was quite ready to take the dinghy and go ashore, have a shower and wash his favourite tee shirt. It was all salt stained. It was black and printed on it in big letters, was "PHUK THE PHANTOM" nice young lad he was. I told him everything that I had seen, and he slightly turning his head and again leaning back said. "Actually, actually, that is not too uncommon in New South Wales." I swear his mother had been quite friendly with Cary Grant.

While in Cairns I aimlessly wandered the town and came upon a brand splashy new, what is it they call it here? 'Flash', Casino, which quite surprised me for my timing was exact, it was their opening night, well polished and long-bodied limos were driving up and dropping of well dressed mirthless people. At the marble stepped entrance to the foyer, two immaculate white enameled and gold braided men were opening vehicle doors. I went up two of those steps, stopped and looked down at my feet. They were bound in sandals, the kind that you can find almost anywhere in the world, made out of old truck tires. My eyes rose to my well tanned hairy legs and my knobby knees, that now had spots on them from what I had just done earlier, an oil change. Dwelt briefly on the safety pin on the fly of my shorts that had a tendency to do the unexpected. I quickly pulled my tee shirt down. I casually stood erect and turning, pulled the brow of my beaten up straw hat down to shield my eyes from the tropic brightness of the hot sun. Yes, I was quite fond of my hat, I had bought it in a little Chinese shop in Suva. There was a small stack of them there, this one stood separate, with a sign on it that said, 'Specal discunt.' It fitted me perfectly, though there was a neatly gnawed hole in the brow. The old Chinese store owner approached me with his hands clasped together, bowed and said, 'Wentilation.' I calmly surveyed my surroundings, still ensuring that my safety pin was out of sight. I was in no hurry, why I could do anything I liked. Why I could go in the casino and check it out, couldn't I ? Thought better and wandered back to Broom.

We carried on through the Torres Straits, riding on the huge swells that were racing up behind us. Two days later we were anchored in front of the yacht club in Darwin. Now, I have to say this about the Aussie customs officers, coming and going, what a pleasant group to deal with. While there I realized that the Australian Operatic society was staging H.M.S Pinafore, my good crew were not familiar with the works of Gilbert and Sullivan, I, on the other hand am an avid enthusiast. I drooled.

That evening before supper I entertained them with a few of the songs from H.M.S Pinafore. I was the cook that night and there is a photograph of me singing while waving a cleaver in the air, perhaps that's why Greg decided not to join us.

A jovial rehearsal for H.M.S. Pinafore.

However, all had been amusing enough for Janice to join me in going to the theatre. The bus arrived at the theatre early and though the doors were open there wasn't a soul in sight. We entered into a large hallway, at either end of the hallway was a grand curving stairway rising to an upper floor, at the bottom of both those stairways were bars. Displayed on the bar counters were wine glasses and casks of wine, open. I took the liberty of offering Janice a glass of wine, she accepted, there are times when I'm really quite generous. When we finished that glass we still had the place to ourselves so we sauntered over to the other bar to check out what they had to offer, and there we had a glass of this and were having a glass of that, when a young neatly dressed man appeared, the bartender.

He smiles, "G'day mates, already for the show." I returned his greeting then added, "We've helped ourselves to a glass of wine, I'll pay you for it," I reached into my pocket. "Forget it mate" he says, "here have another one, no one's watching." We thoroughly enjoyed the performance, for some strange reason we were in the right frame of mind, also, and I'm not at all sure why, but I rather take to the Ozzies. While there we were also entertained by the Essendon Police Women's Band they were hilarious.

Yet, let us not forget the Australian aboriginal, their thin spectral bodies, their cement dusted figures. Early that day as I wandered downtown I had passed them, then I realized that I had, for they were almost invisible. While there an aerial display was put on by a female stunt pilot in a biplane, come to think of it I had a great time in Darwin, sure beats Papeete. Greg left us there and somehow we acquired another crew, Angela a young lass from Tasmania. My passage was Darwin to Durban, I had charts for the major ports but little else. Yes, I was searching, though I never knew what for except I knew I would never find it in nooks and crannies, but felt that I would, in the wide open sea. Needless to say, eventually I did.

Aye, cranny, that narrow street that I spent my childhood in, where the sun seldom shone and that was lined on either side by black soot covered tenement buildings. A dull black cavern where a bird never sang or a plant dare take root. By the time I was fourteen years old I was working full time, then all too soon I was immersed in a cavern of another kind. Caged in by the harshness of severe factory walls and though the roof was lined with glass skylights, they were well blackened by the soot from countless coal fires. Still, there was something that helped to remove myself from the drear, and that was the weak sun that challenged the smog filled sky and shone hesitantly, through a broken glass pane.

As I grew older I worked alone, and my eye would wander to that one particular well sooted broken pane and notice how the beam of light that shone through the crack would settle on the factory floor, and as the day and the season changed so the light would move. Occasionally I would raise my eyes from my chore and seek that beam that had journeyed through the crack, and my eye would happily travel down that sunlit ray that was free from the dull and lifeless black that I felt surrounded by, and my foolish eyes would pleasure in the ray as it settled so warmly on the wooden block factory floor. How pleased I was when I discovered the range of the light, and could pinpoint where the light would land three days before Christmas, and where it would settle just past the middle of June, and there was I, marking the spots with nails driven into the wooden blocked floor. I never knew what my simple discovery meant, or did I know what it was called, and that what I had found on that old factory floor, was Winter and Summer Solstice.

As to my childhood, what ignorant, innocent idiots we were, those companions of mine. There was no pocket money in those days, well certainly not for me, the first earned money that I had I gave to my stepmother who in turn took the money then gave me a small allowance. With that money jingling in my pocket I went to an afternoon movie in the Gorbals Theatre, the first and last time. The place was packed with screaming kids that ran wildly up and down the aisles, fighting and crawling under the seats, no attempt being made by the ushers to control them, not that I blame them. Their parents who no doubt had more money to waste than my stepmother, my father having passed away several years earlier, were happily sitting in the pub next door quaffing a few ales while the Gorbals Theatre did their baby sitting for them.

However, I came from different family circumstance entirely. I had bought my ticket and though I may hate myself for remembering the movie. 'A Night at Earl Carroll's Varieties' an incredibly stupid show for anyone to suffer through, but I had paid my money and had no intention of walking out and feeling that I had wasted it, and in any case there were the cartoons. And that is when the screaming and fighting stopped, for when the cartoons started silence ensued, though being broken by fits of laughter. Then the high light of the afternoon's entertainment, 'The Three Stooges', not a sound could be heard in the theatre as the audience now sat with rapt attention. Aye, well I remember that scene of the three stooges milking a cow, one of them put a milk bucket under the cow's udder's, then another of them yanked the cow's tail up and down. Poor ignorant buggers we were, for no one laughed, including myself, there could have been those among us who had actually seen a cow, but none had ever seen one being milked.

Chapter 10

Awoke before daybreak to that wonderful sound of whales as they blow, and half awake I remember that that's the sound that my good wife makes when she is in a deep sleep, she blows air from her pursed lips. I snore, she blows. Smiling I went on deck and there they were, alternately sinking and surfacing, their huge graceful gleaming bodies sliding effortlessly through the still dark water. You could hear them breathe, and as they exhaled geysers of steaming spray issued from their lungs. There was something gentle and non aggressive about those leviathans of the sea that so calmly cruised by Broom, like a family gathering of cetaceans wandering over to see what this other odd quiet creature was. I stood admiring them then the eastern sky slowly brightened and the shades of black and gray began to fade, and colour bloomed. Then the awakened sun aroused the wind, and the sails gently filled, and Broom answering to the wind's call listed to leeward and the laughter of the sea against the hull could be heard. And the whales lost all interest.

Log: Aug. 11. Had a glorious sail along the coast of Mauritius. Angela, enthusiastic about our landfall brought up her bottle of rum and offered me a drink, the fool that I am I accepted. My attempt to find the entrance to Port Louis Harbour was a total flop, and at the grand speed of two knots we found ourselves on a reef. I wasn't too upset, after all I had a couple of rums in me. I had been suspicious of our position, hence the slow speed, it was beginning to get dark, and now there wasn't a breath of wind. I reasoned that it would be better to wait for morning light then I would lay out anchors and kedge ourselves off, there was one thing however that I hadn't allowed for, a full moon. In the morning, to my utter shock I found that we were now a foot and a half out of the water. We unshipped the dinghy and laid out two anchors and attempted to haul ourselves off but we couldn't budge her. I had felt it was hopeless but worth a try. What do we now do? Wait until the next full moon?

One of the local native boats seeing us came alongside us, a canoe about twenty feet long, five young men in it, powered by a 7.5 h.p. outboard motor. They offered to help us, they would tow us off the reef.

"Well, that's very kind of you," I answered, "and what are you going to tow us off with?" The spokesman for the group stood up and looking indignantly at me pointed down at the canoe and said. "With this." It was probably impolite of me but I started to laugh.

"You're going to tow a 12 ton boat that's aground two feet with a 7.5 h.p. outboard?"

"Yes." Obviously in their eyes this vessel that they had was big, they were very confident.

"Go ahead," I said. Then the spokesman with his forefinger pointing to the heavens said, "$1000 in advance."

He was really quite gifted this spokesman, his finger pointing to heaven like that. For not only would heaven have to have a hand in helping them haul Broom of the reef, it would also have to have a hand in me giving them $1000 in advance. My gentle and cultured Gorbals upbringing however came to the fore. I leaned down to the young man's charming face and said. "In advance?" He smiled, his forefinger once again pointing heavenwards, answered "Yes." In that poor country with the $1000 shared among then they would have been kings. I left them with their pipe dreams while Angela bargained, later they left but told Angela they would be coming back. They did. This time with an old man sitting at the bow, they spoke in their own tongue as they motored slowly around Broom, while the old man carefully inspected the hull, then they returned alongside. The young man who had elected himself in charge spoke. "We can get you off the reef." I smiled and asked. "How?" He spoke in their native tongue to the old man, the old man answered, then the young man turned to me, "he has a secret." "A secret what?" I asked. He again turned to the old man and exchanged words, with an exasperated look on his face he once more turned to me. "A secret way to get you off the reef."

"I see, and this secret way will cost me $1000 in advance to find out." He beamed at me, at last he understands me he thought. I gathered from the look on his face that he thought the deal was made. "Tell your old friend that I appreciate his kind offer of assistance, but to pay a $1000 for a secret, I don't think so." I turned and left them.

There was nothing else I could do, was there? I would have to speak into that idiot box and contact the harbour authorities and tell them that I was on the reef. I began to wonder what I would have done had I been alone, how long would I have to wait? How would the weather be until then? I have been so self reliant all my life, dammit, I hate asking anybody for help, but this time I had to, hadn't I. Rejecting my pride I called the harbour authorities, they wasted no time at all in sending a tug out. Angela and I were out in the dinghy hauling up my kedges when it came roaring up, it stopped about a mile away. This skipper wasn't taking any chances, then its runabout came out to Broom hauling a hawser behind it. When Angela and I got back aboard they were sitting waiting for us. I dropped their hawser over my anchor bollard and no sooner had I done that than the tug was hauling us, and sent me rushing to the V.H.F. not at all hesitant, screaming at them. "Not that way you silly bastards you're hauling me over the reef—this way." My mouth buried in that cursed microphone, my arm outstretched pointing in a ninety degree angle to the direction that they were hauling us, showing that idiot skipper the proper direction. To no avail. Broom climbed over one rock, clatter bang, thud, splash then onto another until she was in deep water, then as she zoomed ahead and slack came upon their line I took the bloody hawser off and threw it over the side, and told that bloody idiot skipper what I thought of him.

Aye, that is exactly how it was. In my dropping kedges to haul ourselves off I had inspected where we sat on the reef, we had only ran on it five feet or so, the passage to get off providing we held the reverse course was easy and clear, anywhere else could have been a disaster, and had I not built in steel, no, not fibreglass, not ferrocement, not wood, not aluminum, but steel. Broom would have been a disaster. The skipper of the tug obviously had no knowledge of the reef or where we sat on it, unless, no, it couldn't be possible, could it? That he was related to the old man. At least they never charged me for the haul. We followed the tug in to Port Louis and they showed us where to tie up and left. Officials were waiting for us but clearing in was all very casual. Directly in front of us were two yachts, one, moored as we were, the other on land, both had police guards. The one on land had also been hauled off the reef, they had found it loaded with drugs. The one directly ahead of us, with the grand title, 'The Nautical Gypsy' had came in to port with two dead bodies, the skipper had shot them and put their bodies into sail bags, we heard more about that story later when we reached Durban, meanwhile, we were in such good company.

That evening I wandered the streets that surrounded the harbour of Port Louis, through dimly lit cobbled lanes lined with low and solidly built buildings built to sustain cannon fire from a time long gone. Dark alleys lined with dismal warehouses shuttered with heavily barred oaken doors that once had held supplies for all the ships that had thronged the harbour, all lay still and dormant. Groups of men hung here and there in the shadows, the glow of their cigarettes showing their presence, not a woman in sight, their murmuring ceasing as I, attempting to appear casual, strolled past. How did Janice, more, how did young Angela handle this, for they were already off wandering, for a woman alone in those streets in the evening could easily be thought of as a certain kind.

Near where we were moored was a large catamaran, a charter yacht, the skipper asked us aboard for a drink, being that I'm quite fond of a glass I didn't refuse. But one drink aboard was enough, he was one of those that you meet, then wished you hadn't. I never stayed long enough, nor was I interested in finding out his nationality, he was white and his crew were all black. One of his black crew served us drinks and while he did so the skipper lifted his eyes to him and said. "When I was up the Congo I slaughtered hundreds of you black bastards." His servant merely smiled, he had probably heard it a hundred times before, but I hadn't and who was he trying to impress? Not I, though he was talking to me, but his eyes were on young Angela. There was a smell of pot in the air and I knew that Angela had enjoyed a joint. I, though having never smoked, tried pot once, and felt that smoke was issuing from every orifice of my body. I wonder how Toad of Toilet Bowl Manor would have enjoyed that. Thankfully, Angela had better sense and left him to his pipe dreams. He was one of those men that I would not have been surprised to hear that his body had been found floating in some harbour, with a deep knife wound in his back.

Log: Sept. 17, 10.30: p.m. Lay ahull for the night off Umhlanga Light, slept for five hours then at 3.30 a.m., hauled sail for Durban. It is always interesting at sea when you get within radio contact of countries, that is, if they speak English. I've never been very good at remembering jokes but one that I enjoy is the one I heard on that radio that night as we lay waiting for daylight. It was being told by a South African doctor and though I wasn't sick, it was the best medicine that I could have had. The doctor had visited a seriously ill patient and said to him. "I have bad news and good news for you, which would you prefer to hear first?" "Oh God," the patient answered, "tell me the good news first." "Well," the doctor said, "you have twenty four hours to live." "Christ, if that's the good news what the hell is the bad news?" "I forgot to tell you yesterday."

Chapter 11

We entered the entrance to the Durban harbour at 7. 30a.m, escorted by the Harbour Police vessel who delivered us to the international jetty at Durban Yacht Club. We were the first offshore yacht in for the season and as at that time sanctions were in force against South Africa's apartheid policies, few yachts were arriving. We were most warmly welcomed, what a difference from Tahiti. The formalities, and those were, asking me to sign a paper stating that we had no socialistic material aboard, if they had only checked my book shelves. Clearing with customs and the port doctor was most pleasant. The commodore of the yacht club came down and invited me to the bar of the Yacht club where I was plied with beer and meat pies, quite enjoyable. Tahiti had been high on my list to see, Africa mainly because of their political system had been at the bottom, overnight all had changed.

The Afrikaners were charming and polite, although there were those, like the woman who told me that the poor blacks can't help being like that, it was not their fault that they were born lower on the evolutionary scale. I cringed. There had been, and probably still were those in the U.K. who thought because of my accent that I too was lower on the evolutionary scale. I have met those of my own age, and with the same accent as I, that have adopted, that is when they remember, an English manner and idiom in their speech. While there I met a white female university professor who would only teach at black universities. I asked her was there much difference between the white and the black universities, she answered.

"There's a large difference, the blacks have so little, that is why I teach there." She had no use for the sanctions that were being imposed on South Africa. "What does someone from London or New York know about our problems, it is South Africa's problem and it will take time but we will solve them." She told me of two black teachers who worked under her, each well educated, each from a different tribe, and because of tribal laws, neither would talk to the other. If they wished to communicate with one another they did it through her. "How do you easily correct a situation like that? It will take generations before South Africa will rid itself of its problems but we are well aware of what they are, far more than some foreigner who has never thought of coming to South Africa."

Aye, she was a grand Afrikaner that one, no hesitation on speaking her mind, no stumbling for words, no pussyfooting around, the kind of folk you either like or dislike. I may not have believed in their political system, but I liked them. However, there was one problem that they seemed to have in common, that is except for the few, such as the female university professor, they were blind to the black poor that begged or sold crafts on the streets of downtown Durban. We have become used to the sight of people begging in the cities of Canada. In downtown Victoria, B.C. you will find them young and healthy, with a few old alcoholics thrown in sitting on the sidewalks with their hands out. But the black poor that you found on the sidewalks in Durban were not like that at all, they had arms or legs missing, or were blind. There was one that I would pass, a man of my own age, leg less, selling rough wooden carvings. I'm quite ashamed to say that I never bought one. Yet when I looked in to his eyes, I thought, only by the sheer happenstance of life, that could be me.

I had moored to the end of the wharf to allow myself an easy retreat, a few days later an American yacht arrived and moored in front me, the owners were two rather snobby American school teachers. I quickly found that I had nothing in common with them and we wisely left each other alone. The next yacht that appeared, yes, I did eye it rather closely was surprisingly another Gazelle. Yes, the same design as my own, on which I had added my own alterations. I, of course was looking at the hull and rig but my neighbours were looking at something entirely different, their behaviour made me feel sure that the sky was falling. "He's not rafting up to us" they said, as they cackled and clucked strutting back and forth on the wharf. I wondered what the fuss was all about, and so I asked what was it that that bothered them. "His fenders," they said, "they'll leave dirty marks on our hull!" I had never thought to look at them, but as I looked, I realized what they were, old automobile tires, bloody great I thought if it keeps snobby bastards like them away from me I'll also get them, only to find that in my search they were not to be had, and when I asked why? That was when I found out what rubber necklaces are, I would rather not have known. Pulled down around the shoulders and arms of helpless souls that disagreed with whatever events that may have taken place, gasoline poured upon them and set alight. Aye, what noble creatures we humans are—that are created in God's image.

While in Durban I had Broom hauled out to inspect the hull, not a dent in the hull anywhere. I met many good hearted people there, perhaps it was the Canadian flag and displayed below it Scotland's Rampant lion that brought them down. Among them was a handsome couple who were just opening a clothing store in a brand new shopping mall, they invited me to their opening, and, as they said there would be wine and tasty edibles, I was not about to refuse. He was a charming man, pure white South African and was obviously very much in love with his remarkably beautiful wife. I would have been too if she had given me half a chance. Her poise, manner, her natural grace, the colour of her skin conveyed to me that she was part Zulu.

Sailed over Gratton Seamount hoping to gain from a current and caught a swordfish. It hung, its tail sweeping the deck as my vessel danced with the seas.

I'm not at all fond of shopping malls, but I was not about to miss out on this. Whatever it was that I expected to see this was not it, for the mall certainly surpassed anything that I had seen elsewhere. In the lobby was a fully rigged offshore sailboat leaning to leeward under full sail, overhead, hanging from the ceiling a biplane from World War I and entertainment galore. As to be expected my new found friends store was all hustle and bustle, I ate and drank and wished them well, and wandered here and there, then came across this great grocery store, now that's the kind of shopping I don't mind doing. I had ventured to the top floor when I heard the sound of a marching band, then realized that directly below me was a large court yard. I looked down in time to see a group of bonnie lassies marching in, twirling batons and raising their full fleshed white thighs upwards to the sky, their long blonde hair neatly tied flourished behind them like golden banners. I can honestly say after a time at sea how wonderful it is to hear and see sights such as that. But it was the next sight that really got to me, a prime example of the sheer contrariness of the human creature. For I heard a drum beat, and realizing that it was coming from the other end of the courtyard wandered over and looked down. Older male Zulu's were beating leopard skinned drums while young loin clothed lads with spears in hand, danced, while threatening an imaginary enemy. In the back ground healthy big breasted mothers clad in Zulu clothing egged on their sons. I loved it, what a contrast it was from the over costumed drum majorettes that implied to me not so much of South Africa, but more of the U.S.A.. Yet my ever straying eyes had not seen all, for as I was about to turn away I noticed a far lovelier sight, facing the young lads was a group of young bare breasted Zulu maids, their bodies and breasts swaying to the beat, dancing gracefully to that rhythmic, almost hypnotic sound, and perhaps in a different fashion, egging on the young lads. Aye, I can assuredly say which group my heart went out to.

I had a months free moorage at the international jetty situated right down town Durban and a free membership in the Durban Yacht Club [highly unlikely to get either in Victoria] that had that luxury that all salt stained sailors dream of, hot fresh water showers. They also have a wonderful display of news paper clippings and framed photographs telling you of all the shipwrecks, terrors, and disasters that await you as you make your passage south to Cape Town. The Cape Alghaus current that runs south west to Cape Town has been known to exceed 8 knots, it is also known that within that area they have southerly gales, when, on meeting the opposing current of water cause tremendous seas.

During my time in port I had met a female friend of the port doctor, she was kind enough to drive me around and show me the sights of Durban. She was as direct as the Afrikaners that I had met, and also extremely forthright, bosom wise. One late afternoon she brought over this old friend who had sailed to Cape Town numerous times down to see me. His face rough hewn seemed to have emerged from an old cedar log that a gifted artisan with a chain saw had unknowingly created, a hat rakishly tipped to one side, a gray beard, a hand grizzled like a bear he offered. I grasped it warmly, I offered him a drink, he accepted it, and it disappeared, vanished, he thanked me. Except for thanking me he hadn't said one bloody word. When he had came aboard his eyes had danced everywhere. I had no doubt that she had told him that I had built my boat and that he was looking at my workmanship with a seamanship eye. I filled my own glass and sat in my favourite position with my feet up, drank from my glass and never made a sound. That old rough hewn Boer's aura filled the cabin. Aye, his face might have been crafted by an artisan with a chain saw but his ice blue eyes were the work of a skilled diamond cutter. His eyes surveyed the main cabin, then rested on me. I smiled and refilled his glass and waited.

He spoke and told me of the passages that he had made up and down that coast, the moment his glass was empty I refilled it, and topped up my own. I had forgotten about his bosomy friend. When I said his aura filled the cabin I meant it, apart from introducing me she had said nothing, and I too quickly found myself speaking as little as possible. Of course I knew what he was doing. He was measuring me, weighing me, sizing me. In doing so he was deciding whether or not he could relate to me, or I to him. When I had refilled his glass he had smiled, then as he began to speak his eyes wandered and I had the distinct feeling that he was back once more in those seas that he had once challenged. Feeling again the wind whipped spray on his cheeks, eyeing the dolphins leaping in the bow wave and the sublime glory of the albatross as it soared overhead. Aye, and now that I'm so much older and also have experienced that, how well I understand, and as he saw the past before him his spoken words came from the heart.

His words were of the weather, of the gales, and of the seas on that passage to Cape Town. I listened avidly to all he said. I've often thought about that old bastard, he could have been twenty years older than I was, no pretensions about this man, there was no way this old bugger would hide his Afrikaner accent, no attempt to put on airs, what you see was what you got. Openly, honestly and sincerely. God, he was an admirable old bugger. I've met enough of those who rate a man's stature by his accent, his education, his money. Here was a man who gave little thought to either, he had lived his life fully, had no regrets, and was quite capable of expressing his thoughts and feelings in an articulate manner. His advice was remarkably short and simple, and I remembered it, and the water spouts.

Log: Oct. 30. We were twenty miles offshore from East London, barometer read 30.05 inches, slowly falling, wind Force 4 NE. clear skies. By noon the barometer had dropped to 28.4 inches, wind increased to Force 5 NE. And there was I standing in shock looking at my compass needle, as it slowly went round and round in circles. I gazed intently at it, it had now stopped circling, no it hadn't it, it was going around circles in the opposite direction. I had no idea what to make of it, what if it should continue like that? I raised my head and there on the distant horizon were—water spouts. I had no thoughts at all on what was happening with the compass needle, but I recalled the words of the old Afrikaner and I reckoned what was likely to take place. The sails fluttered, then all to soon they hung slack. I looked at the compass needle it was still spinning merrily. Then suddenly we were surrounded by the water spouts and the wind hit us. I did as he had advised, turned tail and headed for the shelter of East London.

Log: Nov. 13. We entered Cape Town harbour at 7:0 a.m. The single handed around the world yacht race was on and the entrants and their yachts were mooring across the harbour from us. Hordes of volunteers and well-wishers stood waiting for a racing yacht to appear. They never noticed us. We moored, and later I shopped, returned and went aboard Broom, lit the stove, placed on it a pot with two cups of water and a cup of rice, opened a can of diced tomatoes, a can of meat balls and gravy, put that old beat up Mozart tape of mine on, cracked open that cheap bottle of wine that I had bought, thought of those single handed hero's and their yachts, and, where did I fit in, if at all. Then thought once more of that old Afrikaner, how I would have loved to have heard what his comments would be, on the other hand, I only bought one bottle.

Log: Nov. 18. Cleared customs and left Cape Town with Janice being my only crew. Log: Dec. 6. At 5.0: a.m. we sight St. Helena of the starboard bow, by 6.0 p.m. we were anchored off the jetty in Jamestown, St. James Bay. The anchorage is not at all good, being too deep and giving little protection, there was also the problem of landing your dinghy. There was an old stone wharf that had a series of steps leading down into the sea, those were the same steps that Napoleon had clambered up, again I was in good company. At the top of the steps was a gibbet like structure from which hung a block and tackle and hook, their purpose being to haul your dinghy out of the sea. A constant swell sloshed up and down those steps, and in order to get ashore you first had to fend off your dinghy, then jump out and dash up the steps and grab the hook, then dash back down the steps with hook in hand. Attach the hook to your dinghy and haul it out of the sea and on to the old stone wharf—nae bother. Especially if you're young and agile, which I wasn't. We managed. The port doctor and the custom official were pleasant, the people friendly. It was an interesting quaint old town though there was little there for the young to do.

Went to a dance, 'The Dance of the Bottlecork's' so I named it. It was mostly an older crowd, those well past fifty and many passing sixty, outside and gathered around the windows and peering in were all the younger folk. The women were built alike as peas in a pod, though in this case they reminded me of inverted bottle corks. It was like something out of Alice in Wonderland, the musicians wearing an older style of dress, playing with musical instruments that came from another era, even the music they played came from a long gone past but most especially it was the women. Old corks that's how they appeared, extracted from jugs of red wine and turned upside down and with arms reaching out from their tapered bodies they wrapped themselves around one another, and those appealing old corks danced gracefully around that floor in that old hall, while the musicians with their ancient instruments played a minuet. There was something very pleasant about it.

Dec. 8, hauled sail and cleared James Bay. I had charted a course over Gratton Seamount hoping to gain some advantage from any current that may be there, and realizing that we were over a sea mount, decided to troll a line. I caught a swordfish, he or she was as tall as I was, not counting the sword. It was easy to measure for the only way I could haul the poor bugger aboard was to drop the mainsail and use its winch. The swordfish hung, its tail slowly dragging back and forth, sweeping the deck as my vessel danced with the seas. But that pleasing stage of my mind didn't last long for this creature was far healthier and fitter than I am, yet I invaded his domain and killed him for what, a few pounds of his flesh. And so I sliced a few pounds of his flesh, then removed his sword and the curvature of the skull that surrounded his eyes, the rest went over board to feed smaller fish. Later when I caught another and realized that it was as big, I cut the line.

Chapter 12

Log: Jan 17, 1987. 1.30: a.m. Lying ahull of Needham Pt. Barbados, the quietude broken by the roar of a passenger jet circling the airport. At 4.00: a.m. we are approached by the harbour police boat and escorted into the customs wharf. We were moored to that uncomfortable wharf for five hours, one reason being that I had air in my diesel supply line and I couldn't find out why. The other, that I expected the customs officers to descend on me, after all they knew where I was, but no. I had to go and find them. To make it even worse, I found that their office was only two hundred feet away. Eventually we cleared customs and headed for Carlisle Bay, and again the engine was not at all happy. Between trying to keep the engine running and tacking back and forth in order to sail in to the anchorage, I had little use for the power boat that came roaring alongside. There were two teenagers in it, they were telling me that the Harbour master wanted to speak to me and that I should switch on the V.H.F. Well, I'm not at all fond of using the damn thing so I ignored them, but the buggers kept insisting so I switched it on. The Harbour Master then told me that my wife had just been in the office looking for me. I tell him he must have made a mistake, he assures me that it was my wife, I don't think so I said, but I thanked him and hung up. We were now almost close enough to the beach to drop the hook. I looked for a clearing between the yachts then noticed someone on the beach waving, being curious I picked up my binoculars, shit, I couldn't believe my eyes—it was Marlene. Later she told me that she had been on the jet that we had saw preparing to land, and me getting to that beach, why that was the quickest dinghy ride I ever made. We hugged each other then one of the locals strolling by said to us. "Shouldn't you two get a room?"

Log: Jan. 28. With Marlene aboard our first stop was Bequia where we anchored in Admiralty Bay and where I managed to get our prop tangled by our dinghy line. I dove over the side and freed the line but the prop having variable pitch was seized. While there Marlene and Janice visited an old whaling village, there was a ceremony taking place, it had to do with bringing the whales back, so, I suppose, that they could slaughter them once again. During the walk they met some cute little coloured girls all dressed in white, the little girls asked them for money. They never gave them any, the little girls unhappy about that told them to go and do something to themselves. Aye, it's true no matter where I go the Gorbals is always with me. Meanwhile, I, as usual sat around scratching my head. The engine of course was unusable, wherever we were going we would have to sail out off and into, on Feb. 3 we cleared customs for Rodney Bay, St. Lucia.

Log: Feb. 9. We sailed into Castries Harbour, St. Lucia. The bowsprit was fully operational for we tacked all the way up to the travel lift, we moored and the next day got hauled out. I've always found it interesting that the places that you think would be interesting, are not all what you expected, and those places that you have no interest in going to, are great. I was interested in going to Bequia, afterwards I wondered why, whereas in going to St. Lucia, which I had given little thought to, we enjoyed so well. While there I took the variable propeller apart, dressed it, greased it and reinstalled it, cleaned the hull, slapped some anti-fouling on, the work was over. Now we could enjoy Castries, as usual our first stop was the market place, which I have always found enjoyable. In the basement of the market the meat was as fresh as you can get it, for they slaughtered it before your eyes. Cut into the concrete floor were channels where a combination of blood and water constantly ran. Here everything had to be fresh for they had little refrigeration. Outside of the market were a group bagging and selling charcoal, and that group were as black as one could get, and it wasn't because of the colour of their skin.

Log: Feb. 18. Weighed anchor for Martinque. 2.00 p.m. Anchored in Fort-de-France, and though the French officials were more humane than those in Tahiti, the prices were the same. The taxi stand was alongside the harbour and there the warm stagnant air reeked of urine. Close by I bought a bottle of Martinque Rum, the quality being such that neither Marlene or Janice would drink it, but someone had to. We visited a beach that was packed with French tourists all in various stages of total undress. There were those that were so determined to get a tan, that they lay with their face buried in the sand, their skin the colour of boiled lobsters. Perhaps they had drank, of the vile local rums, whilst the Sun, it scorched, the poor buggers, bare bums.

We sailed that chain of islands until March 12, when we anchored in Groot Baai, Philipsburg, on the island of St. Maarten. I especially remember St Maarten, for two days later it was my birthday and what a contrast it was to my last one in Dunedin. On the day of my birthday Marlene and I heard this wonderful music coming from a bar, always ready to enjoy ourselves we danced in through the entrance and up to the bar. To the utter delight of the entertainer who played a piano and sang, trying to cheer up a crowd of gloomy tourists, he egged us on and we were only too willing to comply. Marlene told him that it was my birthday, he immediately sent us over two black Russians. Until then I had thought that black Russians were Negroid communists. We must have cheered the place up for before us appeared two more black Russians, and yes, two more, coming from the folk around the bar.

We left the way we had entered, this time dancing out of the door. Directly across from where we stood and now lit with flashing neon's was a gambling casino. Taxis were arriving and the elegant elite, or, those who like to think they are, were disembarking. I noticed as they opened the door and stepped out that they were very careful about where they placed their feet, as we came closer and we too stood under those bright lights, I understood. My heart went out to those folk, for, indeed it must be very hard to think of being one of the upper class when you have just squished a cockroach the size of a pregnant mouse under your $200 shoes. Of all the faults that I have gambling is not one of them. Marlene was more interested than I on entering. The well dressed upper class were thronged around the gambling tables, not a smile among them. Their sedate and sophisticated faces carefully eyed what lay on the tables, while sipping on Negroid communists that they paid twice the price of what the bar across the road charged. Considering the condition that I was in I was quite patient watching how the creme-de-creme so solemnly enjoy themselves. Marlene after wandering around the tables went over to one of those one arm bandits, bet .50 cents and lost, after that she came over to me and said. "That's enough, I'm outta here," being the obedient husband that I am, I followed her.

Log: March 15. Weighed anchored 7.30 a.m. I was quite surprised when I read that in my log, considering it was the day after my birthday. March 17. St. Patricks Day. We anchored in Road Harbour, Tortola. Returning from the market the three of us arrived at the roadside bar of the marina, where we had left our dinghy, and there hanging above the entrance was a banner stating, 'For all those wearing green—drinks are half price.' We stopped and eyed each other, none of us were wearing green, then I remembered. I reached into Janice's backpack and withdrew from a cabbage, three leaves. Handed one to each of the ladies and stuck mine behind my ear, we entered and seated ourselves at the bar. On my port side was a young couple from another yacht, anchored in the harbour. Marlene and Janice were quickly in conversation with the folks on the other side. I sat quietly, but not for long.

Aye, they must have waited for one like I for they couldn't wait to tell me of this wonderful recipe that they had just discovered for deep fried canned sardines. Now I like sardines, it was the deep fried part that bothered me. I tried to ignore them and had another ale, but they were not going to ignore me. "You boil the fat" she said, "and don't worry if the last time you used it, it was for french flies." Realizing that she had slurred her speech the young woman giggled, whether it was the smell of the hot fat, the french flies or the ale that had caused the trip of her tongue. I never knew. However, it was not quite noon and the thought of long dead wee fish soaking in boiled oil, did not at all sit well with me, however my hesitancy to listen to their recipe in no way disconcerted them. I had no other choice but to listen. I calmed myself and tried not to hear. Until that time I had never thought of the gentility of my aging stomach, I did then. Afterwards, I asked them if they had ever they tried Martinique Rum, they hadn't. I suggested that the next time they have their deep fried canned sardines simmering in hot fat, to have a good glass of Martinique Rum, it could be just the right companion.

To soothe my senile stomach I quickly took my attention away from them and became very interested in what the bartender was up to. He was fiddling with a little brass cannon that lay a foot away, then he took his eyes to a clock on the wall, it was just about noon. I hadn't the slightest idea of what he was doing. When the second hand reached twelve, he pulled a trigger and that bloody cannon damn near blew my ear drums out. Now, I really am a quiet gentle man, but between those deep fried fat soaked sardines floating around in my gut, and the blast of that idiot cannon ringing in my ears, well, what can I say, except, that a glass or two before noon, even at half price. I'd rather not.

However, it was in Tortola that I heard the story of Nelson's Blood, of course it's true. When Nelson had died they had placed his body in a cask, filled the cask with rum, then sealed the cask. His body now pickled in alcohol would be in a fit state when they returned to England to give it a proper funeral. Very practical I thought, how wise of them. The only problem was, that when they reached England and unloaded the cask they found that a series of holes had been drilled in the bottom of the cask, and the rum had leaked out. I am quite sure that the rum did not go to waste. I just hoped it was not from Martinique.

Log: March 26. We were anchored in Culebra, a small island with an excellent harbour a short distance from Puerto Rico, there was a ferry service that ran back and forth. When we had been anchored in Soper's Hole in the British Virgin Islands, I had been unable to clear my fouled anchor. In the anchorage was another Canadian yacht with diving cylinders on deck, I went over. There was only one aboard, a man a few years older than myself in fit condition. I told him my problem, he was only to willing to help, he ignored his cylinders and with mask, snorkel and flippers came to our rescue. He really didn't have to make it look so easy, for with his head down and his flippers up in the air he dove, then quickly reappeared and told me to ease off on the anchor chain, then he dove once again, came back up and said. "You're free." I mean, I could have done that, if I could have held my breath long enough, and knew what I was doing. He was quite modest when he realized how I felt, he said. "I've been doing that for years." How much should I pay him I thought, for two minutes work, but the ladies looked after that, he was invited for supper and afterwards became a good friend of Janice.

April 1, Marlene has gone, I shall miss her, Janice who can leave any time she wishes to is still aboard. We have cleared customs but the wind has swung to the south, we are entrapped in this bay. Next day the wind changes and we leave.

April 8. It was late afternoon and we were on deck, spread out before Janice was a selection of coloured remnants, pieces of discarded clothing. On her lap was a magazine, the opened page displaying a photograph of the flag of Panama. She held a pair scissors in her hand and was quite happily engrossed in cutting up her old underwear to make a flag. We heard the noise of a plane and on looking up spotted it approaching. It was the U.S Coast Guard, soon it was circling overhead. I think the pilot was trying to tell us something, as always I ignored him, he left and quite soon a Coast Guard cutter appeared on the horizon. Oh dear I thought, I suppose I better put the idiot box on, no sooner had I switched it on then over it came. "Sailing vessel identify yourself."

I gave some thought to that request and never answered, how could I? Then they rephrased it. "Captain of the sailing vessel of our starboard bow identify yourself." Now thought I, I could answer that, I replied. "This is the captain of the sailing vessel whereof you speak, I am six foot tall, blue eyes, my hair is getting rather thin on top, however, I do keep my beard neatly trimmed. I'm actually quite distinguished. I have been informed that I have a slight accent and also that in certain situations I am rather quite charming." Total silence, I'm quite sure that they thought we were smoking pot and sampling the drugs that we had aboard. Then over it came again, "Sailing vessel of our starboard bow identify yourself." I replied.

"This is the sailing vessel Broomielaw, sailing under the Canadian flag, registered in Victoria, B.C." Silence, then came the reply.

"Permission to board your vessel captain."

"By all means, it has become rather boring." The Coast Guard cutter drew close, in minutes a rubber ducky loaded with six well armed young men appeared with an officer at the bow, as they drew close I went forward to grasp their mooring line, the officer with a brush of his hand, dismissed me. I stood aside. They leapt aboard and the officer politely introduced himself and asked to be shown below. I led the way, one of his boarding crew followed. When the three of us were below he turned to me and said, "If you will excuse us, we would rather be alone." I started to chuckle at that and could not help but reply, "I guess you two never get a chance to be alone aboard the cutter." I went back on deck.

Chapter 13

Log: April 12. 11.0 a.m. Anchored in Cristobel harbour, Panama, cleared immigration, however our transit of the canal will not take place until April 23. Here they have a yacht club, which we quickly availed ourselves of, moored the dinghy and as we did so watched the iguanas bury themselves into holes along the sandy shoreline. I wandered downtown, although we were advised not too, muggings had taken place close to the yacht club. I poked my nose into a bar, its confines dark and cool. I stood just inside the doorway, my eyes adjusting themselves to the dark. My pupils slowly responded. In one corner of its sheltered confines were two passed out drunks, and seated at the bar were three young women displaying their fit and healthy thighs, and other gentler parts. They eyed me up and down, voraciously. I returned their gaze, as I too, in turn weighed them, with my blue eyed icy stare, which quickly turned to warm water, my testicles quickly scurrying to where I once wished my toe should be. I let the door swing behind me and returned to the hot sunlight.

Eventually they changed the date of our transit to April 21. I had the unpleasant task of acquiring line handlers, four were required and I being the skipper could not be one, I had to find three others. The locals were volunteering their services for $40 U.S. plus food and drink. Considering how low their wages would be, I thought how generous they were. With help from other crews waiting to go through, and a young Norwegian lass, Angela, who was travelling these parts with a friend, by bicycle, I managed. She told us of the narrow escape that she had with, as she called them, bandidos. Waving a shotgun they had stopped her and her girl friend on the road and made it clear that they had to get off their bicycles and come into the bushes, a car slowed down but when they saw the shotgun they took off. Giving little thought to it, Angela and her friend pedalled like hell. To travel like that she's got more guts than I.

The yachts would be going through in a convoy and on reaching the locks, pairs of yachts were wedded together. Broom was mated with a large expensive fibreglass American yacht, the owner was quite in favour of the match until he discovered, with shock, Broom was built of steel. A look of horror came upon his face, he disappeared and spoke to the pilot. The marriage never took place, instead Broom became engaged to a Swedish vessel, a wooden yacht named Nordstern, the skipper was Swedish and his lady friend Irish, they were not at all concerned about Brooms building material.

Log: June 5. For four days I've sailed, my sextant close at hand, my eyes ever searching the heavens seeking the shy and hidden sun, and yet have not been blessed with a sight. Overhead lead bellied clouds dominate the once blue skies, the sparkling sea has aged and on its tired brow, gray wrinkles, flourish, and like the sun the coy horizon is unseen. We have again struggled through the doldrums, that place on the sea where the winds hibernate and you must have the patience to let them once again arouse. Whistle if you will, but they will pay you little attention, and if they do, you may be regret that they ever did.

Before me lay an odd scene, for it appeared as a low lying island, except that it undulated with the gentle swell of the sea, nearing it I realised what it was. We are slowly sailing towards fields of small sponge like jelly fish, who, absorbing the warmth of the sun sent little curved sails rising gracefully from their gelatine bodies. Their bodies reacting to the warm rays of the sun caused their opaque jellyness to disappear, and their bodies became iridescent and colourful. We were only making two knots and Broom was not cutting a path through them, but merely pushing them gently aside. As they slowly slid past the hull I reached down with the bucket and scooped some out. Instantly their scimitar shaped sails collapsed, their iridescence vanished and they returned to their opaque jelly state. They were, the noted, 'By the wind sailors.' I found them extremely appealing, they were as a mountain meadow flower, its blooming period extremely short and the moment you pick it, it is dead. Unlike flowers on land those blooms of the sea could move, was that what attracted me to them?

Let the sea rage and the wind howl what did they care, they would disappear from the ocean surface and wait the storms out, and when the sea had vented its anger and the wind grew hoarse they would return to the sun blessed calm sea, hoist their little scimitar sail, soak up the warmth of the sun's rays, and like a flower blossom with richness and colour from the sun's warmth and its radiant glow, and come fully alive. Bless the little buggers. What was this metamorphosis that we had sailed through, this sea blessed changing that was taking place? Was it because of the temperature of the water, the upswelling of the oceans depths, the current of the sea, or could it be that in those islands of 'By the wind sailors,' could it be—mating time?

I was coming home from a voyage around the world, and in those full blessed morns, well before the golden sun had yet awoke, my eyes would stray ever eastward, and joyfully I awaited it. Aye, those days, so alive, so brimful of life and energy, while I, well aware that old age was quickly approaching, was yet filled with a remarkable youthfulness. Aye, and the white spume streaked combers as they ran happily alongside my iron steed, how they lifted my imaginings and freely they inspired me. And the blessed pristine air, cleansed by the oceans spray, filtered by the demanding wind, and with it, I filled my lungs. Aye, I celebrated it and how well it pleased me. And as the Sun retires from its brazen voyage and leaves the moon, the planets, the stars, free to travel their resplendent journey across the darkened sky, I, with ever heavy eyelids, admire their brilliance, and bow to their splendour. How I loved those glorious skies, those ever changing heavens, and those incredible seas. It was all so incredibly rich, when I felt so incredibly poor in my ability to put my thoughts to words. Yet, there was more than that, for there were sights and feelings and emotions, that I had never given thought to, that were now only simmering in my mind, and there were words, brewing and waiting to be formed.

We motored slowly through the heavy fog, and the fog in no need to hurry, leisurely rose. We sat dead centre in a circle of clarity that extended around us in a radius of fifty feet, past that, the fog once again blocked our vision. I raised my eyes and the fog hung, suspended, and like a layer of icing on a cake the shimmer of the sun danced on that damp gray blanket that hovered two feet above my head. I reached up and the sight of my hand became ambiguous and ethereal, as if my hand had entered another dimension. The damp chill of that gray cloud slowly entered my fingers tips and drew warmth from my hand. I lowered my arm. The circle that we sat in had increased in diametre, the fog slowly rising was now halfway up the mast. Overhead the heavy dark grayness was disappearing, it was becoming lighter, then hesitantly, unwilling sparkles of light appeared as the moisture in the fog reflected the sunlight. There was a dream like quality to it. I felt incredibly happy.

As the strength of the radio direction signal became stronger I reckoned that we could be within eight miles of Cape Beale. I turned the engine off. Then unexpectedly, as if in answer to a prayer that dew soaken mist that now hovered overhead like a silver cloud, instantly, became translucent with light, and as if it was all just a game and a magician was merely plying his trade, he flicked his wand and the silver veil was gone. And there before our eyes were mountain peaks capped by last winter's snow, a large bay dotted with rocky tree bound islands, serene blue water its colour reflected from the cloud free sky lay calm and still, and Cape Beale light house stood, seven miles away, staunch, secure, poised confidently on a pile of rocks. Barkley Sound lay before us, sublime in all its pristine magnificence and—omnipotent. And I—humble.

Chapter 14

Sept. 2, 1990. I was off again, this time heading down the coast to Mexico, but to me it really didn't matter where I was going, it was as if the sea and I had some unfinished business, for there was a happening, a circumstance that had shyly escaped my searching. There was something out there that I had yet to face, perhaps more so, there was an experience out there that I was needful of, but what was it? And why was I so needful of it? Perhaps there wasn't a large pot boiling in the imaginings of my mind, but there certainly was a shallow pan simmering, there in the cooking-pot scullery of my brain, something as yet ill-definable. What ever it was, part of it had to do with that morning of our glorious landfall at Barkley Sound. Of how my finger tips had seemed to dissolve and fade away as they entered the fog barrier, and the fog as if reacting to my touch, vanished, and how awed I was of the scene that lay naked before my eyes. How awakened I had felt, and for the first time began to conceive the meaning of soul. From that experience, I had become more assured of the path that destiny had directed me to follow. Yes, I had tasted a long time dormant brew that had slowly aged in my mind, and like a devout drunk, I wanted more.

We left Tsheum Harbour in Sidney and anchored off Cadboro Bay then dropped Marlene off and continued sailing to Port Angeles, Washington. In San Diego she would join me and who ever else who might still be aboard. My crew was my good friend Charles, a friend of his, a lady, and a man who was at that time a Turkish friend. We spent the next night moored to the public dock in Port Angeles where we stocked up in diesel fuel, and I stocked up in beverages of the alcoholic variety, and received a U.S cruising permit. That evening I became a hero, yes, I've always wanted to be a hero. I had just poured myself a glass of rum, the salesman that I had purchased it from did not approve, he had called it rot gut, but I had already tasted rot gut, yes, from Martinque, this certainly was far superior. Then I heard the sound of a little girl crying, it troubled me. Stuck my head out the hatch and along the wharf was a wee lass about four years old shedding tears, with her was a woman that could have been her mother, and an older lady, perhaps her grandmother. Emptied my glass then walked down to see what the fuss was about. Her mother was wiping the tears that were running down the little girl's rosy red cheeks. "Is there something wrong?" I asked. The mother never taking her eyes from the child answered. "It's her cat." I looked into the water thinking that the cat may have fell in, then the grandmother spoke, "No, it's on the pilings, under the wharf." Raised my eyes and there it was, a white fur ball clinging to a black tar soaked piling, every now and then giving a plaintive poor-me, meow.

I'm not particularly fond of cats, recalling the smell of the toms who so thoroughly marked their territory in the close of the tenement building of my childhood, remembering when my children were young and we acquired a cat, and the cat gave birth and when I told my work mates they replied, 'just hold their heads in the toilet bowl and drown them.' I thought I could manage that, I did for one. The poor wee bugger struggled for breath under my grip, well, I couldn't take it out half drowned. Or is it the time that I sailed with my daughter and her husband who had just bought a 30 foot sailboat, they snuggled into a berth alongside the engine and I slept in a berth alongside their galley table. They had a cat. I had gave no thought to the cat or to the litter box, or where it might be. They had placed it on the galley table. I awoke in the middle of the night smelling that vile urine smell, then, scratch—scratch, and found myself covered in kitty litter. No, I'm not at all fond of cats.

Went back aboard and lowered the dinghy, and it and I went under the wharf, no, I didn't care if the crabs would be dining on that creature tomorrow or not, but the tears rolling down the cheeks of that wee lass bothered me. Under the wharf I shipped the oars and manhandled my way to that snowy white pussy, by this time the dinghy was covered in streaks of tar and my hands could do with soaking in a gallon of rot gut. I reached for the poor wee creature who hadn't a spot of black anywhere on its white furry crab trap body. Grabbed it by the scruff of its neck, expecting at any moment it would hiss or piss. Got back to the wharf, by this time quite a crowd had gathered, life must be quite exciting in Port Angeles. Again I grabbed that spotless white cat and placed it in the hands of the beaming little girl. Her grandmother leaned down to me and patting my hand, said. "You've made a little girl very happy." I looked at the attractive mother of the little girl, and quietly answered, "I'd rather have made her mother very happy." Went back and tried another glass.

Log: Sept.15. Anchored in Santa Cruz, there my male crew members left ship. Next day we were anchored off the beach in Monterey, where if you are a fan of John Steinbeck is the place to go. Spent the day ashore, next day I was quite willing to weigh anchor and move on, for though I found the sight of pelicans pleasing, the noise and stench of the sea lions was over powering. Log: Sept. 25. We were off Santa Catalina where we watched a U.S Navy helicopter drop an object astern of us in to the ocean, the pilot when he saw us must have reported our position for we were quickly approached by a U.S Navy cutter, who on seeing us warned us, yes, I had to put the V.H.F. on, not to go south or west of our position as we were in an unexploded weapon dumping ground. I checked my chart and that area was marked as. 'No longer used unexploded dumping ground.' So much for that. Following day moored to the Harbour police dock in San Diego. Spent five days at the Police transit dock, there met my ex-Kiwi crew Janice who was sailing with our new found friend Fritz, then Marlene, happily arrived.

We visited much of what there was to see in San Diego then popped down to Tijuana. Walked across the border expecting at any moment to come face to face with well decorated Mexican officials, with bandoleers loaded with gleaming golden cartridges slung over their shoulders. Not so, no one cared, that is, except for the most definitely North American entrepreneur who was sitting at a table selling walking tours in English of how to get to Ensenada. You'd have to be off your head if you couldn't get to Ensenada, the road that led you there was lined with stalls. Behind his table were taxi drivers leaning on their cabs smoking cigarillos, they would drive you there for $5, they were cheaper than the map. But none were as cheap as we, who walked for fifteen minutes and were downtown Tijuana.

We enjoyed San Diego but by Nov. 5, I was ready to move on, but not quite yet. I had found out that local yacht chandlers threw a party for all yachts heading offshore, the party took place when the hurricane season ended, for it was only then that the insurance companies would carry a policy on those yachts. I never carried insurance, but that wasn't to say that I wouldn't join the party, the wine was free.

We sailed happily down the coast of Mexico anchoring where ever our fancy took us. The wind being consistent in doing that which we rather it didn't, for in the early morning it would be soon blowing 25 knots. It would ease its labours in the afternoon and quickly stop by supper time, with little wind during the night. The result was that the seas, never quite knowing what to do, would leave a lumpy sea which left you rocking and rolling.

Log: Nov. 30. Early in the morning we sailed through throngs of rental fishing boats that hovered around the western edge of the tip of Bahia. As we rounded the point we could see yachts anchored in the harbour of Cabo San Lucas, we made our way there to join them. At the entrance to the harbour there is a small sandy bay where birds flocked, just past that it is a jetty, that jetty contains the only fuel dock. A yacht was anchored by the bow directly off the end of the wharf, rolling in the swell, from its stern was another line leading back to the jetty where it was secured to a bollard. A fuel hose was being lowered from the wharf to the stern of the yacht. A line had been tied to the end of the hose which one of the crew of the yacht was trying desperately to grasp in order to pull the hose aboard. I was so glad that my diesel engine merely sipped fuel, and all I had to do was take a five gallon container over by dinghy to have it filled.

By noon we were anchored in that lovely protected little harbour, how pleasant it was, and how different it was when I returned alone on my voyage north, for then they no longer allowed yachts to anchor inside the harbour. They had placed mooring buoys outside the harbour which you could moor to, how nice of them, except it cost you $20 U.S. a night. On my return north I anchored among them and wondered why anyone would want to stay there, for as the evening fell the swell of the sea came in and I spent another uncomfortable, rock and roll night. While in the harbour we took our dinghy over to the fuel dock and had our container filled, then visited that little sandy bay. We had no sooner gone ashore, then, as if waiting for our arrival they landed around us, a flock of vultures. I can assure we were more scared of them than they were of us. There is something eerie about those bare headed creatures who grow red warts where feathers should be. They walked around us, their heads darting here and there but their eyes always dwelling on us. We eyed them suspiciously. I had the distinct feeling that they hoped that at any moment I would have a heart attack, of course they were really quite harmless, then again I never had a heart attack.

Two days later my female crew member boarded another yacht, captained by a lone sailor that we had met on our passage down the coast. Now it was Marlene and I, how liberated I felt. She had little love for the sea, except for admiring it, I wasn't too sure that I was in love with the sea, though I was certainly beguiled by it. When Marlene became uncomfortable with the sea, she would fly home. When I became uncomfortable with home I would haul sail and go to sea, meanwhile, we enjoyed what life had so generously bestowed upon us. We spent Christmas and Boxing Day there, which was our anniversary, then on Dec.27 we weighed anchor and sailed, bound for Puerto Vallarta.

We crossed the Gulf of California in unpleasant weather, that being the reason why we were boarded by fellow travelers. They were most welcome, if only they would clean up the mess they left behind. Our first arrival was a little tern who fluttered about our bow, making a great decision on where to land. Then locating a spot that seemed secure and comfortable, found it, under the jib and close to the anchor winch, and there settled himself in for the night. Our next arrival was a Frigatebird, who with its long forked tail and a wing span of close to eight feet had no intention of landing on deck and wanted a spot where he could keep an eye on things. He chose to roost in the centre of the triatic stay that ran from the top of the mainmast to the top of the foremast. It was most entertaining to watch the determined actions of this creature as he attempted to get hold of the stay. Broom, rocking and rolling in those seas with the tops of the masts in a constant state of agitation, the bird being buffeted by those winds until his patience was exhausted, then with neck outstretched he grabbed the stay firmly in his beak, then getting his claws firmly clasped onto the stay, released his beak, then casually ruffling his feathers as if someone was watching, which we were, settled down for the night. Then two brown boobies landed, one on the dodger over the aft cabin hatch, which he immediately proceeded to defecate on, the other in the middle of the main boom gallows. There, close by our shoulders they perched and ignored us.

The reason that those large birds had received the name boobies was that they were considered not too bright as they were so easy to catch. I quickly doubted that explanation. I had decided that it would be safer heading offshore during the night which meant going on the other tack, however, if I did the boom, that only cleared the gallows by just over six inches would swing over and hit the booby and—send it—flying. Well, I am not about to harm any creature if I can avoid it. I approached it with a towel over my arm and did exactly as Janice and I had once done with a pelican, placed the towel over the birds head and lifted the bird off its perch and placed it nearby its fellow passenger. Then I removed the towel, and that bird, unlike his companion, who ignored all that was happening, screeched vocally at the top of his lungs, then with great indignation fluttered his wings and landed exactly back on his original perch, then with his beak held high in the air, totally disregarded me. "Okay you silly bugger just don't blame me," I said as I spun the wheel, Broom tacked and went on the other course. I stood watching the boom as it swung over, then my eyes wandered to the boobie. The bird was looking straight ahead, standing pompously erect on the gallows, his head stretched out, acting as if it owned Broom and I. As the boom reached him, he slowly crouched down and it passed harmlessly over its body, then he stood erect, and that was when I wondered, which of us is it—that's not too bright.

Log: Dec.29. It had rained in the morning but by noon the skies had cleared and there was a 5-10 knot SE wind that gently sent us on our way. Then the wind picked up and Broom reacting to the wind's song tucked up her skirts, leaned, and danced joyously to that air, we zoomed along. Minutes later my fishing line sang like a well-tuned guitar string and the moisture that had dozed comfortably on it all day, flew. The rubber snubber that I had hooked on the line was stretched to its limits, we were about to have fish for supper. We passed Las Tres Marietas, and as we rounded Pta Mita we lost much of the wind but with the last of the breeze we sailed into anchor. We dined on fresh fish and after a most pleasant night we headed for the comforts of the marina at Nuevo Vallarta. I reckoned we could afford the seven dollars a night.

Log: Jan. 31. Bahia Navidad, spent over a week there and during that time Marlene had met at the telecommunication centre, an Irishman, now an American citizen. Sidney, a man quite a few years older than myself who spoke fluent Spanish and had been a great help to Marlene in her troubles in that office. She had asked him to visit us. Later that day a dinghy from one of our neighbouring yachts came alongside and informed me that there was a doctor trying to get us on the V.H.F. "A doctor?" I said. "Yes" and pointing to shore, said, "that's him waving." Then I remembered Marlene's words. We rowed over to the beach and picked him up, meanwhile knowing that all of the folks on yachts would be wondering why this doctor is visiting us. I had no intention of spoiling their scuttlebutt.

Sidney was a Doctor of Music, one of the oldest tenors in the world to retain his voice, tenors he told me are the first to lose their voices. I have a fondness for sailing in and out of anchorage's, this was a prime morning for that. With Sidney aboard we hoisted the foresail and as Broom began to take up the slack on the anchor chain, we began to haul the loose chain aboard. The clatter of the chain caused heads to appear from the adjoining yachts. Then we started singing, the 'Volga Boat Song.' "Yo ho heave ho—Yo ho heave ho heaving ---, " with the anchor shipped we hauled all sail, "—labour unending onward we're bending toiling toiling—Yo ho heave ho" and with sails bent and slowly drifting past the anchored yachts, we sang. "Hey bonnie boat like a bird on the wing over the sea to Skye, carry the lad that's born to be king over the sea to Skye." By the time we had left the bay, the silly buggers we were, we were damn near in tears. Standing at the bow singing our hearts out, both of us trying desperately to dam the flood from our eyes. There couldn't have been a better day, a better place, a better time for two sentimental old fools to have sung those songs. Each of us far from the place of our birth, he from Dublin and I from Glasgow, there, where we had spent our young manhood, where we had learned the songs and the words, and each of us recalling that time—as we sang. Singing like that as we slowly sailed out of that silent bay, where the only sound that could be heard was our own voices as they echoed back to us from the surrounding hills. Aye, we must have entertained the folks there.

Log: Feb. 7. Anchored in Manzinillo another typical poor coastal Mexican working class town, an extreme contrast to the luxury hotel, Las Hadas, that lay directly across the bay. We anchored off Manzinillo, cleared customs, and wandered through the town, the next day we sailed over to Las Hadas. There we anchored off the beach and rowed our dinghy through the entrance into Las Hadas Private Yacht harbour, that was filled by expensive American yachts. As opulent as the grounds and the pools were, I'm afraid that the dissimilarity between the Haves and the Have nots was a bit too much for me. There had been a movie filmed there, as all that were there were only too willing to tell us, but by the next morning my plebeian ways had got the better of me and we weighed anchor and sailed back to Manzinillo.

We were now heading back north to La Paz, with stops here and there in the places that we had enjoyed on the way down, Bahia Navidad being one. In La Paz Marlene would fly to San Diego, then home, when Marlene was gone I would be heading homeward. With that wonderful wind behind us Broom flew down the harbour into La Paz, leaving all those anchored yachts rocking in our wake. I never had a chance to look at the chart and realize that there was a sandbar in the middle of the harbour. Not that it really mattered, for she ploughed into it and cut a path through it. It slowed us down somewhat which gave me time to notice something rather strange, the wind was directly behind us, but those yachts that we had passed were not facing the wind, their sterns were to the wind and their anchor rodes were stretched out in front. Why, this is all contrary to how it's supposed to be. Yes, it did take me a minute or two to figure out what was going on. Why, it's a river we are anchoring in, a river, and the tide must be going out and the wind is blowing us in, but there it was again, my poor mind being challenged, when I drop the anchor where will Broom eventually sit.

I steered for the roomiest space that I could see and lowered anchor. We waited, the anchor grabbed, we lowered the sails, Broom lost headway and swung with the flow and almost sent her ass burying into this cute little fibreglass sailboat, embellished so prettily in shining brass and polished teak. The kind that you see in yachting magazines with vases of flowers and plate glass mirrors, and a lovely lass wearing a bikini and high heels. I waited, Broom driven with the running tide sheered, I tugged at the anchor rode and freed the anchor, Broom ran with the current. I quickly lowered the anchor, it grabbed. I looked around and gave a sigh of relief, but, how would we be when the tide changed? We waited, the tide changed and all the yachts as if in some orchestrated dance took a different position. We were sitting fine.

Marlene had flown home and I was heading that way. Cabo San Lucas was now closed for anchoring. I dropped the hook between the 20$ U.S. a night mooring buoys. There are so many great places to anchor in Mexico why would anyone want to spend anytime anchored there. Went ashore and stocked up with those supplies that I enjoy and was all too ready to leave. It is the law in Mexico that when an offshore yacht enters a harbour or anchorage where they are Mexican authorities, the yacht must clear in, but by this time I had no intention of doing so. It had been head winds all the way to Cabo, and being a hopeless optimist, expected that those southerly winds would stay after I had rounded the tip of the Baja Peninsula, they did for one day.

Log: May 17. Same strong head winds, same seas, and I've been a total of 160 hours of being hove too. It wasn't so much being hove too that bothered me, it was that the wind and seas were blowing me back. Why, that was like finding out that you had a hole in your pocket and all your hard earned money was falling out. Then I recalled an article by an American naval designer, he had an idea that sounded quite plausible. His concept was basically, why go to all that bother of carrying sea anchoring paraphernalia with you. Why not just lower your anchor with all your scope, and the resistance of the drag of the anchor and chain will bring your bow in to the wind, the vessel will then sit more comfortably. What a great idea, it's so sensible, and in one of those half dead gray cells of mine, I tucked it away for future reference. Which was now. I dashed up on deck and dragged up from the chain locker 300 feet of chain, then lowered the chain and my 45 pound plough anchor overboard. Then I waited with great anticipation.

It did not make the least bloody bit of difference. Broom ignored the whole exercise as being rather silly, and sat exactly the same way and still kept drifting back. So much for listening to that idiots advice, then promptly the truth of what I had done struck me. Oh Shit! The weight of my useless sea anchor! I am quite sure that you probably have some idea of the weight of a 45 pound anchor. Now, about the weight of 300 feet of chain that hangs straight down. Now, let me see, the chain weighs 1.5 pounds per foot, and 300 times 1.5 plus 45 equals 495 pounds. As for a power anchor winch, that's another thing I don't have. I am a great believer in one's ability to laugh at himself, but that afternoon my ability was sorely tried.

Log: May 26. Sailing on Tofino Radio beacon and after 42 days I can see the welcome sight of land. Entered the calm water of Uclulet harbour and moored to the wharf at 9:30 a.m. Phoned Marlene, then phoned for custom clearance, yes, there are certain things more important than the other. How pleasant it was to hear Marlene's voice, and how pleasant it was to deal with a customs officer who wasn't filled with their own self importance. But it was the sights I noticed, after the gray dry dusty landscapes of Mexico to find yourself in the luxuriant damp green rocky tree blessed landscapes of British Columbia, my eyes devoured the scene. I welcomed this feast that my senses had of the sights and the smell of the land. I reveled in it. Yes, I knew where the grocery store was, and where the B.C. Liquor store was. I strolled in their direction. Then my masculinity raised its head, for as I had become accustomed to the landscape of Mexico so to my eyes had become warmly ensconced by the graceful femininity of the Mexican women. However, here in Uclulet, I wasn't too sure, for here men and women wore the same clothes, both wore earrings, both wore pony tails, some shaved their heads and still wore pony tails. I wandered back aboard with my arms loaded with fresh meat, vegetables and the odd bottle of spirit. I shrugged my shoulders and wisely said, "Ron you can't have everything" But I did. The last words on my log were. "Life is wonderful."

Chapter 15

Log: May 15, 1995. I was off again, with a paying crew but how long they would stay, I had no idea. The crew, my son in law, a young Canadian lass from Quebec and an American lad, David. David had answered an advertisement that I had placed in a cruising magazine. He wanted the experience of offshore sailing. We spoke for a few minutes then he said. "My trouble is, I'm thirty two and I think I'm sixteen," my quick reply was. "My trouble is, I'm sixty four and I think I'm fifteen." We were bound for, Hawaii, thence Papua New Guinea and afterwards only time and good fortune would tell. Broom was now equipped with G.P.S., I had also changed the rig and added to the height of her masts. I had no concern as to her ballast. She was now rigged as a stay sail schooner. Originally I had rigged her as a junk schooner but I had not cared for the mainsail feeling that it over powered the vessel and though the junk foresail was excellent down wind, more sail area was required forward of it. This rig allowed me to have two head sails, the larger one outboard, the smaller one inboard. It was a bit like the Javex jugs. As always I had timed our leaving so that we could take advantage of the strong ebb tides and with the tide and the engine we were at Cape Flattery in no time.

On the last of the ebb tide and without a breath of wind we rode an elevator ride on the enormous swells that were now coming in from offshore, we slowly climbed up those steep waves, and without effort, slid down, and dolphins surrounded us as they joyously crisscrossed our bow. My young American friend David must have noticed a look of concern on my face for he came over and asked me what I was thinking. I mentioned about there being no wind and what if the engine failed. "Oh" he said, "we'll just drop the anchor." Then, fortunately, he rushed to the bow to get another look at the dolphins, yes, it was better that he never noticed my expression for once his back was turned I lowered my head into the palms of my hands and groaned. For regardless if the anchor reached the bottom or not, Broom would turn broadside to that quick steep sea, and everything below would go flying, and we, all of us would be leaning over the side emptying out our inners, not worrying whether we were going to die, but feeling quite sure that we would rather.

Log: May 29. Becalmed all night and morning, huge swells from the north west, sea is like a desert. This starts the fifth day of calms. The G.P.S., aye it's a grand tool, but there is one problem with it. For there is the temptation to cut corners, for it so easily tells you the shortest route. An example would be the route from the Juan de Fuca Strait to Hawaii. I'm afraid that after a few days I succumbed to that very temptation and landed too soon in the Doldrums. However, days later the mountains of Hawaii came into view and as the evening wore on we lost the wind and eventually motored into Hilo, it was 10: p.m.

I am not at all fond of entering strange harbours at night but as the visibility was good, we did. We anchored in Radio Bay and cleared customs the following morning. Grand little harbour Radio Bay, sort of prepares you for the hustle and bustle of Hawaii. Especially as it is close to the airport, two days later the crew and I were at the airport, they being confident that Marlene was on this flight. I being hopeful. Then Marlene came striding down the landing stairs. Aye, and that evening; I remember well, was hot—otherwise there would have been no reason for us to lie naked in the comfortable aft cabin of Broom. The port lights hung open catching the last of the gentle evening breeze. I, lying patiently by Marlene's side, having risen to the occasion hours ago, or so it seemed, and having learned patience, waited, Marlene bless her, talked a light year. I listened and it went in one ear, and out the other. I smiled, trying not to let my eyes dwell too long on her comely form. Then I admit—the heat got too much for me. Two days later our daughter Dawn, flew in, Broom was now fully crewed. A few days later we left for Lahina, one night there was sufficient, for that place was far too busy for me. We left for Molokai with a good tide but with little wind, that is until we reached Molokai Channel, there the wind blew so strong that it ripped the clew out of my large head sail. We sailed past the anchorage in Molokai where the few yachts that were there were rocking and rolling, and with that favourable wind continued to Honolulu. We hove to during the night and with dawn entered the harbour.

We spent two pleasant weeks moored to the first finger as you entered the marina. Nothing blocked our vision from our deck, before us lay the panoramic playground that the sea had to offer for locals and tourists alike. I sat there in the early morning hours, dawn just breaking and the sun barely clearing the eastern horizon. My first coffee in hand, while the surfers, both male and female, were already out, lying belly flat on their boards waiting for the breakers to arrive. On my second cup I realized that there was a second layer, then slowly a third and a fourth, for farther out, out rigged canoes surfed, and farther out still, sailboats were leaving or arriving in the harbour and at the edge of the scene, Love Boats cruised. Layers of people one after the other enjoying the sea in their own particular fashion, each wrapped up in their own world and quite unconscious of the other were all spread out before me like pages in a travel magazine. The town behind me lay half asleep and silent, while I absorbed this early awakening of my morning spectacle, a scene that I felt that I alone was seeing, that I alone was aware of, as if all that was taking place was for my own personal amusement.

I was hiding under our sun awning cranking on the handle of my many times blessed sewing machine, as I replaced the clew that had been torn out of the headsail.

We had been moored for a few days when a small steel Canadian yacht came in to the marina, the lone crew being a pleasant young lad. At that time I was hiding under our sun awning cranking on the handle of my many times blessed sewing machine, as I replaced the clew that had been torn out of my head sail. Fair skin and red hair, the sun and he were not close companions, he was a likable and entertaining lad, which I soon found out when we shared a drink. He had bought a used Genoa and had cut a piece from it and had made a sea anchor, he had lots of material left over. He was hoping that I would sew him an awning from part of that left over material, and wondered if I would accept what was left of the cloth as payment. I inspected the sailcloth it was excellent, it was one of the best deals that I ever made.

David alone was continuing with me, however, he had met two enthusiastic young Austrian lads. I was tempted to say German, however they had made it quite clear that they were not German, but that they were Austrian. I had no problem with that, for I have met those that because of my accent think of me as a Brit, or heaven forbid as English, I like to make it quite clear that I am neither. When the sun came close to the yard arm I would pour myself a glass, the musician would join me, and we would sing. He told me that he knew that one day he would be a multimillionaire. I eyed him, then speaking tenderly, and, taking a deep breath, said. "Pray tell me young lad, as you have told me a stranger, you have also told your father?" "Yes," "And what did your father say to your comment." "Nothing," then he added, "however, you have the same look on your face as he had when I told him." We also acquired a charming young Canadian lad, James, he and David got on well, David was fond of commenting that they both came from the same side of the track, a comment meant to infer that the Austrians came from better circumstances, and, were better educated than they, and I add—and I.

Log: July 17. We left, bound for Tawara Lagoon, Kiribati. I estimated the distance as being approximately 2250 miles. By noon James was not at all well, no, it wasn't the sea, it was the bottle of vodka he drank last night. Soon he was accompanied by the Austrians, however, they were most definitely sea sick. As for the vagaries and caprices of the crew, the two Austrians are as punctual as I thought they would be, if their watch starts at two they are right on time. James, however, is a another kettle of fish entirely. If his starts at two he might get there fifteen minutes later, which of course led to the Austrians having words with him, since then he has cleaned up his act. As for the kettle of fish. Caught a fine big tuna just as it was getting dark, cleaned it that night and cooked all of it the following morning. Ate it that day, and the following day, and the following day. Pickled the first day's remains in vinegar and placed it in a clear square plastic container and sat it on the shelf above the sink, where it looked like something out of an old Frankenstein movie. For some reason I was the only one eating them. I was not too surprised that the Austrians did not eat fish, for I soon found out that they never ate vegetables, when we had them, or beans, peas, lentils, oats or rice. They both would be quite happy with two pounds of raw meat daily, and a packet of Cocoa Puffs for the ski instructor, and a packet of Corn Flakes for the musician. The Austrians have told me that they are leaving in Kiribati, meaning no disrespect, but thank goodness. James is indecisive. I admit I'm ready to be alone. I wonder what David will do?

Log: Aug. 3. Crossed the date line. In my stocking up in Honolulu they had on sale something that I'm rather fond of, egg noodles. While checking the water in the bilge I realized that two of those packages had landed there, the packages were holed, fortunately none of the crew noticed as I removed them from their damp abode. Shall I tell you what had happened to the egg noodles, of course I shall. Down there they had transformed themselves into a rather gooey mixture, very similar to gyproc drywall filler. I cut a hole in the top of the bag and squeezed this substance into the same plastic container that I had kept the pickled fish in. Had I cleaned the container—hmm. Then I placed the container on the shelf above the sink where it sat in the sunlight for two days, the mixture, dramatically, grew.

We had taken turns baking bread, that is except for the Austrians, the concept of them baking bread was far beyond their imagination. I emptied the container into our bread making bowl and instantly my nostrils were assailed by this captivating aroma of Parmesan cheese and eggs, added three and a half cups of flour, yeast and water, kneaded it and put it in our cast iron pan and covered it with a tea towel [at that time the towels were quite clean] let it sit for an hour, then placed it on the stove and lit the low burner. Later when I was removing the pan from the stove one of my Austrian crew came down, sniffed the air. "Ah, that smells vonderfull is it a different recipe?" I can assure you that I wasn't making fun of his use of the English language. However, the sun was already over the yard arm and I was the one that had baked the bread. I answered.

"Jah mein herr, It is an old Keltic recipe it contains eggs and cheese and I promise you they are no wegetables or legumes of any kind in it."

"What do you call it?" "The name is pronounced somewhat like, bilge."

"Ah, like bilge in a boat?"

"Why you're right, I never even thought of that, isn't that interesting?" Need I say that the bread was such a success that two days later they were two more bags brewing in the bilge.

Log: Aug. 8. Tawara Lagoon, after a 23 day passage we anchored in Port Betio. David and I went ashore on the dinghy and were fortunate to meet an Aussie, a retired volunteer who was employed in the local technical school. Folk like that are a wonderful source of information. My first question was the availability of drinking water, his answer was that the water should be boiled, for it was rainwater that was collected in shallow pools. As for the local diet, fish and rice, though some of the natives raised their own pigs. There was little produce grown on the island, practically everything was imported. He directed us to the customs office, as we walked to it we surveyed the village. Garbage lay piled high on street corners, and among it children happily played, and within it, rats undoubtedly prospered. Electrical power was supplied by a diesel generating plant, around the circumference of the plant were pools of diesel fuel and around the plant were the homes of the people of the village, with their washing hung on clothes lines to dry while chickens scratched in the black soil. Always conscious of food supplies I checked out the small grocery stores, all of them had large open bags of rice and flour, in all of the bags weevils flourished. One of the stores had a shelf loaded with canned food, on the shelf was a sign reading 'Special Sale.' All of the cans were swollen. Yet everywhere we went we were greeted by happy smiling people. Oh, how my heart went out to those poor but happy people, when many of us have so much and are miserable. And this was where I had to tolerate this pompous strutting idiot of a customs man. He made it quite clear that he had to come aboard and inspect our vessel, there was only one reason for that, which later he made quite evident. He was quite upset when he realized that he would be going aboard in a dinghy— with oars. We approached Broom, and the Austrians as polite as ever welcomed him aboard. I was voiceless. He told us that when he goes aboard ships or yachts they present him with a memento of his presence. David gave him two dry crackers which the silly bastard ate, I would have gave him strychnine, if we had any. The Austrians smiled congenially to him. He was not so much interested in our passports, as he was about the number of stamps that they had. I had just renewed my passport, they were no stamps on it, he asked me where is your old passport, I answered I scrapped it, he asked me what do you do? I answered, "I'm retired." I was quickly rejected. The Austrians had hordes of stamps on their passports. When he asked the musician what he did he lightly dismissed it, but when he asked the ski-instructor what he did, he drooled.

Log: Aug. 12. Weighed anchor Port Betio. Gorgeous sailing. David is ill, he says it's from drinking the water from Kiribati. I'm not too sure. I think he has something on his mind, which he informed me off two days later when he got off in Rabaul. As for myself, and I have no problem admitting it. I'm not keen about sailing through the Dampier or Malaysian Strait alone. Alone at sea is one thing, in those busy shipping lanes, it is something else. Yet, it wasn't the ships that troubled me, as it was the smaller craft, like the fishing boat that I had close company with when I neared Darwin. Going hell bent he was, heading right for us, exhaust pouring out of his smoke stack and when I put the binoculars on him, not a soul at the wheel. Auto pilots are such grand tools. There was also the heat and the humidity that seemed to sap my energy. It's also true, I was getting old, the energy that I had thoughtlessly assumed would be my constant companion was fading. So there it was, I decided. I would, as I always have, let my spirit lead me.

Aug. 28. Anchored in Rabaul. I was interested in seeing Rabaul, it lies on a large natural harbour surrounded by active volcanoes. In 1937 it was heavily damaged by volcanic eruptions. It was a major Japanese base in World War two and was destroyed by Allied bombardment. Almost a year ago I had read that Tuvurvur, one of the volcanoes that surrounded the town had again erupted so we had no idea what to expect as we approached the port, or whether the port still existed. As we rounded the point of land we could see the desolation caused by the volcanic eruption. I had not known what to expect but simply reasoned that the town would probably look as if it had been bombed, but it wasn't like that at all, for all lay buried under the sheer weight of the ash that had slowly fallen from that windless sky the day of the eruption. The desolation was beyond my imaginings.

We entered the harbour and motored over to where one lone sailboat flying the Aussie flag sat at anchor. Then I noticed protrusions, they appeared, then disappeared as if they were floating just below the surface, then I recalled what I had been told, and what they were. They were the tops of the masts of sunken sailboats, overloaded by the weight of the volcanic ash had sunk, and with the gentle movement of the water in the harbour showed the positions of those vanished hopes. While David lowered the dinghy my eyes wandered from mast top to mast top, we were anchored in a graveyard of lost dreams, aye, among corpses in a battlefield of a different sort. We anchored off, what I gathered was at one time the yacht club. We rowed over to a dilapidated jetty, the remains I think of a rather grand one that had landed far grander yachtsmen than I. From the end of the jetty and running twenty—thirty feet inland was an overhead roof with a width of seven foot, holding the roof up was a series of steel posts. There was something strange about it that roof, but what was it?

As we entered the structure I looked overhead. The curved shape of the roof had given me to think that it was modeled as a pagoda, but no, it was as one would expect in more northern or southern climes. A simple peaked roof, the frames of the roof angle iron, 2 inch by 2 inch, the centre of the roof being roughly a foot higher than the outer edges. Within that eight foot width the angle iron had buckled from the weight of the ash. There are 40 foot steel sailboats with a beam of 12 foot that are built with frames lighter than those roof beams. How much weight was there on that roof? How high must the pile of ash been to have caused those angle irons to bend and buckle like that? Had it rained afterwards and the ash had absorbed it? And what was it like then? In that modern day Pompeii. Closer to town and on the shore of the harbour is a monument. It commemorates the men and women who were taken as prisoners of war in Rabaul by the Japanese. They were loaded upon a Japanese vessel and were being shipped to Japan, the vessel was sunk by an Allied ship, all were lost. The town had shoveled the ash away from the base of this sad memorial that only reflects on the stupidity of war. The ash around it is over four feet high.

As I wandered from where the yacht club had once stood groups of natives from the hills and the mountains had gathered, they never saw me, I don't blame them. The men, austere and savage, aye, the noble savage, well built proud fierce looking bastards. I wasn't about to ask them for directions, their women stood by their sides, their labours were over for the day and they had eyes only for their babes as they breast fed them. It was their toddlers who stood quietly by their sides, wide eyed and innocent, who stared at me. An open truck was driving around picking up those natives, they passed, silently, hired from the hills to clean up this shambles that the town's people at the price that was being paid, wouldn't do?

As I walked away from that area and towards the town the ash was less. Businesses were functioning and all seemed well. David joined me and we met those from the Aussie yacht, with their dress and their arms filled with groceries they were quite noticeable. The natives were sitting at street corners hawking coconuts and balls of something wrapped in banana leaves. I eyed those balls suspiciously. David bought a coconut and a leaf wrapped ball, he unwrapped the leaves, took a bite, then handed me the ball while he drank from the coconut, he damn near had to twist my arm to get that ball back. I was hooked, it was tapioca. The customs officer, a young man, was fair but stern, confirming to us what the Aussie's had said. He told us most strongly that we had to leave P.N.G. within 48 hours. I cringed at that for I had the full intention of visiting Madang, but then he gave us our passports back. Then I noticed he hadn't stamped my passport, with that, I gave a quiet sigh of relief. As for what may take place in Madang, well, I'll cross that bridge when I come to it.

David helped me fill the water tanks then we said our good-byes. He was a damn good crew—as long as he wasn't the cook. Exactly 48 hours from when we had anchored I weighed anchor and left Rabaul. It is a mere 408 miles from Rabaul to Madang, still it took me ten days to sail that distance, though I did have an interesting stop over. The trade winds that had captivated me with their dependable power was like the continuity of the orbits of the planets. Yet this sailing weather was quite different, it seemed totally related to the rising and setting of the sun. Also I was all too willing to be alone, to accept this weather for what it was, a respite, however had that been true I should have been more prepared for what may lie ahead, I wasn't. I was doing something I had never done before—living one day at a time.

Chapter 16.

'Gie me a spark O natures fire that's aw the lesson I desire and tho I trudge through murk and mire, wae plough or cart, my muse tho hamely in attire may touch the heart.' Robert Burns.

It had been far more than a week since I had last sailed at night. I had left my sails up, hanging limp in those windless nights and slept with my willing ears praying for that delightful sound of the sea gurgling happily against the hull, but that sound never blessed my ears in these waters. I would be on deck before dawn with a mug of coffee and watch the sunrise over those far distant shores and as the sun rose the breeze would awaken, and the flatness of the sea would be replaced with tiny wavelets and my sails would slowly curve, and fill, and we would once again make way. And that warm breath from the land would keep my vessel making its own path whilst I whiled away my indolent hours under my sun shelter, until, the sun having shed its heat, kisses the horizon and sleeps.

'Twas only then that I could remove myself from the protection of my awning, then slowly, that gentle breeze would die and I would willingly stride forth and luxuriate in the coolness and quietness of the coming of the night. The contrast from day to night pleased me. When the first light from the drowsy and half awakened sun disturbs the darkened night, the stars slowly hide, and the sun arouses it self and with courage strides forth and its blazing light stirs the wind, who in turn provokes the sea. Yet I, though a willing adherent to its travels shy from its life giving and burning rays, for I

128

come from a colder clime, where the sun is ever welcomed, but carries little heat and is seldom seen. And so my happy daylight hours would slip past, until, the sun, tiring, sleeps, and evening appears in a dark and cloudless star studded sky, and I would once again become entranced by the magic and mystery of those nights. And the light from those long dead stars would light my motionless path, and its soothing dream filled rays would beckon me and will my eyelids closed.

It is night, and as nature calls my water splashes on that black still ocean and the sea in response becomes alive with phosphorescence emitting from all those living organisms and creatures who had rose from those fathom less depths when darkness fell, much as I had, when I had came out from under my sun shelter when the sun had finished its daily voyage. As my last drip left my body, their light faded and I would reach for my flashlight and shine it on the still sea, and the sea once again came alive and as far as my light would shine, shone the luminosity of those creatures reflecting their light back to me. Strange, I never felt … alone.

How I loved sailing alone, alone with the sea and the sky, and a lonely star to steer me by. That is if I can keep my eyes open in those starlit nights. Aye, it's a romantic I am, and I'm not talking about two in a bed making three. No, I'm talking about me and the sea and the sky. Aye, its true, when the wind journeys across the water and carries my wee boat and I steadily on our course with my hand never feeling a need to touch the wheel, how I loved that. And when you are out there far from land, with only the Sun and the Moon and the Planets for company, traveling on their long ordained journey, why, it makes you feel that you too are part of them, when you realize that you too are traveling on your own ordained journey. Silly isn't it, for you know that you can't know, still, it brings peace to my heart, what more could one wish and how it pleased me.

But nature has a way of altering circumstances and had created for me what would best be described as an odd day. A day when I was out of character, a day when I didn't follow my primordial instincts. You wonder what do I mean? I didn't listen to myself, oh I had my coffee and the toilet bowl quickly called me but that's not what I mean. Yes, it was strange. I was approaching land why I could see it. I lifted my arm and stretched it out, and with the flat of my palm shading the sunlight from my face, I let the sun rest on the top finger and counted the fingers between the sun and the land, four. The light would be gone in an hour. Still, I left all alone and sailed on, oh I admit when I get a good wind I can't let it get away, a little bit like having money in the bank, oh, I've said that before. Still, me doing that, that is not obeying my natural instincts, why it's incredulous.

So there I was knowing only too well my habits and blinded by God knows what, then almost instantly I realized the Sun was disappearing, and I, knowing that I was far too close to an inhospitable shore to hove to, I would have to find a place where I could anchor. Did I not already tell you? Well let me tell you now. I am a practical man, I don't mind making decisions, it's the quick ones I don't like.

By my side was an open bay, for a place to spend the night, no, I don't care for open bays. Yet it wasn't only that that bothered me for as my eyes swept the area I saw how those steep cliffs that surrounded the bay promptly plunged into the sea. Aye, for they told me that it was a deep bay, the kind that are a hundred feet in depth until you're twenty feet from the shore, then abruptly, ten, then two. No I didn't like the look of it. It's true, I would have far preferred the open sea than to find myself entrapped in this open bay. Could you imagine how it would be if the wind came up and swells were running, and the surf breaking, and I attempting to keep my balance on the bow, while I, with my hand powered anchor winch hauled in a hundred feet of chain and a forty five pound anchor.

No I didn't care for it at all, then I noticed it, a red smear a hundred feet offshore and near the centre of the bay. Even in the last of the day's light it was easy to see. I suppose it was the contrast between the golden sand, the green palms and the red wreck. Aye, it was a long abandoned vessel on the beach. I trimmed sails and in the last of the dying breeze headed for its leeward side. It lay tipped at a thirty degree angle, the leeward side of the deck was barely a foot above the sea, its windward side inclined and pointing to the heavens. Aye, if the wind did decide to blow it would give me shelter and moorage. Its bow may have been on the beach, but its stern was in a hundred feet of water, I didn't hesitate but carefully headed closer. Threw my fenders over then lowered sails and slowly came alongside. Opened my deck box, hauled out my grappling hook, threw the hook, it locked on the ship's gunwale, I dragged Broom alongside. My harbour for the night secure I put a pot of water on the stove for my rice, sipped my rum and dreamt of supper, rice with a half a can of diced tomatoes, half can of corned beef and a teaspoonful of curry.

Woke at dawn, put my coffee pot on then stuck my head out the hatch. The new day's sun was awakening the heavens as it sent its messengers across the sky, silver streaks heralding the coming of the morn sped across the firmament, and my eyes drawn to the eastern horizon saw the searching fingers from the golden orb caressing the gray sea. How I love the early dawn, and when anchored close to land, the cry of the multicoloured birds would arouse me with a song that my jaded ears had never heard. And those idyllic days at sea, when the sun woke the wind and sent us gently on our way, and when it set, there would be I, barely managing to keep my eyes open from the star lit splendour that faced me. And in the middle of the nights for I could never break that habit of rousing and sticking my head out the hatch, I would be become fascinated by clarity of the heavens. Aye, those many times when all seemed so perfect and I felt that I could reach out and touch the stars, but

I'm a fool, so pay little attention to what I say, for there was also those times when the ocean raged, and I on that rolling deck, reefing sails and taking them below and repairing them, but what else did you expect, still how wonderful it was.

I could have left that early morn, yet, for some reason I hesitated, I was in no rush to go and the wreck somehow drew me. Had breakfast then boarded her, had no idea what to expect so I suppose it was just to satisfy my curiosity. Clambered over the rusted bulwarks, leaned as if I was climbing a church roof and wandered the deck, the covers for the hold long gone they gaped like opened maws. Thought briefly if the hull was intact it was possible that I could have a badly needed fresh water warm bath. Found a rust encrusted hatch lying wide open, grabbed the rungs and climbed down. Streaks of the morning sun shone inquisitively through a jagged hole that lay on the waterline. Fish swam innocently, in and out, aye, but it was the bottom of the bilge that intrigued me for it was alive with seafood, my God if you were stuck here you would never starve to death, oh sure, you may get fed up eating seafood, but you would never go hungry. My eyes dwelt on the opening and thought, why I have my own fish trap, for even with the little tide that was there, what ever swam in could easily be trapped, and as for the shellfish, they were there for the picking.

Now, can you imagine an area with a dimension of twenty by thirty feet, the depth of the water three feet and crystal clear, and above, an opening where a blue sky shone on all that lived below. Just below the opening colourful frangipani flourished, their blossoms scenting the air and the iridescent plumage of the birds that flew in and out, added more colour to the resplendent scene. Then slowly, for I was in no hurry, the light of the rising sun eased and no longer shone through the gaping hole but rose to the heavens, and its golden light now shining from above sent its warming rays blessing the flourishing pool. Now easily seen was the profusion of colours of the sun blessed fish, the butterfly, the clown, and the feather like fronds of the anemones, as they wafted to and fro with the gentle current. Crabs scuttled on the bottom, dining on the clams and oysters that had found a happy home there among the proliferation of the plants that flowered and grew wildly on the bottom of this old hold. Oh how it pleased me, ah but you don't understand so let me tell you, damn it I've told you already, no matter. I was raised in a climate where the weather is gray, the buildings are gray, the birds are gray, and the fish are gray, this colourful scene, this sea garden of Eden pleased me greatly.

I have no idea how long I stood there grasping the rungs of the ladder gazing at this Eden, for that is exactly what it was. To my right and about two feet above the water a steel grating ran across the width of the hull, on one side of it was a handrail. I gripped it then putting my feet on the angled grating walked across the pool. I felt as an invader, a Mongol, a Hun, trespassing upon this idyllic sea garden, especially when I thought of food as I eyed this well stocked supply. I am fond of sleeping, after all I'm so good at it, and eating I find is a close second. Yes, I felt guilty standing there, my hands firmly gripped on the rail looking down, then I noticed a large fish dining on a smaller one, and the crabs that seemed quite happy digesting on all that they came near, then I felt slightly better for I knew that I would do what I have always done. I've never like the idea of canning, that is taking more than what is required for the day. Never really thought about it until I saw the fish, and the crabs, doing exactly what I have been doing all those years.

I was in no hurry at all, as I with my bare feet, my well worn shorts and sporting a tattered tee shirt explored the vessel. I found myself in the companionway to the engine room, the steel fire proof door hung open. And there was I, as I stood in shock, long neglected and rust encrusted it may have been, but I recognized the engine, it was a triple expansion steam engine. I was seventeen years old and at that time was serving my apprenticeship in Fairfields Ship Building and Engineering. You don't understand, I'll tell you for with engines like that it was obvious. The three different diameters of the engine cylinders, high pressure, medium pressure, and low pressure. I had totally forgotten that time and here it was awakening all these forgotten memories. Silly how it pleased me, yet I ignored these foolish thoughts of mine, it couldn't possibly be the same engine and continued my meandering. Quite enjoyed exploring the wreck, though there was that odd feeling I had about it. Couldn't figure out what it was so disregarded it, and kept my eyes open for something that I could use for a spear. I found it.

It was lying among the wreckage in the galley, an old broom with most of the bristles long gone, but it was the wreckage that got me thinking. That the cupboards had been stripped that I understood, but not the smashing of them. Drawers littered the floor, and the enclosures where they had once lain, why, it looked as if someone had taken an axe to them. It didn't make any sense, if there were natives on the island they wouldn't have created this shambles. They would have taken the drawers with them, perhaps even the cupboard doors, but they wouldn't have caused this useless devastation. I withdrew my knife from its sheath, turned a drawer on its side and sat on it, then picked up the broom. I cut the last of the bristles off then trimmed a point, meanwhile my eyes wandered around the galley. Something shone beneath one of the drawers, taking the broom handle I tipped the drawer over and there lay all the ship's cutlery. No, it hadn't been the natives for they would have taken them, even if they didn't know what some were used for.

With my new found spear in hand I ambled back to the crew and officers quarters for another look, the havoc that had been created there was less than the galley, mainly I think because there was less to damage. Found the stairs to the wheel house and climbed them, didn't expect to see much up there. It was a riveted hull and with the steam engines I reckoned it had been built no later than the forties, and in that case there wouldn't be much there in the way of electronics. Anything electric was smashed, looked for the ship's log but never found it, papers and charts lay scattered, picked up part of a chart and a course had been laid on it, from the Bay of Bengal to Singapore, thence North East, but after that the chart was torn, couldn't find the other part. The chart table beside the helmsman seat was wrecked, but the seat surprisingly, was fine, and more importantly the ship's wheel, a fine five spoked affair of bronze and teak. The teak handles still glistened from the sweated hands of the steersman, and the bronze wheel had already attained the green patina of verdigris. It was held to the steering shaft with a large capped brass nut. I eyed it voraciously. I sat on the seat and realizing that it turned, I turned. Opposite the chart table was the doorway that I had entered, and on the wall beside it was a heavy brass commissioning plate, it too was covered with a green verdigris. The printing on it was indecipherable, all I could understand was *'Bengal Engineering and Shipbuilding' 1935*.

Bengal, but Bengal is in India, what is a coastal steamer built in India doing in the South Pacific? And what had happened to the crew? How did it end up on the beach with a hole in the hull? I turned around and looked out of the wheel house window, little could be seen of the island for the bow being on the beach blocked my vision. Left the wheel house and went back on deck and out to the end of the bow. Directly below was the sand beach, fifty feet ahead palm trees flourished and the ground lay littered with coconuts. I quit thinking on what may have happened and instead thought of my happy hour, and how well coconut milk would go with rum. Cut a piece out of a net that hung draped over the side, went down on the beach and knocked a few fresh coconuts down, piled them in the net and took them aboard Broom.

I was sitting on the grating above my water garden, my feet just clearing the sun dappled sea. The opening in the hull lay directly below me. I was waiting. Another thing I have found about getting old is that I have acquired patience, at least to my way of thinking getting old is the only way I could have got it, for in my younger days I would not have had the patience to calmly sit there, waiting for that special moment, and here it was. She came swimming in through the hole, a nice big fat tuna. I wasted no time but quickly drove my sharpened broom handle into its sleek body, flicked it up in the air and landed it beside me. With the flat of my axe I stunned it, thanked it, then gutted and cleaned it. Its guts fell through the grating and crabs rushed over to dine. I put the fish aside and eyed the largest crab, knowing that I would never be able to drive my spear through its hardened shell, I hesitated, wondering how I would manage, then the crab decided for me. It reached up with its powerful claw and grabbed the end of my spear and refused to let it go, I lifted it up, flipped it over onto its back, laid it on the grating, picked up my axe and with one swoop split its belly open. Thanked it, got another one, cleaned them and their guts fell into the pool where all were happily dining. I had enough for tonight's supper and tomorrow's breakfast.

I was quite happy sitting there on my deck box, my feet up on the binnacle, my well patched awning shading me from that hot sun, aye, that hot sun that has began to bother me as I have grown older, and why shouldn't I be happy. With my glass of coconut milk and rum, my pasta just about cooked, my crab legs boiling away and my fish in the frying pan waiting for me to light the flame. Aye, life was grand, one drink and I had forgotten all about the enigma of this mysterious wreck, two drinks and I was thinking about my wife and kids. She, my wife was very fond of the sea, that is providing it was only for looking at, as for my children, I just wished that they were living their lives as I was living mine. I'm not a poor man, neither am I rich, oops hold on a minute, not too sure about not being rich, look around, what do you see. Ah, but you can't, so let me tell you.

The sun is going down, look, it's slipping behind the palm fronds that wave to me in the last of the day's dying breeze, and can't you see just behind them, how that well blessed orb slyly goes to bed. Look around, no twilight in those climes, overhead the stars are shyly appearing soon to be over anxious to show you their sparkle, and watch, over there, can you not see how the horizon somehow gleams, and, don't take your eyes away just watch—there it is, the moon slowly rising to be once again resplendent in the silence of the heavens. Now stop, and listen to the cry of the sugar bats as they descend on the trees for their nights slumber. Sorry, I have to eat, and soon, sleep.

Next morning rose as usual with the sun, made my coffee and heated my leftovers from last night's supper. Had already figured my chores for the day, one being my attempt to remove the ships wheel, aye, I don't mind telling you that I rather fancied that ship's wheel, though I reckoned that it would take quite a bit of effort to remove, another was to have a better look at the land around the wreck. Couldn't get the idea out of my head that the damage done wasn't random, that whoever had done it was looking for something, and what about the crew? What had happened to them? So there was I equipped for my first chore, with my axe, a piece of wood, my big pipe wrench and a length of pipe. I boarded the wreck and went up to the wheel house. Placed my pipe wrench on the brass nut that gripped the ship's wheel, slipped my pipe over the handle of the pipe wrench to give me leverage and pulled—and damn near fell on my ass. The damn thing was loose. On my knees with that piece of wood in one hand and my axe in the other, I laid the wood on the bottom of the wheel and with the head of the axe started to tap all around. Shit, the ship's wheel popped up. Shocked that's what I was. Why is it when I think it's going to be tough, it's easy, and when I think it's going to be easy it's tough. No matter. I could see myself home, the ship's wheel hanging over the wood stove while its embers glowed from the blasts of the winter winds blowing up the Strait, and my feet up on the coffee table and I sipping rum. Meanwhile drool making odours came from the kitchen as my wife cooked supper, and sang happily, off key. I removed the wheel and a piece of paper that was trapped underneath fell out. I ignored it for I was far too pleased with my new possession, yet my eyes glanced at it, it was about a half an inch wide. I picked it up, it was cut in a circular fashion with a hole in the middle to go around the steering shaft. I had thought that it was just packing until I realized that there was writing on it, on a single line it read.

'octftblwlxxftaftpt.'

Well, what could I make of that, aye I laughed, in any case I was far too pleased so paid little attention to it, hesitated, then stuffed it in my pocket and happily lugged the ship's wheel back to Broom. Dumped it in the fo'c's'le then wandered the island. Really didn't expect to find anything, for whatever it was that had happened, had happened some time ago and all signs would have long disappeared. The beach didn't extend too far for all to soon I was surrounded by palm trees, there was a noise every now and then, a thud, the ground was littered with coconuts. I raised my eyes and quickly stepped aside as one came crashing down, ready to return to the dinghy when I noticed something white underneath a pile of fallen coconuts, brushed them aside. Lying on the ground, the colour almost gone from it was a well weathered cross. I picked it up, barely decipherable on it were the words 'James Brown 26 years old 1942'. Placed it erect then used a coconut to drive it back into the ground. Brushed coconuts and dead palm fronds from the ground and found two more. 'Peter Murphy 32 years old 1942' 'Jimmy Ramsay 45 years old 1942'. Stood both crosses erect and drove them into the ground. Knocked down a few fresh coconuts then with them in hand, and in a somewhat sombre mood, wandered back to Broom.

Had another look at the ship's wheel then placed it under the mattress in the fo'c'sle. Picked up my fishing gear then hesitated, took the paper out of my pocket and had another look at it, shook my head, laid it on the bookshelf and went back to catching my supper, and that night I fried the fish in coconut milk. Lollo I think they call it in Fiji, or is it Lolo, no, I remember Lolo, I smiled, then mixed some Lollo with my rum. I picked up that piece of paper that I had found and with my feet up on the binnacle sat mulling over the writing. *'octftblwlxxftaftpt.'* Reminded me of those cryptic crossword puzzles that in those land bound mornings of mine when I sat with coffee in hand and the days local paper spread out before me. After I had scanned the headlines my fingers would quickly flick the pages to those cryptic puzzles that would get my mind awake, and functioning. Aye, and with the rum reminding me, it made me think. 'Course, I thought it's all Greek to— *'octftblwlxxftaftpt.'*—no it's Roman—oct is eight—could it be—ft—blwl—xx is twenty—aft—pt.—'8 foot below water line 20 foot aft port'!!

I gulped my rum down, what the hell is eight foot below and twenty foot aft on the port beam. Went below and turned my stove off then boarded the wreck. Went as far forward as I could then walked aft twenty feet, on either side of the hull were two tanks. On the top of the port one were two valves, from the forward valve a copper line went overhead, I reckoned that it was for ventilation, the copper line that left the other valve ran towards the engine room. Thought it strange that there were no clean outs anywhere on the tanks. Walked over to the other tank and found that that was exactly the same, shrugged my shoulders and made my way aft. Old fool I thought, getting my head all wrapped up with something that happened all those years ago, what's that to do with me, bugger it I said. Climbed back on my dinghy and rowed to the leeward side of the hulk. Dragged the dinghy up on the beach and appraised the wreck, six inches above the waterline barnacles prospered, and little red crabs ran back and forth reaping their harvest, and I the old fool wondered what I was doing. The vessel lay tipped and twenty foot from the bow and eight foot under could be, of course I was just guessing, that what ever that was there would be, two foot under the water.

Went back to my rum, cooked my supper and just before climbing into my berth glanced at the barometer, it had fallen, stuck my head out the hatch, overhead storm clouds were already gathering. Expecting the worse and hoping for the best I returned on deck and removed my awning, then eased the sheets that held me to the wreck and climbed back under my blanket. Awoke two hours later with rain pounding the cabin top, turned on my side and went back to sleep. Woke an hour later with the wind screeching, but that wasn't what had awakened me. It was something else. I lay hearing, a moan, what the hell was that, there it was again only this time it was louder. I began to get that very uncomfortable feeling that I get when I know things are not going well. There it was again. I sprang out of my berth and opened the hatch, the wind howled and raging seas pounded against the windward side of the wreck, overhead flashes of lightning crossed the sky and angry black clouds hurdled past. My eyes dropped to the beached vessel. Again there was a groan. I gazed at it, it moved and slowly began to topple towards me. God it was tipping—how far would it go? Then it stopped.

Before dawn the sky had cleared, the wind had died and the seas were slowly calming. I spent the morning raising my awning. The edge of the ship's hull was now flush with the sea. By noon it was dead calm, I went round in the dinghy for another look at the port bow. The crabs were leaving their high and dry quarters and the bivalves, squirting their excess water were going out of business. The spot that I had eyed earlier was now above the sea, spent the afternoon clearing barnacles then found it. A half inch thick round flange about two foot in diametre was bolted to the hull, with a brass plate in its centre and when I got it clean it read, 'Location for Bowthruster'. I laughed, stupid old fart, all this bloody fuss and all you find is the place where they were eventually going to install a bowthruster. Daft bugger, still I laughed, they sure were planning ahead and whoever had placed that message under the ship's wheel must have been just as nutty as I am. Went back to fishing. My fish stew with rice and canned vegetables was simmering while I drank. Damn it, it didn't go down well with me, and I'm not talking about the drink or the fish. It didn't make any sense, the bowthruster idea had happened after the vessel was built, a sort of after thought, yet even at that, bowthrusters in a ship with a steam engine, oh come on. I dined and knew what toils I would be up to tomorrow.

Coffee and breakfast over, the sun now filling the eastern sky, I loaded my dinghy with my axe, pipe wrench and pipe, a heavy chisel and headed for the port bow. Took far more effort to loosen those nuts than the one on the ship's wheel, one stud rusted solid to the nut sheared. Drove the chisel into the surrounding edge and eventually the plate loosened. God knows what I expected to see in there. I levered the plate off and with a splash it sank into the shallow sea. Sufficient light reflected from the sea shone in the opening. I looked in and saw eighteen metal World War Two ammunition boxes, eighteen bloody metal ammunition boxes! And my imagination soared.

Shocked, yes, the sort of shock you get when your mind stops functioning and you gaze opened mouth and realize what lies before you. The sort of shock that makes you have serious arguments with yourself. Ideas were entering that infertile skull of mine and I didn't like any of them. Thoughts were sprouting in my head like eyes in a rotten potato and none were what I wished, and in any case I wasn't too sure that I wanted to know what was in those boxes, and, what if someone should come along now? Yes, just at this moment and see me hauling those boxes out of there, and what if those thoughts that I had were true? What then? I mean it wasn't as if I was in it over my head, whoa just a minute, you bet your bloody life I was. God knows why but I rushed back into the wheel house and picked up the scattered papers and charts. 'Course I was searching, if I only knew what for, then I found the other part of the chart, and there on it was a small cross just north of Hue in Vietnam. Not that it was any help. Still, I had no other choice had I? Went back to the opening for the so called bowthruster and hauled one of the boxes out, took it ashore and, dreading what I may see, opened it. It was filled with clear plastic bags that held a white powder. I closed the lid and sat on the box and remembered.

Was it twenty years ago when the school bus that Malcolm had used to transport his family and furniture west, was parked in our spare lot. He had it up for sale and two men were coming to see it, he had to work and he had asked me to show it to them. They came on motorcycles, complete with leather jackets, tattoos, and beer in their pannier bags. I got on quite well with them, though I remember my daughter not approving of me being in their company. We entered the bus and they drank beer and handed me one. Then one of them took a clear plastic bag out of his pocket and opened it, it was half filled with a white powder, he withdrew his sheath knife, stuck it in the bag and placed a heap of the powder on the tip of the blade then he passed the tip of the blade to me. I had no idea what it was, though I felt sure that it wasn't sugar. I smiled and shook my head, he lifted it to his nose sniffed it, placed it back in the plastic bag, reheaped it and passed it to his buddy. I reckoned I knew what was in these ammunition boxes. So what do I do?

I unloaded all the boxes and checked their contents, they all held the same packages and were packed in the same manner.

I reckoned that each bag was about a pound and that one box held fifty, eighteen boxes at fifty pound a box, it wasn't the numerical weight that bothered me, but its worth. So what do I do? Sail away and leave it there, do you realize how much money is there? Madang was four days away, that's by sail, but what do you think would happen if one of the custom officials just happened to pass by in a power boat and found me here, then noticed what I had strewn on that sun blessed beach. What do you think might happen to me? Aye, it's a coward that I am for I hastily loaded the boxes aboard, untied my mooring lines, hauled sails and left. Make no mistake I had found what they had been searching for, how long ago that had been I had no idea, some of them could still be alive and if they had came back for a second look while I was there, it would have been— Goodbye Ronnie.

My going deeper in the keel had gave room for my extra ballast and after I turned the boxes over so that the handle was down, they looked like part of the steel hull, why with a little bit of bilge water over them they would look fine. I felt so much better noticing that. I had a grand argument with myself as I sailed off. The conclusion was I had to go in to Madang, I needed to fill up my water tanks and pick up more supplies. If the customs agent was like the one in Rabaul, great, bless him. Aye, it's true there are many things that I lack in my mental makeup but confidence is not one. As for my memory, well, that is one of those things that I now lack for it is not at all what it once was, for I can quite easily forget what I had for supper last night, yet unwillingly recall parts of my past that I'd far rather forget. So soon I was back in my old sea going ways.

Chapter 17

Log: September 7, 1996. Hove to ten mile from the pass into Madang, Papua New Guinea. Rose before dawn and hauled sails, and with a mug of hot coffee in my hand watched the newly awakened morning air send gentle ripples dancing across the still slumbering sea, and the sails, aroused from a balmy night's languor would slowly stretch and fill. There is but one entrance into Madang though the chart shows two, one being over a reef. With that that in mind I made the best course that I could, then noticed ahead the turbulence and swirl in the water, and my optimism like a burst balloon, deflated. Close hauled and with the engine ticking over pinched my way up the coast, to starboard a congested wall of rich green vegetation stretched for miles, and to port was the blue and open sea. Aye, that sea appealed to me. The land, an impregnable jungle of stalwart palms and thick twisted vines that aggressively flourished to the salt water's edge, then abruptly that seemingly impenetrable coast broke and there before me was the pass. I entered. On my right openings appeared through the matted jungle and glimpses of the sea came in sight, then suddenly and easily seen was the churning water of the reef infested pass. Then the pass opened up and there in its pristine clarity was one of the most picturesque and fully protected harbours that I have seen.

Aye, the colour, the beauty, the richness of the tropics draw me. How I love their plant life, the colours of their ever blooming flowers, the Bougainvillaea with their showy rose red petal-like bracts that hang drooping from their branchlets.

The Tropicbird that welcomed me as I approached their seas, their glossy white plumage, their long pointed wings and their wedged shaped tails. The Frigatebird, black crested and hooked bill, God given so that with it they can grasp triatic stays on visiting yachts, and the males, flaunting their masculinity as they blow up their scarlet coated bagpipes to impress the ladies. And in some sheltered anchorage where I had early settled for the night the sulphur-crested Cockatoo would descend among the treetops, then as the evening wore on and they left, a contrasting flier would appear, a flock of black winged Sugar bats. Who, reaching up with their jagged claws grabbed those same branches and dangled and slept upside down—how I loved it—it was all so alive. Yet there it was, the one major drawback that I have, for as I grow older and each year slips past my resolve weakens and the ability for me to realize my dreams fades, for the hot humidity relentlessly draws my energy from me and leaves me weak and drained.

I motored around that harbour using my ill loved but useful radio, trying to gain attention, but no reply. Nary a yacht or recreational vessel of any kind were moored, I had passed a small stone jetty with old truck tires for fenders. Over it hung a sign, ' MADANG FISH and GAME CLUB'. I turned Broom and motored back to that jetty. As we neared the shore the crystal clear water became shallow, every now and then a jagged rock would rear its hull piercing head aggressively from the sandy floor. I moored but the place was deserted. I approached the back of a restaurant and bar and a grizzled elderly native came out. We spoke. He told me that he was the caretaker, that it was off season and that it was okay for me to stay where I was moored until I had cleared customs. At least that's what I thought he said. He was good enough to lead me to the customs office. He left me there and I tipped him, something I never do, that is not if I can help it. However, this was a different world entirely and under these circumstances, it made a lot of sense.

I liked old Michael. Though he did mix English with his own tongue, which is exactly what Pidgin English is. It meant little to me for half the time I never knew what he was saying. He left me at the customs office but there was no one there, it also looked as if there had never been anyone there. On the other side of the building was a gate that led into the custom warehouses, they were two security guards at the gate. I approached the guards and told them where I was moored and that I required customs clearance, and would they inform the customs officer when he returned. They smiled pleasantly and nodded their heads, then went back to drinking coke. I had this nagging impression that just perhaps, that they understood English just as well as I understood Pidgin. Meandered the town, found the post office and picked up two letters, one from Marlene and one from my ex-Kiwi crew. Then feeling responsible I again returned to the customs office, again there was no one there, went over to the guards at the gate. This time there were two different guards and this time I made sure that they understood what I was saying, or so I thought. On my wandering way back to Broom I came upon the overseas telephone office. I popped in.

Geezus, there was a long line up, waited briefly then one of the staff noticed me and called me over. "Are you paying cash?" she asked. "Yes," I answered, "one moment please." Then she directed me to phone number five. They were five phones mounted on the wall, no cubicles, and all within elbow contact, no privacy here. Amazingly got through to Marlene right away, told her that I was alone and that the heat and humidity was getting to me. I'll spend a few days here then I'll wend my way home, I'll drop you a line. A few short and sweet words. On the way back I passed the local brewery store wherein with relish I picked up a case of cold beer. I should mention that my enthusiasm for those cold beers rapidly waned over the next twenty four hours, that was when I realized why the Aussies called the beer, cold piss. I was back aboard and sitting comfortably, rereading my mail when there was a knock on the hull, then a voice shouted, "Customs". Aye, I remember that quiet sigh of relief I gave when the customs officer in Rabaul handed me my back my passport, unstamped. But what if that customs officer in Rabaul should unexpectedly appear in Madang, what then? And what if? Oh God no, let's not think about that. For now I will deal with this officer. God knows how he would be.

Black well shined shoes came down the companion way stairs, beige knee high socks, beige shorts, beige shirt with identification tag. Cocky, handsome, middle thirtyish, big smile, outstretched hand, "Welcome to Papua," he said. I was in a state of shock. I've never had such a welcome from a custom official. I thanked him and presented my passport and ships papers to him. He took a casual glance at them, then asked me how long I was going to stay. I answered probably just a few days. "Oh that's fine" he said, "I'll pop down and see you again." I offered him a beer he drank, and left, leaving me in a state of utter bewilderment. No comment on twenty four hours, not a word about one hundred dollars. Was that because this wasn't a port? Did no one ever come here? I have never had a more casual clearance. Well, I thought if they don't bother me I won't bother them. Still?

That hot blinding burnished globe had not yet reached its zenith, and although I had kept as much in the shade as I could, beads of perspiration that had gathered between my shoulder blades became rivulets of sweat as they ran trickling down my back. I was standing in the middle of the market square in Madang, around me and sitting on that dry arid ground were the natives. Spread out before them was the produce of their toil, mainly vegetables, although they were a few selling jewelry and carvings. There was little shelter for them from that blazing sun, and although some had attempted to shade themselves with makeshift awnings, most of them patiently suffered that sweltering heat and sat stoical. And as usual I forgot what I had intended to acquire and found my attention being captured by the people.

There sat sun wrinkled and aged women, with younger neighbours with children playing by their side, and younger women again with babes in their arms, and all, gossiping and giggling that hot afternoon away. On one side of the market place sat a long house, being some three times longer than it was wide, at either end of that building was a doorway. My curiosity aroused I made my way to the nearest entrance and found myself looking down a long narrow passage way that ran through the middle of that hot tinned roof building. On either side of the passageway ran an extended table covered with banana leaves. Sitting on the top of those banana leaves lay one continuous and very orderly row of small brick shaped objects, composed of a rather white translucent jell. Behind those tables and sitting shoulder to shoulder with their backs against that well seasoned timber wall, well polished by all those who had gone before, were all the young maids from village and town. I entered the doorway and gazed down that long corridor and as they noticed me, all those young heads turned and their girlish chatter subsided. I have no doubt that somewhere in that long corridor they were two old crones keeping an eye on things, but I never saw them. Aye, and I can honestly say that there was that about the scene that really appealed to me.

For all that lay before the eyes of this old bald pated curmudgeon was a bevy of young virgin maidens, lined on either side like tropic flowers blooming on a garden path, that this old fool, unconsciously, and most happily had strayed on. They ranged in years from twelve to sixteen, their skin golden to nut brown shone with good health, their hair like a raven's wing, glistened, their eyes all big and brown and innocent. They questioningly looked me over, some curiously, some shyly, all with interest. Perhaps it was that the Aussies who worked in the offices around the town never went in there, and yes, I could believe that, or perhaps it was that I was a head taller than the natives, perhaps it was my gray beard. Whatever it may have been that made them seem so interested in me, I'm afraid I tend to think that what it was, was that looking back into their young and innocent brown eyes, were a pair of sullied and aged blue ones. I started to walk down that long corridor and all those eyes followed me. How pristine and beautiful they were.

It was the kind of garden path that only an old codger like I could blissfully wander. How well I knew that if I had been the age of the oldest lass and had found myself in this Islamic dream, my testicles would have disappeared and like an ice cube in that hot sun, I would have melted and vanished. But I wasn't. I slowed my steps, there was no need to hurry, was there? On the contrary there was a great need for me to take just one step at a time. I slowly turned my head from side to side, absorbing and smelling the flowers as I dreamingly strolled down that narrow passageway. Like an old bee foolishly sniffing the nectar of those succulent blossoms, or an aged butterfly who vainly flutters from flower to flower, musing while he dreams? No, just an old fool who remembered how life once was, and yet was not quite old enough to let it easily slip away.

I stopped and turned to my right, and found myself face to face with this wee nut brown lass. I leaned over to her and nodding my head to what she was selling asked her, "what is it?" She fluttered her long black eyelashes at me, lowered her eyes and turned her head shyly. I had already figured out what they were, however as I have acted pretty daft most of my life and have been quite successful at it, I felt no reason to change. It was probably her older sister who sat on her right, that leaned over and said. "Tapioca," "how much?" I asked "10 cents" says she. I bought one, from the wee lass with the long black fluttering eyelashes. I walked out of there smiling at the lassies on either side while I tucked into the finest dessert known to man. Now I want to make it clear that I am not one of those souls that believe in heaven, for to believe in heaven is to believe in hell, and if they were to exist, I know where I shall end. However, I could be wrong and someone could make a mistake and if that should be the case, I would like it clearly understood that for me heaven would be in that hot tinned roof long house with all those lovely nut brown maids, and their delicious tapioca. Providing .... we had an air conditioner.

Wandered back to Broom and spent the afternoon sewing patches on my well worn sails. Aye, I mused and pondered as I had hid there under my sun shelter, cutting pieces of sail cloth, sticking them on my worn sails with contact cement then sewing them on. Yes, there was that that troubled me, my supposed customs clearance, there was something wrong—it was all too easy. I ignored that thought and gave my mind to my other tasks. The filling of my water tanks, and the filling of my spare fuel container. I had also to pick up extra provisions, and on this task, I failed miserably.

The harbour being quiet and deserted when I had came in I had never really noticed the bay, until now. I was moored to the outer side of the quay, on the inner side there was sufficient depth and room for two twenty five foot cabin cruisers. Ahead of the end of the quay and directly of the tip of my bowsprit was a twenty foot opening, that opening allowed entrance to the inner side of the quay, and enclosed by that opening was a sandy circular bay. It was filled with dugout canoes, they lay half out of the water, in a neat and orderly file on the sandy shore. They were twelve to fourteen feet long and about fourteen inches wide, with one small out rigger, in front of where the paddler sat was a wooden shelf. The market was closing. I noticed that the women with empty arms paddled their dugouts out to the reef, to fish? The others with unsold produce, and those with children paddled directly home to their village across the harbour. Their day's labour at the marketplace may be over, but now their evenings toil was just beginning, was there any happy hour for them? Slowly the dugouts left the bay and the bay again became quiet and deserted.

I awoke before dawn with the laughter of the crows singing in my ears then as I made my morning coffee the sound of voices traveled across the silent harbour. With a mug in hand I went on deck, across the harbour women and children were emerging from the village pushing their dugouts before them, they loaded them then climbed in. All were women, though some were mothers with babes on their laps. There also appeared little school children of both sexes, happily climbing into smaller dugouts. I found it quite engaging viewing this armada, yet it was the children that somehow touched me. How enthusiastic they were as they piled into their little dugouts and started paddling, happily, across the bay. They had school satchels over their shoulders, much as I had carried over my shoulder when I had gone to school.

And my retentive mind, too emerged, not from under palm fronds but from smoke encrusted tenements, my eyes dulled by dust laden memories, still I remembered, when I was young. And there was I, skipping down the whitewashed stairs of that soot stained tenement building with a satchel over my shoulder such as they had. Hopping over cracks on that old sidewalk on my way to Abbotsford Public school, while overhead a weak sun struggled through the smog laden gloom, then my mind refused to remember, and stopped.

One canoe caught my eye, it was of the same design as the others, yet it appeared more conspicuous. It seemed to be carrying extra baggage but what it was I couldn't quite tell, when it came closer I realized what it was. It had the customary shelf piled high with produce, and there sitting with his back against the produce was a small boy about two or three, he was facing a young woman who was paddling, between the young woman's arms and sitting on her lap was a child of about a year old. I quickly remembered and waved her over and dashed below.

My son in law has this particular talent for finding things, cast offs, odds and ends, and I do admit that some of the pieces are rather unique, though I have often wondered about his ability to acquire them. During our short stay in Honolulu he managed to find a table, a chair, an ice box, sad but empty, and an attractive plastic toy. When he left us, the table, the chair, and the ice box all went in to the garbage dumpster. The toy I kept. It consisted of a tricycle, and upon it sat a huge black man, and upon this black man's back sat Mickey Mouse. I had kept it, waiting for an opportunity such as this. I grabbed Mickey Mouse from his prominent place on the bookshelf and rushed back on deck, by this time the young family were nearing the end of the jetty. I waved to the young woman to come closer, she smiled shyly and came close enough so that I could hand to her, Mickey Mouse. "For your little boy," I said, coyly she answered, "Thank you." I went below and forgot all about that young family, until my somewhat unwilling, but precipitous departure.

I went shopping on Saturday afternoon. I had seen frozen lamb in one of those stores, I had also promised myself a glass of rum, but it was now time to dally down the garden path and get my daily fix of tapioca, and whilst dining on that, I bought my lamb, next was finding the rum. The liquor outlet was part of a large cement building adjacent to the market, there was no exterior door that I could see but merely an opening in the wall. Your purchase was made through that twenty-four inch by twenty-four inch iron barred opening, the gap between the bars being just sufficient for a bottle to pass through. Buying was achieved by pointing at what you wanted from their very poor selection, then passing your money between the bars. Then the salesman would then take your money, remove the bottle from the shelf, put it in a brown paper bag, then pass the bag and its contents back to you.

I felt that I had gone back in time, I was in the Bastille. I had just bought a dead rat from one of the guards and now I was looking furtively over my shoulder, lest one of my fellow inmates should covet my delicacy. I hid my prize under my shirt and skulked away. Not quite, instead my warm rum kept good company with my frozen lamb, and I wandered of in good spirits. On the way back to Broom I found waiting for me my customs officer, however was this the same man? Gone, was the previous confident cocky charming personality, here was a man who had just gnawed off all of his finger nails, a man frightened by his own shadow. In a way it was most fortunate that we met, perhaps more so for him than I. It had gone through my mind to seek him out and tell him that I was leaving on Monday. It had also gone through my mind not too bother. Now that I had met him, I told him, was that a sigh of relief I heard.

Back aboard and soon my lamb and onions were simmering, mixed myself a rum and cordial and went on deck. The sun having shed its heat was slowly sinking behind the dark purple hills. Soon the heavens would again come alive with the brilliance of the stars, but for now something much more practical, a cooling breeze blew. The bay was now empty of dugouts, and standing alone by the water's edge was an older gray haired woman wearing a rich red dress with a floral pattern. Was it her colour, her dress, her gracefulness that touched me so. Why is it that those rich and dominating colours look so natural and are so becoming on dark skinned women? She held in her right hand a bundle, and as I watched she twirled it over head then threw it with perfect ease, and the bundle flew out over the bay and expanded into a gossamer web that fell gently on to the surface of the water, and for the first time I noticed the disturbance on the calm surface of the bay. The water throbbed as if under the surface a giant heart was beating, then slowly the water became calm and still, and I realized what it was.

Yet, it was the woman who held my attention, she was totally oblivious of me sitting there on the fore deck sipping my rum, watching her. There was a wonderful air of quiet dignity about her, her lithe movements as she cast the net, retrieved it, and how she would shake it gently as she folded it over her arm in preparation to throwing it once again. It all seemed so beautifully gracious. It was as if she were performing a ritualistic dance that had been handed down to her, and she, being completely unaware of the simple majesty that it held, made it for me all the more compelling. She was taller than the average native, her gray hair pulled back from her forehead, her dark skin blending so well with the long dress of vivid and opulent colours, and yet those colours and her, and the scene seemed to merge in to a harmonious whole. I sat there on the fore deck sipping my rum while the scene embedded itself into my mind.

The sky was clear that night and because of the breeze I had decided to sleep in my hammock on the aft deck. The loud voices and the sporadic laughter that had emitted from the club had died, for they too had tired. I lay there with the stars for company and again felt that stir of excitement, for soon I would be leaving, the anticipation of going to sea for me being as provocative as the land fall. When I had spoke to my good wife I had told her that my course would be due north to forty degrees Latitude, then east to the Juan De Fuca Strait. If because of conditions that was impractical, I would head for Guam. There I would spend time so as to avoid the worst of the winter in the North Pacific, however, if I could avoid stopping in Guam I would continue on to Victoria. Ever the optimist, I said I should be home before Christmas. I had estimated the approximate distance as being 6500 miles, and as I had averaged in long hauls 100 miles a day, why that meant I should be home in the middle of November and with good fortune would miss the worse of the winter's storms.

Tomorrow being Sunday the stores and the market would be closed. Tomorrow I would take it easy and make it a day of rest and Monday morning when the vegetable fleet came in and passed my bow I would use up the last of my Papuan money, I would call them over and buy up all their stock. I slept that full night away. After breakfast I wrote a letter to my wife and mailed it. When I came back I had a shower, and clothed in a towel, I sat at the chart table poring over a chart of the Carolines, when there was a knock on the hull. Visible through the portlight were two pairs of legs, one pair being undeniably Michael's, the other pair belonging to a taller man clad in blue cotton. I went on deck and there stood Michael with this younger man with an identification tag on his shirt. "Good morning, Customs" he said. I answered. "Good morning, how many of you guys do I have to see?"

It was fortunate that Michael was there, for he had been there when the bogus customs officer had came, Michael supported me in my contention that I had indeed seen a customs officer. Michael and the customs officer then had this spirited conversation in Pidgin and I haven't the slightest idea of what was said, then the officer paused. He looked away, then turning to me said. "If you stay there is going to be a departmental investigation" he paused, "you have already exceeded your time limit had you been cleared legally, while this investigation is going on you will be in jail." He paused, and carefully weighing his words, added, "I strongly suggest that you leave." I could well understand what was going through his head. This situation would undoubtedly be a tremendous embarrassment to the customs office, especially as I knew that there was a Premiers' conference taking place less than a mile from where I was moored. Then almost as an afterthought he added, "If you are still moored to this wharf a half an hour from now my friend, you will be in jail tomorrow morning." I have to say this for the man, all the while his manner was respectful and polite. However, as he turned to go he said, "I'll require five dollars for the paper work," feeling slightly suspicious I handed him five dollars, and as if to confirm my doubts he added, "and remember you have never been in Papua." Whoa, just a minute, what paper work? For as he said I had never been in Madang.

However, I had no intention of arguing with him, and I had no intention of being in jail tomorrow. For, what if? What if? For Chrissake the bloody fool that I am I had forgotten about my cargo. What if they should thoroughly search my vessel? What if the customs officer from Rabaul should suddenly pop down to Madang? Forget about the bloody customs agent from Rabaul what if they should find my cargo. Where would I be then? Sweat gathered on my aged brow, and no, it wasn't from the humidity. A bald gray bearded old fart in prison in New Guinea, caught smuggling cocaine into their cherished land, corrupting their young and innocent children. Off came my towel and on went my shorts and I made Michael very happy for I gave him all that I had left of my Papuan money. I started the engine, untied my mooring lines and left.

I was heading out when I heard a female voice calling, "Good-bye—Good-bye." I turned and standing on the spit of land that led in to the bay was the young mother that I had given Mickey Mouse to, on either side of her and holding her hands were her young children, she released their hands and the three of them waved and called out to me, "Good-bye—Good-bye—Good-bye." I shall never forget how that young woman and her children's voices sang out to me in that still morning air, and this over sensitive old fool that I am, tears came to my eyes and that hard lump that has troubled me before, stuck in my throat, and like a mute idiot all I could do, was .... wave.

Aye, the vegetable fleet hovered in my mind, and the young mother. Yet, what if I had stayed that other day. I with my finger tip upraised beckoning the young mother's to come alongside, and the police arriving, grabbing me by the crotch and hauling me off to unairconditioned confines. And there I was, standing before a scowling black judge wearing a white wig, who at last had a white man in his court, and I saying. "Oh no your honour I just found those boxes and I thought that they were filled with salt, and, well you probably don't know it but there is a great lack of salt in Western Canada." My God, my imagination was pleading my case, but enough. Wasn't that the very reason I chose this journey, and the others, to face those tribulations, to temper my mettle, to sharpen my wit. Did I say wit, yes, that too, for I had reached that time of my life when I could so easily laugh at myself, and that day I did. Yet, there it was, forever buried in my mind, the young mother and her children crying out—good-bye—good-bye.

Like the Bottlecorks of St Helena the clouds danced across that clear blue sky, except, they were not what one would find in a bottle of red wine, but more of what one would find in a bottle of aspirins, with their bottom half cut off, with a very sharp knife. The sea sparkled and a warm breeze blew and I sat happily musing, remembering saying, 'I'd go where the spirit would lead me', then the remains in my bottle of rum entered my head, I went below and poured myself a shot. Then a thought entered my head, and slowly, like a crack in the wall of a dam, water trickled, poured, and the dam burst. My cargo, my cargo. Did I say Guam? That if conditions weren't good I'd pull into Guam? What the hell was I thinking about. Guam? Far better being nabbed in Canada, than the U.S.A.. I rushed below and raised part of the flooring, they looked like, the keel. Why even when the U.S. coast guard boarded us of Panama, they hadn't looked in the bilge, and with a cursory glance, all would be well. Except, if they were suspicious, and they had dogs. I emptied the last of the rum. Yes, I don't like quick decisions, in any case there was no hurry, was there?

It was my kind of sailing—well almost. This would make a wonderful holiday if you were content with traveling fifty miles a day. With no wind at night, no shipping of any kind in this area, and providing you were conscious of the areas of strong currents, why you could drift along like Huckleberry Finn. Huckleberry Finn—Huckleberry Finn, I had forgotten him. He flooded back into my mind and—took me back to that day those long years ago when I sat on that huge cast iron bollard watching the River Clyde washing all before it to the open sea, and wondering, would it also take me. What was it that I had wrote, 'past all the ships being built and under repair, past all the giant cranes that leaned hungrily over them like great praying mantises, to where I imagined myself—like Huckleberry Finn on an imaginary raft, drifting on that enduring tidal stream to the great adventure and trials that the open sea would hold for me.' What a silly old bugger, Huckleberry Finn. Aye, but that's how it was.

Now to the weather, no, I didn't put my short wave radio, I was well aware of the conditions that I could be sailing into, instead I went to my bible. 'Ocean Passages for the World' page 13, 'tropical storms generally originate between the latitudes of 7 degrees and 15 degrees', an area that I was heading for. On page 12 there is a graph showing the months when tropical storms dominate. 'Western North Pacific, June to November, the worst months being, July to October, twenty two typhoons a season. The South West monsoon fades in September, that's when the North East monsoon gives birth'.

And there was I, this old fool voyaging at a time when the weather couldn't make up its mind. A time when the challenging monsoons either sleep, or vie for supremacy of the sea, while I traveled through them to the birth place of the typhoons. And the last thing that I needed was to read the works of Edgar Allen Poe.

Log: Sept. 14. Something is troubling me and if you were to ask me to explain what I mean, I couldn't. Yet there is a heaviness in the air, the sky of blue has completely gone and in its place is a sky of a dark an ominous lead. No, reading Edgar Allen Poe doesn't help, his narratives dwell on the dark side and I find myself becoming personally involved in the tale. Also, as I think of it, that is what there is about the sky and the air, it was as if I was sailing in an atmosphere of gloom, and surrounding me lies an overwhelming sense of foreboding.

So whether it was all in my imagination or not it affected me sufficiently that by the late afternoon I had lowered the topsail, bagged it and stowed it below deck.

That night after three hours of sleep and half awake I climbed out of my warm berth to view the horizon. I opened the hatch and was blinded by a flash of light, and it is amazing the conjectures that the human brain can come up with in that fleeting period of time when my eye caught that brief flash, and the still black and silent aftermath. I gazed around at the darkness that encircled me, had I imagined that flash. Can there ever be a blackness on land such as I saw that night under that coal black sky, when astride on my Iron Horse I rode over that still and sombre ebony sea. Yet, it was not just the uncanny black of the night, it was also the deathly silence, as if I was afloat in eternal space, a floating time machine that was carrying me, where? Could I have imagined that flash? Was I half asleep? Or is it you Edgar, playing with my imagination?

Then instantly, blinding flashes of lightning haphazardly blazed their way across the heavens, then again complete and silent darkness, or was it .. did I hear a faint roll of ... thunder. Aye, suspicious I was, for I went down two steps of the companion way stairs, turned, closed the doors and with only my head and shoulders above the hatch, waited. Ahead a blinding flash lit the sky and as its light died emerging from dark sombre mist slowly appeared a black cloaked cloud, was that what had discharged it? and for the first time I noticed the huge swell that now dominated the once flat and calm sea. Then once again blackness flourished in the heavens. Aye, it is you isn't it Edgar? Playing bowls on those ebony coated thunderheads and setting off fireworks, trying to scare an old Scotsman or is it Canadian that I am, for I've never been too sure. Yet another flash of illumination blinded me, followed by a roll of thunder that was so much louder. Then quick, a flash this time to port, then another off the stern. We were completely surrounded by flashes of lightning, and yet if the

Gods, or Edgar were angry that night, they were not noisy, for there were no thunderous claps from the lightning's bosom companion. I wasn't too concerned for as you know you can tell how close the lightning is by counting the seconds between the flash and the thunder roll.

Still, it is eerie standing on the deck of a boat at night, in the middle of a great sea while overhead the sky is ablaze with lightning flashes, and as there is no harm in being overly prudent, I disconnected the antenna wire that ran in to the back of my V.H.F. Radio. The radio antenna was located at the top of the main mast, if it was hit by lightning the charge would run down the wire and ground in the radio, and the radio, could it—explode ? The mast being made of aluminium and the hull being made of steel, if the lightning bolt hit the mast it would then ground out through the steel hull in to the sea. It should. Shouldn't it? I disconnected the wire and was closing the hatch when I was simultaneously blinded by a flash and deafened by an ear piercing crack. The atmosphere crackled and my ears were assaulted by the loudest thunder clap I have ever heard. My nostrils sucked in air that reeked with the pungent odour of ozone. I stood there, my eyes now tightly shut, both hands fiercely gripping the hand hold on either side of the companion way stairs. I waited, there was another strike, I counted two seconds then I heard the thunder roll. I have no idea how long I stood there, before I had the courage to bring my head above the hatch and look. And realized, that all was well.

Log: Sept. 15. Last night the barometer started falling and the rain came pouring down in sheets, by midnight it had settled to a steady downpour. At dawn the sky, a dull leaden gray scattered with lines of squall ridden clouds marching in formation like so many storm troopers, and there, just above the horizon was one forming and heading directly for us. Then as I realized how fast it was approaching, wondered, how much wind is there in that damn thing? I left the main cabin, closed the fore hatch and doors, opened the door to the aft cabin hatch and entered then closed the doors. I stood halfway down the aft companion way stairs, my head and shoulders just above the hatch, overhead a storm dodger. With my right hand resting on the ship's wheel, I waited.

The black squall struck, Broom hit by the wind careened, the port gunwale plunged four inches into the white frothed sea and the rain came pouring down in torrents, the driven rain that had flooded the mainsail poured off, streaming down and overflowing from the dodger. Aye, I could feel Broom answering to the wind yet all my eyes could focus on was the port gunwale as it sank ever deeper in to the sea. Slowly the bow rose and I swear that I could sense the ass of Broom as it settled itself down in to the churning water, but should she turn too readily in to the wind my head sail could flog it self to pieces, but Broom, more secure than I, also waited. With her port gunwale buried under the surface of that foaming sea, her sails iron hard, her masts and rigging straining, she also sat, biding her time.

Like an old dog crouching in the wind and rain she sat, its head cocked, waiting obediently for an order from its master, but I was not its master, not at that time, no, the wind was, and the old sea dog waited and I watched. The gust eased, and slowly the old sea dog raised her ass, stretched her weary limbs and leisurely began to right herself, she shook her fur, and the last of that torrential rain came pouring off the mainsail and on to the dodger, then as if with some unheard command, the bow of Broom slowly turned and the old sea dog plodded faithfully back on to her original course. Aye, how fulfilling I found it, how satisfying it was to create this vessel and take it to sea, and realize that it was more capable than I to face the arduous labours that the ocean would place upon us. That I could, with sense, leave it to do that, which it knew better than I how to. It was of immense satisfaction to me, and that was when I got the idea that, which of us was the tool, and which of us was the voyager.

From my position my fully reefed main and reefed stay sail were fine, it was my large head sail that I couldn't see. I removed the safety line that I kept hooked on the binnacle and wrapped it around my waist, left the shelter of the hatch and closed the doors and hatch. I reached the foremast and sat on the forward starboard edge of the trunk cabin, braced my right foot against the gunwale, then attached my safety hook to the hand rail. I ran my eyes over the sail, there was a three foot rip in the centre of the head sail where a seam had parted. The only reason that the sail was still in one piece was that I had sewn a rope completely around it. I had to lower the sail and repair it. Originally I had it on a traveler that ran down the bowsprit, to remove it was to pull the traveler inboard, the trouble with it was when I was on a windward tack I could never get the luff tight enough. How I wish that I had left it on the traveler. My smaller head sail of many colours, I would first haul up to steal the wind from the larger head sail and making it easier to lower.

The squall having passed and the wind gone had left the seas behaving unpredictably, wild and capricious they ran, colliding with each other and sending their salted spray flying skyward. What could I do but relate it to being in a pub in the Gorbals on a Friday night. Surrounded by a bunch of enthusiastic drunks all determined to have a great time, all with one too many, swearing, pushing and shoving. Then the grand melee where fists fly, but no one really gets hurt, mainly because they are all too drunk, and there we were, Broom and I, stuck in the middle of this inebriated mob—Cold sober. Which was just as well.

I hauled the sail out of the sea and piled it on the net under the bowsprit. To remove the head sail I had to climb out over the bow, step down on to the eight foot bowsprit, then straddle my way out to its end and there, unhank the head sail and bring it back aboard for repairing. With hands on either bow rail, I squatted on the bowsprit and stepped down into the net—where, seven feet below sea foam sparkled and the white sea boiled. On either side of me ran a three eighths nylon line from each bow rail to the end of the bowsprit, and with either hand grasping on to those lines, I inched my way forward to the end of the bowsprit. The bow dipped and white churning sea that now rose to greet me was two feet below my apprehensive feet. I was at the end of the sprit, and heard the sea roar, I turned and realized that another black storm trooper was approaching. I cowered, closed my eyes, and tightened my grips on the nylon lines. The wind hit. Broom heeled, and I went sliding to leeward, my left foot digging into the sail, my prehensile toes burying themselves into the openings in the net, my right leg curled snugly around the bowsprit, my right hand pulling furiously on the nylon line. And Broom with the sail area forward now halved, turned more readily in to that rolling sea, and the sails now filled with that driving wind sent her ploughing in to them.

And there was I, on the snout of the Iron Horse, who, as if trying to get a true scent of the sea had purposely buried her nostrils into those raging combers, and I, who had never ridden on a horse now found myself on the bare back of a wild bucking bronco. I've lost the reins and someone has dumped a load of wet washing around my legs, and I, the old fool frantically pushing it out of the way so that I may throw my arms around this mad stallion's neck. Aye, there was I, with that snow white crystalline foam bubbling just below my aged knees. Yes, it was like that, but it was also something else for my mind had ceased to work, and each part of my body was acting independently of the other, as if each part knew instinctively its purpose and my mind was not needed. When those seas hit the bow and the bow climbed the crest of the wave, my lungs would fill, and as the bowsprit rose my thighs would strengthen their grip around it, my toes more firmly bury themselves in the net, my hands tighten their grasp on the bow rail lines, and my eyes, fastened fanatically on the tip of the bowsprit rose with it as it climbed heaven wards. But when we came off the top of the wave, and the bow sank, the bowsprit now directed my eyes to the seething sea and the frosted spume rushed to embrace me, then my eyes would tightly close, and the bow submerge into that white turbulent water while I, half buried in that white foaming sea held my breath until the bow again rose and brought me up and I could once again, breathe.

If I think therefore I am, on that eight foot journey on the bowsprit there was no am, no id, no ego, no mind. My body functioning as nature intended it should, doing the necessary tasks for its survival and governed only by its energy and spirit. If there was an I, it was a singled cell amoeba, a wet human like spectre that had slowly and painstakingly made its way to the end of the bowsprit. Mindless, and yet strange as it may seem—so fully alive.

Chapter 18

The best laid plans of mice and men gang aft a-gley. Burns.

Log: Sept. 17. Squall has again changed to a storm and had blown me south 10 miles before I awoke, but was it really dawn, for with those sombre funereal skies it was hard to tell, and it didn't really matter. I ignored the tarpitched blackness and the clock, my innards said coffee time therefore it was. Fumbled my way out of my berth, three short steps forward, two to the right, my right hand reaches the bookshelf and there I grab the lighter. My ass now firmly pressed against the bar counter, I face the stove. Over the stove hangs the oil lamp, my left hand finds the lamp glass and flicks it back, my right hand finds the lighter, and flick ... the flame licks the wick and there is light. I light the stove and make coffee, and with a mug of coffee in hand take it back to bed, got myself comfortable then a machine gun rattles as hailstones arrive, bouncing off the deck, pattering against the portlights, and just when I thought they would never stop, they did.

Are they gone? Those beautiful days that had once given me so much pleasure, when I had sailed so joyously before the trade winds, when nature and I were in such perfect harmony, but alas all had changed for the last few days have been a continuance of what had passed before, northerly squalls, with the wind reaching storm conditions, then becalmed, then light east winds swinging to the south, then becalmed, then again, the same unpleasant squalls and wind. 'Ocean passages for the world' tells me that where I now am there can be twenty two typhoons between July and October, fortunately you can't have raging typhoons that bring with them those deathly silences and the monsoons with there bloody squabbling squalls at the same time. Yes, I was entering the area where, 'tropical storms generally originate' though I'd much rather not have known, and if all of that wasn't bad enough, the equatorial current was taking me west.

Checked my sails and noticed one of the seams on my stay sail was no longer in good company with the other, their marriage was falling apart and it was my job to reunite them. With about twelve inches of sewing to be done I could remove my wet stay sail and take it below, and there do a good job repairing it. And also get my already damp cabin wet in the process, or, I could do a poorer job sewing it where it stood and only get myself wet in the process. With a light drizzle falling from that murky grey sky, half squatting and half kneeling, my left hand bringing the sail together my right hand applying the needle, I managed to do a half decent job, and got wet in the process.

Clear skies at last, becalmed all night and at dawn a light southerly, also at dawn the last land mass that I would see until I once again saw the shores of North America. Fifteen to twenty miles from me lay the island of Truk. What wonderful land' falls those mountainous islands make, so unlike the coral islands where with cautious eyes you search the horizon for waving tree tops. Truk, however, has a surrounding reef and I am tempted to enter, that is, if, I had a chart, or if, it was not this particular time of year, or if, our passage had been more expedient, but there was far too many ifs. In any case Broom made up my mind for me by gently sailing by. I took advantage of the sun and brought up my bedding and towels to dry.

Sailed past the edge of the Northern reef in the afternoon and it was easy to see where the reef lay, for there with her bow high up in the air and well aground was a freighter. I stared at that freighter in shock, then laughed. I had forgotten all about my extra ballast that was firmly ensconced in the bilges. For the next two days the weather was pleasant and I had no sail repair or chores to do, and I sailed happily and filled those idle days, dreaming.

Aye, I dreamt and so found myself idly pondering on my extra ballast. How my mind happily wandered to the thought that I could do a lot of good with that money, though I really didn't know how much was there. Doctors without Borders would get a nice sum, and with their advice build a few hospitals in the more needed areas of the world. Of course it would also be a disaster in the lives of those poor fools who injected it into their veins, and what about the contacts I would have to make, and the people that I would be dealing with. And so I argued as the pro's and con's of those sun blessed days happily slipped by. I can assure you there was no lack of time for me to muse on those questions as I daily became closer to home. And that night after supper, my head filled with fancy, I slept and dreamt.

I was dressed entirely in white except for the red cravat that I wore around my neck, my wife looked sumptuous, she was also dressed in white except for the red sash that she wore around her slim waist, and that woven hat she wore with a red ribbon around it, my gosh she looked good. Her eye lashes somehow have grown and not only that, had proliferated. Toby is waiting for us, he's a young South African, dressed in a beige shirt, a little tag on it said, 'Captain,' beige shorts, knee length socks and beige shoes. Handsome chap, we board our jet, it's really quite small, we only have one hostess a young coloured woman who at one time could not possibly have had this position. She approaches us and making sure that my wife has all that she needs, asks me. "Sir, would you like cordial with your rum or would you prefer coconut milk". "I'll have the coconut milk, providing it is fresh." She returned with a leaded crystal glass, waited till I had tasted it then asked. "The coconut milk was fresh sir, is your drink all right sir" "Yes dear, it's fine." Is it acceptable to address your servants as dear? She turned to my wife. "Madam would you care for anything?" My wife answered. "Yes, Renay I'll have a small glass of Pinot Noir," now where the hell did she learn about Pinot Noir? Was that what she was up to when I was gone? In any case what is Pinot Noir? "and Ma'am we have some fresh pheasant aboard for supper, or would you prefer lamb?" "The pheasant will be lovely dear." I guess it's okay to address your help as dear, just hope she doesn't talk to Toby like that. What a grand reception they had for us in Malawi, robed dignitaries, their brown skin gleaming, their servants holding huge multi coloured brollys shielded us from the broiling sun. They welcomed us warmly, then we climbed aboard a white stretch convertible limo and drove us to our lately built hospital and school. I waved to the crowd that cheered us as I let dollar bills fall freely from my fingers tips. I love being celebrated.

The next morning with my morning cup of coffee in hand, my oats simmering on the stove, I sat by the binnacle gazing out on the calm sea and my dream shyly, hesitant less it may not be welcomed, entered my mind and the fool that I am, I sat chortling. It was then that I began to conceive that my mind and I were fellow companions. I who had so often said, 'I've lost my mind and I don't care if I never find it' what a fool. The next day was another pleasant one, I put up the awning and did these chores that I thought necessary. No, I wasn't the least bit interested in reading Poe. The sun went down, I added a half a can of corn beef to my left over lentil stew. Ate, slept, and again dreamt.

I was sitting in my car in an alley in Vancouver's east end, it was raining, it was midnight. I had tried to make our meeting at two in the afternoon, he had burst out laughing. I gathered he was still sleeping at that time. Midnight, oh God, my eye lids were killing me. I was waiting. A black limo drove up and parked behind me, the driver flicked his headlights, I flicked mine, a black van drove up and parked in front. Three men got out of the car, one stood on either side of my car while the third man opened my passenger door and climbed in. He was a big rough looking bugger, he was smoking a cigar. God I hate cigar smoke. "So what the fuck you got?" I smiled and reached into my pocket and pulled out a small plastic bag that held white powder, I handed it to him. He opened it sniffed it then said. "How good is this fuckin shit?" He was not particularly gifted in his use of the English language, I shrugged my shoulders. "What the fuck are you shrugging your shoulders for?" Aye, his grammar was not that great. I answered. "Would you have believed me if I told you it was excellent?" He smiled, two of his front teeth were missing, it must have helped him to hold that cigar while he talked. "Comon." I think he meant come on. He opened the door and headed for the van, I followed him, we went in. A chain smoking old man sat at a table, beside him was an overflowing ash tray and a conglomeration of scales and test tubes, he handed the bag to him, then sat down beside him. I sat opposite. No one spoke. I placed my hands between my knees so they wouldn't see me nervously picking my nails. The old man fiddled with the powder, then stopped and displayed two thumbs up, his nails were worse than mine. "Really" the big rough looking bugger said, his cigar nearly falling from his mouth, "really—no shit!" he turned to me and said, "How much of this shit you got?" "Nine hundred pounds." His cigar fell to the floor. "Did you say nine hundred fucking pounds?" "No, I said nine hundred pounds." Why did I call this prick?

In the middle of that black rain filled night I awoke, laughing. I ignored the weather and turned on my other side and went back to sleep.

And found myself in William's Head prison looking out of a barred window at other barred windows looking back. I was having a new cell mate. I heard the cell door opening, I turned, he entered and the guard locked the door behind him. He was young, acne had found a happy home on his pugilistic face, "What are you in for?" I asked. "Car theft, how about you?" "I tried to sell nine hundred pounds of coke to an under cover R.C.M.P. officer," his eyes sparkled, he smiled. "Shit, that was you! everybody is talking about you, God damn it let me shake your hand." It didn't seem to matter to him that I had got caught. I was a celebrity.

Sailed past the Northern reef in the afternoon and it was easy to see where the reef lay, for there with her bow high in the air was a freighter, I stared at it in shock.

Greeted on the morning of Oct. 1. by the Grandaddy of all squalls, then just before noon—again hit. The swiftness of the blast sent Broom on her beam ends, and I flying off my seat at the chart table in the aft cabin and ended with me kneeling on the companion way stairs, my hands grasping tightly to the hand holds. Aye, and there I huddled all the while trying desperately to pull myself erect, meanwhile Broom was again burying her ass in to the sea. Was it my imagination, or could I actually feel her strain as she struggled to raise her bow to face that wind, but the wind never eased, but just kept pressing her over—she was getting too close to being knocked down. I had to get on deck and reduce the sail. I opened the hatch and reached for the safety line but before my hand ever found it, rains came, and all I glimpsed before my sodden gaze was an eye blinding deluge. It would have been insanity to consider that I could function in these conditions. I closed the hatch and sat helplessly in front of the closed aft cabin doors. A sea crashed into the bow and boarded us and again she lay on her side, Broom, fighting to rise was hit by yet another blast, this hull, this steel drum that I was in, resounded with the impacts. I, lop sided and half crouched with my right arm stretched, my left arm tightly bent, my hands gripping the hand holds, my eyes firmly shut, sat listening.

Listening .. listening, to the torrential rush of the sea as it pounded and boarded the bow, its mad scramble as it ran madly down the cabinway, over the wheel deck it ran, an attempt to scale the aft deck failed then in despairing anger it expelled its rage and ran through the scuppers and poured overboard. And there was I knowing that there was nothing that I could do—but listen—all my senses were void, but that one—so I sat back, yes, and listened, and my imagination, ever a good friend, reigned. Such it was with I.

The sound, the reverberation, the drums, an arousing orchestral opus, a Les Miserables that reaches a peak then slowly fades, and becomes a soft and gentle rolling and as the last of the wave gathers itself and shyly empties out of the leeboard scuppers, another sea boarded us and the roar once again returned, growing louder and louder as the angry wind aroused the rabble. Fearful I may have been but fool that I am, I smiled, recalling my dreams, a celebrity in prison, now a

French revolutionary, but now, just to sit—and listen—and my mind, free and unemcumbered—imagines. So with eyes tightly closed, I heard the thunderous peal as the wild horde slams into the vessel, the screech of trumpets, the tumultuous clamour of the raging multitude as they clamber over the bulwarks and race madly down the passage between the gunwale and the trunk cabin. The scream as they released their anger on the raised aft cabin, and their rage denied a jet from a fire hose sends water squirting around the aft cabin doors. Then having vented their fury and spent their energy, they pour over the bridge deck and run wildly overboard through the lee scuppers. Aye, that's what my ears heard, and my mind portrayed it all.

The pounding eased, and slowly the storm wind lessened and Broom gradually took a more upright position, but with my imagination still aroused and my head buried in my hands, I waited, for the soothing sounds of violins, but alas, none came. I stood and opened the hatch and reached for the safety line. A huge low lying black cloud lay to leeward, to windward, clear bright blue skies. The wind that had reached Force 8 so speedily, had gone. On deck, my tattered stay sail hung, split right down the middle, held together at the luff by the leach line and in the centre a gap of over two feet. No hand sewing on this one, I let it hang there to drip dry.

Oct. 5. I awoke and before my eyes opened I sensed it, old fool that I was, what is there to sense in the middle of the ocean, there is nothing except ... or is there? I opened the hatch and all had changed, the sky had brightened as if it had gone through a metamorphosis. Those dark and melancholy heavens which seemed so filled with gloom and despair and that I had felt so totally immersed in, had gone. The day had become much brighter, though I'm sorry to say that I was suspicious that squalls will still be my hated but constant companions, yet, those too had changed. They had somehow become separated from the once dark sky and now against the blue heaven, were clear and defined. Line squalls? If so the line that joins them is quite invisible and the blue skies that now lie between those envoys of misfortune could easily lull one in to a mood of complacency. Which I admit I was so willing to accept. It is also worth noting that the distance from where I stand on deck to the horizon is just over three mile, and it is surprising how fast those storm troopers can move, what else can I call them? Yet I feel it is the combination of the blue skies and those black storm troopers that created that spectacular scene, that I was soon privileged, yet hesitant, to witness.

Yes, there was something odd about the formation of those squall ridden clouds. For they looked so much like hard boiled black eggs attached to each other by an invisible thread, as they, one after the other came wildly hurtling across the clear blue sky. Bringing with them gale like winds then as quick as one came, it would be gone, leaving in its wake little wind and boiling, maddening seas. Then eventually dead calm while I waited, apprehensively, for the next one. Such is the sea.

Early in the afternoon the top of one of those black egg shaped clouds appeared on the horizon, the light being so good and the visibility excellent, that black rounded form so well defined, why it was more like it was emanating from the depths of the ocean than merely coming over the horizon. It sat there on the exact edge of the horizon, then as I watched it leisurely grew larger and larger, now it was a half moon, a half black moon sitting astride that defining line between the sky and the sea. Then in the exact middle of that half black moon arose an outline, had I been off the coast of British Columbia I would have thought, a log boom? I went below, got my binoculars and came back on deck and stared at it. It did look like a log boom, copper coloured and flat, afloat in the exact middle of that half black moon that sat serenely on the rim of the horizon.

The last unwelcome yahoo long gone, the sea having calmed lay clear and sparkling, yet my eyes never strayed from the log that lay contentedly in the middle of that slowly increasing black half moon. Then oddly enough the centre of the copper coloured log slowly began to curve upwards, and yet either end remained clinging firmly to the sea, appearing for all the world like a long lost creature that had just emerged from the depths of the ocean, luxuriating as the heat of the sun warmed its body and as the creatures trunk now blessed from the heat became more flexible, it slowly stretched and raised itself. That half black moon grew larger now it dominated the starboard horizon, and the copper log also grew, increasing in size and curve, and yet either end still held their grasp upon the sea. Then I noticed, below the centre of that copper curve another flat log slowly appearing, only this one was yellow and it too, gradually raised itself into that same graceful curve, with either end again never losing their hold upon the sea. Then leisurely beneath it another flat log appeared, this time green, and it too curved and grew and all the while that half black moon shaped cloud became larger and larger, and yet another log emerged, green, curved and grew, and still another, blue, then indigo, then violet, and the old fool that I am. Knew.

When all the colours were present and curved, that black cloud, the mother of that newborn rainbow, broke its union with the horizon and slowly lifted. Then daylight appeared under the cloud and on either side of the rainbow, and the cloud slowly began to dissipate, and the rainbow grew larger and larger, until it filled the Eastern sky, and I, the old fool that I am—found tears, dribbling down my cheeks.

Log: Oct. 14. It is evening and my eyes have grown hesitant to gaze upon the barometer for should it imply that another typhoon is coming coming my way, what could I do, but lower all sails. I had also noticed that it wasn't so much what it read, but far more, how fast was it falling. My eyes settled on it, it had fell and far too quickly. I lowered all sails and laid ahull for the night but I had no sooner gone below when I heard the thunder roll, then the wind picked up. Tried to ignore it, lit my oil lamp and made my supper then ate. Then, as is my habit before climbing into my berth, I opened the hatch and looked out. A full moon blessed the heavens, its light trying vainly to break through those heavy storm laden clouds and they ignoring the moon hurried their witch making way across that black and leaden sky. Occasionally a flash of lightning blazed across the heavens then the thunder rolled, that was not too disturbing, but imagine if you will.

As pitch black as it was, I could see those white caps, aye, I had no problem with that, but it was the hearing of them that troubled me. Listen, just close your eyes and listen. Hark, can't you hear that horrendous brushing sound that slowly becomes louder and louder, as if a giant broom was being wielded and sweeps the sea sending those foam crowned waves higher and higher, piling them atop one another then just when they can be stacked no longer there comes a brief silence when all is still and you think that you have lost your hearing—then, that white ragged crest would break, and that outrageous sound, like children screaming as they sledded down a snow laden hill, the seas roared gushing with laughter and boiling with joy, and—oh how I heard it, with my head just above the hatch. I heard and envisioned.

Then gradually all changed, for the moon broke free from the harrying clouds and what my imagination had conceived, lay before my eyes. Illuminated by the moon's cold and brilliant light the scene that lay before me became alive, and my imagination, stilled. Big enough those seas were in the darkness, when my mind ruled, when all I could imagine in that skull of mine was their eager bubbling froth. But when the resplendent moon free from that black tempestuous sky shone its bright and cold light and lightning flashes joined it and raced across the heavens, all those brilliant and flaunting lights like so many strobe lights, lit the scene. Creating when there was no need to create, emphasizing the shapes and contours of the sea, when there was no need to emphasize, and those foaming white cataracts rushing headlong towards me, now startlingly bright increased in size ten fold.

How small I felt, insignificant, yet, there also a feeling of being privileged, of being allowed to be a witness to such a view, to have that inner sense that enabled me to recognize and to behold so wholeheartedly, this incredible sight. Aye, it's true that's how I felt, as if a right had been granted to me, this working class idiot making claim to a birthright that was far above my class structure. I laughed, what a bloody old fool, this was my class structure, hadn't I been told that the salt in my blood matches the salt in the sea. And the ever working ever sleeping ever changing ever challenging ever amiable, aye, this demanding sea, somehow, reminds me of myself.

And if that was not enough there was more, was it of the sea, or was it of I, all quite silly, yet when that happened yesterday I should have responded quicker. Instead I just stood there, my mind wandering, my thoughts easily triggered, and I, mentally carried off yet when my attention came back to where it should have been, it was too late. Of course it is all quite laughable. Still—something did happen—yesterday.

I was doing the last of the sewing on my new one hundred and twenty foot head sail, but the barometer had been slowly falling and at noon it read 28.8 inches, after seeing that I thought I'd better go up on deck and drop the stay sail. I rushed up on deck and lowered and lashed down the stay sail, then hurriedly went back below, less than an hour later that stay sail was kicking up its heels and wildly thrashing over the cabin top. Disgruntled, I pushed my sewing aside and dragged myself again on deck, and there with one foot on the cabin top, the other on the deck, crabbed my way along the stay sail boom lashing down the angry flapping sail. It was only when I had well secured the sail did I casually raise my eyes to the sea. Then I understood why the stay sail had cast off its lashings, and thankful that it had and brought me up on deck.

Directly astern and dominating the curve of the horizon from east to west, was an enormous turbulent black cloud and where it met the horizon, a streak of white grew, and I knew what that white foam meant. I had to get my main sail down as quickly as possible. I released the main sail halyard, climbed on to the cabin top, and with one arm wrapped firmly around the mast, clawed down the sail. Crossed the bridge deck and hauled the sheets in snug, then with one foot on the raised aft deck and the other on the binnacle whipped a lashing around the mainsail and was at the wheel—more with good fortune than with efficiency, just before the foam laden breath of the thunderhead struck Broom.

The wind roared and like a whetted knife the sea cut through those newly made crests and sent their scud, now level with my ears whizzing past like frosted bullets. All I had up was my new seventy-five square foot jib, and my one hundred and twenty-five square foot sail of many colours. That wind and those sails made this twelve ton boat pick up her skirts and fly. I could feel her ass as it first began to sink, then her bow rose and I could swear she was planing, and as much as I would have loved to have gone below and switched on the G.P.S, to see how fast we were moving, I felt that I couldn't possibly leave the wheel. How exhilarating it was, Broom soaring along with its bow lifted high, the hull almost halfway out of the sea. Oh, it was thrilling with those pieces of sea foam scudding horizontally past my ears. A quick glance on either side and I could see that we were riding on the bow wave, another quick glance and I realized that there astride us—was that giant Thunderhead. Like some angry God finding me a nuisance and determined to brush me aside, treating Broom like those seas that he had so easily piled up. I was running wing on wing with those two head sails and I felt that I could not take my attention off the steering for a moment. We were simply going too fast, and yet that whirlwind was sending us North, the direction we wanted to go, those two little sails, belly full and pregnant were flying us along. Terrified I was, and at the same time ... ecstatic.

We flew like that, and after a time it was like I was sensing the wishes of Broom more that actually steering, touching the wheel this way then that way, keeping my two head sails wing on wing. Aye, acting like I was mesmerized, like Broom was telling me what to do, like I was out of myself. I have no idea how long I stood steering like that, feeling somehow removed from myself, then I began to notice on my sail of many colours, where the sheet was attached to the clew, a thread or were there two, stiffly fluttering as if they were not too sure which direction to point. I looked, saw, and began to realize, and quietly I murmured, 'Shit'. Then that four lettered word disconnected Broom and I, a switch was flicked, my brain changed gears, my mind wandered off and all I could conceive of, was the heavy concentrated brown solid sludge that was accumulating in my inners. Is that what constipation does to you?

My mind at last responded and my attention raced back to the storm jib, and I saw thread by thread break free from the cloth of the sail and watched them, as they did that same rigid fluttering act and like a movie filmed in slow motion the clew on my sail of many colours slowly began to come apart, piece by piece. I left the wheel and was halfway up the starboard deck when it literally exploded and pieces of the sail flew off and joined the white scurrying foam. I released the halyard and crawled forward, with my hand on the down haul I attempted to haul the sail down. All too late. Aye, it's a fool I am, I have no doubt about that for why else would I find myself on my knees on the fore deck, the sea crashing over the bulwarks that salted ocean totally saturating me, and as the last remnants of the sail flogged haplessly, I hand over hand made my way back to the wheel, murmuring a eulogy to the sail. "Good bye old friend, you've sailed the world with me, my shipmate in many a storm, I've patched you and have known you, and so many times have sewn you—Good bye." The bow dipped, a breaking sea came sweeping over the bow and inundated me. I eased the wheel and thankfully, the Thunderhead having well exercised his irascibility and appeased his anger, no longer glowered over my shoulder. Later that night I recalled what I had said, and smiled, the words had left me so easily, though they did remind me of something Kipling had written.

Log: Nov. 1. Sea has wiped out the solar panel and rail and removed one of my navigation lights. I am again rationing food. With one cup of rice a day there will be sufficient for fifty-five days, that means that unless I curb my appetite, by Christmas the rice will be finished. Coffee for three more days. Tea, two bags a day for forty-six days. Water at four litres a day, sixty days. Stay sail being repaired, when finished will only be left up overnight in fine weather. Which seems unlikely? All sails must come down with falling barometer. Lack of thread and needles. Before supper the barometer had started its downward tumble, before dark all sails were down and we were lying ahull. I had, over time learned to sleep with the howl of the wind in the rigging, and the sound so close to my ear of the ocean's roar. I had got used to the slap and splash of the seas that came streaming over the windward gunwale, the sound of a river running over my head and the gush as it poured out of the lee scuppers, but there was a noise now that was quite different. Again I awoke to the sound of something clattering and banging against the hull. I lay wondering on what it was? An oil drum washed off the deck of a freighter, I had met them before, if so, it would clatter and bang its way along the hull then be gone, but it didn't.

No, it wasn't the dinghy, for it was secured over the skylight, it wasn't the sails or the rigging. There it was again that clatter and bang. I took my flash light and made my way through the engine room into the aft cabin. Lifted the floor boards and checked the steering, everything seemed normal, and yet, every now and then I would hear that same crash and bang. I opened the hatch and shone my flashlight around the deck and all appeared as it should. I had no intention of wandering around the deck searching for the cause of the noise, however, the sea not content with letting me go Scot free sent half the ocean over the gunwale and the heavy spume saturated me before I had a chance to close the hatch. I went below cursing the bloody weather. It was two days before I felt that it was safe enough to venture on to the aft deck and find the cause. On that morning, lying prostrate with my arms reaching down and over the stern, I hauled aboard the aluminum pipe that held the solar panel and stern light. The stainless steel bolts holding the pipe rail to the davits had sheared, the heavy electrical wiring I had used for the power supply had allowed it to dangle as it swayed and banged into the hull, yet had kept it secure.

I had not the slightest doubt from what I had been experiencing that had I sailed around the Horn the weather could not have been any worse. Yes, I had been keeping a weather eye open on the barometer, but I also had begun to feel that if I paid it too much attention, I would become a nervous wreck. There had been times that the barometer had hovered below 28 inches and it had been dead calm. At that time it would have been quite easy for me to convince myself that I was a speck in the eye of a typhoon, and I probably was. There was one consolation in all of this, and that was that I was now out of the west flowing North Equatorial current, and had entered the east flowing North Pacific current, and with time, that current alone would take me to the shores of North America.

Yes, I am now in the Western Hemisphere. All is well, the day is fine, the sea is gentle and I'm smiling. Having started this on a more optimistic note do not be misled, an occasional change in the weather required no doubt to keep my spirits up. However, I am becoming fed up writing about anything as boring as the weather, so, I have decided today to write of something, well, equally as boring, but far closer to my heart. My bowels. Oh for goodness sake I know, no ones interested, but I am, my bowels and I have been close companions for many years and I'm not at all willing to ignore them because someone doesn't want to hear about them.

First, let me reminisce. I remember coffee, had my last cup Nov. 6. I remember our house in Victoria. I remember the mornings. Two cups of coffee and the morning paper. I would be half way through the cryptic cross word puzzle when nature would tell me that I had to sit on the toilet. I would only be on it for ten seconds, well, perhaps a little longer if it was a particular silly crossword. No fuss, no pain, no bother, my waste was easily disposed off. I really don't think the crossword puzzle had anything to do with it, my regularity that is. In those days I hardly needed to flush the toilet, a cup of water thrown in the bowl would have amply washed my softly formed discharge, over the neck of the toilet and gracefully down the sewer. Now today, well that's another thing entirely, for I'm not too sure if I have to go or not, and that was true for yesterday, and the day before, and etc. At first I tried, now I don't bother. I got fed up sitting there and nothing happens, though something did happen, a few days ago though when I looked in the toilet bowl it was empty. The reason I know something happened was that I was sitting patiently waiting when there was a great splash, as if I had just dropped a one inch diametre steel bolt in to the toilet bowl. The cheeks of my behind were wet, I stood up and looked into the bowl, it was empty, except for some of the remaining water.

You will of course gather that the care and feeding of the hand primed toilet pump is a matter of prime importance. Attempting to pump a one inch diametre steel bolt, though my personal belief in my case, soft lead would be more correct, through the pump and overboard would not be a good idea. After drying my wet posterior I timidly approached the pump. Gently I applied pressure, the handle thankfully moved, then it stuck, rock solid. Yet I am a patient man, with gentle words of persuasion and caressing strokes, I did eventually get that unwelcome and leaden projectile that had so unwillingly left my body overboard. Where it assuredly fell with ever increasing velocity down those fathomless depths, leaving behind a trail of stunned fish and undoubtedly causing a colony of bottom feeders, a slow and agonizing death. Now that wasn't too bad .. was it?

Chapter 19

Much had taken place, and much of that, was I. I was half starved and any energy I had was easily dissipated. It was the first time in my life that I, who had always been active, found myself willing to be idle, which with my lack of food was fitting. The little sail area that I had left had to come down at the first sign of rising winds, when the winds began to shriek and the seas reach those incredulous heights unseen by me before, it was far too dangerous to be on deck. I was becoming resigned to my fate. The days were becoming shorter, and as I lay, cold, wet and hungry in my damp berth in what seemed to be eternal darkness, I waited, and found myself ever listening. Yet it wasn't the clamour of the seas my ears now shuddered from hearing, or their relentless pounding on the hull, it was the scream from that cyclonic wind that raged around me, that in surpassing seventy knots plucked from the shrouds a sound blessedly unheard of on land. Aye, hideously it sang and the tumultuous seas, flayed by that wild wind sent their crowned crests eighteen metres high, cursing the waters arround me.

And the Broom and I like so much flotsam climbed those high crests, then on reaching the top, sank in to a seemingly bottomless crevasse, was it that action that spawned the insane harmonic in the rigging, that caused I lying in that hellish blackness to feel as if Broom and I had been transported in to some Stygian Shakespearean nightmare.

The raging angry sea, brutalized by the wind and white with foam and spray. Broom, barely afloat on this boiling broth of a witches cauldron and the witches up there in the rigging, with their claws plucking the shrouds as if they were strings on the devil's base, and I who now knew, waited for the first bar of Danny Boy. Had I had gone mad, no, though I would have, if they had played all of that lovely Irish air but most happily for my mental state they only knew the first bar. "Oh—Danny --- Boy." Then there they would be a pause. Then again. "Oh—Danny—Boy." I reckoned the pause was when Broom sunk down in the crevasse and the seas towered over us, or was it being played on the way up, I don't know, nor, do I know if at that time there was the odd witch up there, plucking at the rigging.   When first hearing that harsh, yet harmonious sound my curiosity became overwhelming, I opened the hatch and looked. With my eyes but five feet above sea level, those crests towering over me were at least sixty feet high. From the top of those froth laden crests and down in to the sunken hollow that lay between, was a wide valley that had been created by the strength of the wind. Wavelets had been swept clear and lay piled high atop a white mountain of spume and spray, that was rushing towards me. I can with the utmost sincerity inform you what a grand magnificent, awesome, and fascinating sight those seas are to behold. Providing it is not for long.

There's not a cloud in this sky of sheer blue and the reflected blue of the sky is barely discernible under the sea's cover of white seething foam. The seas are continually sweeping the cabin top and finding places to squirt cold sea water below, the result is that everything below is either wet or damp. On either side of the trunk cabin are five port lights. Since the beginning of November I have became concerned about those seas, for should they break when meeting Broom they'd send tons of water crashing in to the hull, though it wasn't the hull that concerned me but the portlights. I had taken my sail covers and stretched and lashed them down, one on either side of the trunk cabin in the hope that should the portlight glass break they would stop most of the sea from pouring below. The forces of those seas hitting Broom were enormous, and when I saw the amount of water in the bilge I gave thought to the integrity of the hull. I lifted the floor boards and scrutinized the bilge, no, those buckets of sea water were coming from above.

The main cabin has a skylight, it is sealed with a rubber gasket, stored on top of the cabin roof and covering the skylight sat my nine foot hard dinghy securely lashed down. Regardless how water tight that hatch appeared to be those seas hit us with such force that the dinghy gave little protection. I stood almost under the skylight with a safety belt wrapped snugly around my rapidly slimming waist, allowing my hands to be free to cook, yet when one of those seas hit a fine spray would come shooting out from under the hatch gasket. Even with my sail cover protection around the portlights, they too when hit began to dribble. They also had a rubber gasket all around and except for the two around the cooking stove were also caulked and sealed on the inside.

My once warm and pleasing cabin is now dark and gloomy, with the dinghy over the skylight and the sail covers over the portlights, there is little light, and what there is comes through the tears that the seas have made in the sail covers. When the wind screams the ragged cloth flaps wildly and those rips tap an indecipherable message on the glass, then light, hesitantly flashes in. As everything seems different at night and our imagination far more active they were times that I lay there in my damp berth and thought. Had the witches grown tired of their melodic efforts up in the rigging and were now on deck and there, with their clawed fingers and blackened nails, trying to attract my attention by their irritating—tap—tap tap—tap, on the glass. Or, were they just trying to warn me? I lay in the dark and noisy dampness and did my best to ignore their efforts. On either side of the trunk cabin and beneath the portlights ran my bookshelves. Those shelves are now barren.

My books that had once sat there had become waterlogged, and I, not too willingly threw them overboard. Gone was

Slocum, who kept forgetting to button up his fly, and Voss who with great fondness admired sea anchors. Goodbye to dear old Hiscock, who when telling of stocking up for cruising, says, and a pound of rice, and lest you be mistaken, adds, for rice pudding. Adieu to Moitessier, who, though doing well in the ocean race dumped a load of stuff overboard, and changed his mind. So long to Tristan Jones, burgoo, and his vivid imagination. To Poe, sleep well, and to Robert Louis Stevenson, 'will you no come back again'. Fare thee well to the Norton Anthology of English literature and Robertson Davies, who had a heck of a time trying to ride a bicycle. I do hope he can swim, and many others. Splash, they were gone. The few, such as the Roberts of Burns and Service, and the Ocean Passages for the World, I stowed in the driest place aboard, and that, apart from the stove's oven, was the ice box.

With winters approach darkness came earlier, and though I had electric lights, I used them only when it was really necessary. I would not risk having a flat battery when I needed to start the engine. As for my oil lamp, I fed it like an Old Scrooge as I grudgingly eyed up its container, constantly assuring myself that the kerosene that I had would last as long as I. Its Golden Glow was my solace, not bright enough to read by but warm enough to almost dry my socks, gloves, hat and matches. Its lowly simple and warm light secured me from those hideous nights and helped to remove my mind from my noisy and tempestuous companions, no electric light could have possibly given me the heart felt comfort that it did.

I had hung my stainless steel colander, that no longer looked as if it had ever seen a stainless steel factory above my oil lamp, and when night came, as it did all too soon, I lit my oil lamp and that rusty colander became my handy man's all purpose dryer. Inside it lay my matches, while daintily festooned around its outer edge hung, my gloves, socks, and hat. But it's true, regardless whether I had light to read by or not, I had no interest in reading. My mind was not concerned on deciphering someone else's meaning, my mind was coming to grips with those thoughts of my own that had long awaited a time such as this, where concepts had once been formed from casual speculations, and now there was no need to venture, for now there was ample time to ponder and to muse.

All was a mess below, what was once my snug and cozy quarters was a disaster. The port bookshelf that was also a handhold and had once sheltered books, was now split and broken. We had been assaulted by a particularly vicious breaker and I had been violently thrown against the shelf, breaking the shelf then with the reaction of Broom to the sea, thrown forward and hit the galley counter, and there found myself laying prostrated over it, gasping for air and trying desperately to draw breath. It was the first time in my life that I had been hit so hard that I couldn't breathe, it was also the first time in my life when I found myself giving thanks, and that particular realization grew daily. This voyage, this very personal fragment of my journey through life was gradually changing from a physical adventure to a spiritual experience, it was becoming much more than I would ever have thought, it was not just that I was struggling with the sea, I was also struggling with a bog that lay under my balding pate. A morass that surrounded my mind, and that I, had always taken for worth, until I had met that wild and cleansing sea. And to add to all that, was that I had began to acquire a pain at the bottom of my tail bone when I lay flat on my back, so that to sleep I had to lie on one side or the other. I had no intention of getting a mirror and dropping my pants and looking, first, it was too bloody cold, secondly, it was probably salt water sores, and thirdly, I really didn't want to know.

Barometer had fell to 28.0 inches, has risen now to 29.1 inches though the wind is quite unaware of this. Just realized that I've been at sea for 75 days and according to my reckoning sailed 3887 miles, again reckoned we have another 1931 miles to reach the Juan de Fuca Strait—if we kept that same mileage we would be home by Dec. 29. It's possible I could get home for Hogmanay—what a party that would be. Then unexpectedly my cargo popped into my head and for a short while I was off dreaming and forgot the weather, until, we were hit by a sea that wildly came crashing aboard. I had no doubt that it was another angry Greybeard. I was thrown against the salon table and everything that was not firmly affixed went flying. Those things that I had stored on the starboard side, changed places with those I had stowed on the port. Part of my stove disappeared. My tapes that I had thought securely stowed under the tape player on the port side, landed on the starboard book shelf, the rest in the bilge. Sea water came pouring out of the bottom of the oil heater. I had two deck boxes bolted to the deck, in the morning when I looked out of the portlight, there was only one.

The sea that had taken my deck box had also swept up the side of the aft cabin, entered an air vent and shorted out the fuse panel. This was the cause of my electrical problems, but I only found that out later but until then I was forever fiddling with the panel and bypassing fuses in order to get the electric's working. Not that I had many. My radio/tape player, V.H.F. radio, depth sounder, cabin lights, navigation lights, G.P.S, and probably the best companion of the lot, my little portable Radio Shack short wave receiver, that even when it was sent tumbling down into the bilge still worked. As I neared the Juan De Fuca Strait freighters would begin to over take and pass me, I would have to keep well out of their way. I knew that I could be navigating Juan De Fuca Strait, Race Rocks, or Victoria Harbour, in the dark, without navigation lights. I could only hope at that time there would be little traffic. I did not want to warn shipping of my lack of navigation lights for I knew the coast guard would be listening and would soon start telling me what I had to do. I had, surprisingly though it might be, managed, I would like to continue what I had started.

The little light bulb that was built in to the compass has become a bit of a nuisance as I was never too sure whether it would light or not, so I went to the trouble of rigging another light only to realize that I seldom required it. For the nights when the sky was clear I rediscovered the Milky Way, what a unique visual pleasure there was when those heavy rain filled clouds went their way and I again saw the brilliance of the heavens. Many a night I never looked at the compass, but would merely stick my head out of the hatch and let the Big Dipper and Cassiopeia point my way to the Polestar. Ah, how romantic those nights were, when I could so easily discard the compass, the G.P.S, and sail in the manner of the seafarers of the past, gazing on the heavens and letting the planets and stars guide my way. There was something so incredibly joyful about doing that, standing there with only my head above the hatch, my body sheltered from the challenging icy wind and my eyes surveying the cold and brilliant heavens, and I, happily ignoring those modern navigational tools.

Yet, as everything in life comes with a price, the cost of the clarity of those skies was the bitter cold that I suffered, though I never doubted that had I more food in my stomach and had my clothing been dry, the chill would have affected me less. Still, how comforting it was to gaze on the star filled heavens as I made my slow daily Northward progress, and each night notice, Polaris becoming higher and higher in that lustrous firmament. Then in the morning with a mug of hot water where a well used tea bag barely floated, look through the tattered sail cover on the starboard portlight and discover day break, and there to the east see the rising sun that was now slowly wending its way south to its winter's solstice. How I loved it.

Log: Nov. 24. A change has came over the sea, there's now a steepness to it, those high white capped mountain peaks who lorded over those low broom swept valleys below had closed their ranks. When the sea elevated us to the top of those foam soaked crests and I gained enough courage to open the hatch. I would look out, then down. It was as if I was standing at the edge of a snow capped peak in the Selkirk mountains, and directly below my feet ran a steep ravine cutting its way down into a deep and narrow crevasse, covered in soft fresh snow. Except, as I watched, the snow moved, and I moved, for I slowly slid down over the frosted snow in to that white crevasse. Eventually I stood at the bottom, and shielding my eyes from the cold biting spray I looked up, and my enticed eyes fastened themselves on that great white mountain that magically grew before me. Tilt your head back and look, no higher, higher yet, and there, towering overall it appeared, like a great white pompous God with a white curling pouting lip. Over my head it hung, this hoar frosted avalanche piled high on a white crowned peak that could at any moment break its union and unload its heavy winter's harvest upon my bone chilled limbs.

But I wasn't in a valley looking up at a snow capped mountain peak. I was in the middle of a great ocean, and the union that would break was not of the land but of the sea, and it wasn't snow. Yet, how incredible it is that the wind can stir up that sea and create those mountainous white peaks that are laden with white foaming froth, that is almost, and yet, not snow. And there we were, Broom and I, now on our elevator ride up, up on our way to meet that avalanche like wave that was as capable of doing as much damage as one of snow and ice. My eyes never took their awestruck look from that great pouting lip as we climbed higher and higher, then miraculously, I realized that we had reached the summit. It passed under us and I turned my head from starboard to port. Then as I watched, that great curling lip of the Greybeard, now sixty feet to leeward, broke. I could hear the thunderous roar as that great white over hanging billow parted company with the sea, how well I visualized that mad frenzied mass as it cascaded its way down the other side of that billowing sea.

Yes, we were lucky, but would our luck hold. It would have been quite easy to have been on the other side of that great curling lip, where we would have went ass over tea kettle, head over heels, spinning and corkscrewing our way down that cold and roaring vortex. Yes, Poe's Maelstrom.

By the time the last light from that weak winter's sun had gone I would have devoured the last morsel of my hot evening's meagre meal, and with my hot drink snug between my chilled thighs, blow out the warm and comforting flame from the oil lamp and the cabin would again be enclosed in darkness. And with the enfolding dark came the sounds of the night, and though in my short sleeps I brushed them aside when I awoke, they were always there. The sounds, no different than those of the day, except as I lay there blind and surrounded by this damp dismal environment that had so easily enveloped my unwilling spirit, my ears though tuned were hesitant—yet I waited for the ominous plucking call of the witches. And if the rain was not coming down in torrents, I would gain courage and open the hatch and look around the horizon.

What horizon, there was naught to see except those white foaming suds mounted on stampeding seas. Those were the nights when the cloud cover blanketed the star studded heavens. Those were the nights when I wondered that I could I see those foam coated raging seas at all. But wait, they were other nights when I hesitantly raised my eyes and saw the splendour of what lay above. If you have been entranced by the sparkling firmament as you stood gazing from your vantage point on some dark hill top in a crowded city, you will be moved a thousand fold more as you stand alone, out there in the middle of this great angry Greybeard sea with over a thousand mile of ocean separating you from the nearest land as you gaze, in awe, to that glorious firmament that filled the heavens.

Why was I moved so? Was it the pristine clarity? Was it those unfeeling seas? Was it just that I was there? Was it my hunger and the cold? Was it all of those things that made me so receptive? To find myself feeling so deeply, to somehow be all absorbing, like a radio receiving signals from outer space and yet not able to make sense of it. They were times that I felt that I had been transported, yes it's true. Silly, isn't it, feeling like that, time was of no consequence, I never knew when I left. I just knew that I had, and it would somehow slowly enter my dull skull that I was back. Standing there with only my head above the hatch, that furry hat from Nepal that my daughter had given me, firmly and snugly pulled down over my head and ears. The exposed skin on my face stung by the black needles of the icy sea spray that flew blindly and relentlessly out of the dark night. I saw, yet heard not a sound, though the seas pounded Broom and the wind howled. After a time I would come out of my trance, is that really what it was? Then I would close the hatch and in the darkness grope my semiconscious way to my cook stove, there I would pause. With my left hand firmly gripping the edge of the galley sink, my right wiping away the moisture and condensation of the glass on the portlight. I stood in silence, looking out into that wild sail cover whipped night. I always paused there, but why? No, I wasn't deep in thought nor was I meditating. Funny isn't it when we start using a certain word, then we think there is surely a better word, in this case the simple word pause, then we find there isn't any. You see all I could think that what I was doing there was, that I was offering a silent prayer to a God I don't believe in. Strange, quite strange, isn't it.

As I've mentioned my bowels were not happy with me, in the last week my bladder has decided to join them in showing their displeasure. Unlike my bowels who were just on strike my bladder was working all the overtime it could get which caused me to have great arguments as whether or not to have my bed time hot drink. Yet, my argument was ever easily settled. I lit the stove and put my half filled kettle on. My sodden gloves surrounding that hot flame were close enough that steam rose and I could smell the leather as they singed.

My hands first being placed on the kettle, then as the kettle became hot, hovered over as if in supplication to the flame, then removing my hat from my bald pate placed it on top of the kettle like a fur covered tea cosy. The coffee and tea long gone, I flavoured the boiling water with a touch of spice, and took a mug full under the tarp and in bed with me. Have you any idea how much pleasure I received from that hot drink, could you not conceive how I felt as I held it so adoringly in my chilled hands and with tender love, would bury it in my crotch. Aye, how I relished it. After enjoying the warmth of that mug, I would be, given the man I am soon fast asleep. Ten minutes later I would awake feeling that my bladder was about to burst. I'd given up hope of being able to make my way to the head and instead kept a large empty coffee can in close proximity to where I slept, jammed under the oil stove. But first I had to untangle myself from the tarp, and blankets, and by the time it took me to dig through all I wore and search for my now terrified and bladder frightened limp member, it was almost too late. The result of this grand exercise was, and regardless of how hard I tried not to … I squirted.

Log: Nov. 26. Awoke to the sound of a rattling halyard, slipped on my raingear and buried my bare feet in my gum boots, and went on deck in that black, wind howling rain soaked night, and found out why the halyard was rattling. About four foot from the top of my fully reefed main was a rip running from the leach to the luff. Its use as a storm sail had ended. Aye, another big hand sewing job awaited me, lowered the sail and with a handful of sail ties and one foot on the aft cabin roof and the other on the binnacle, and hanging on as if a grim death awaited me if I fell, which it did. I tied the sail ties on that flogging sail and quickly went below. My hands back to their frozen state, my bladder bursting, I closed the hatch and quickly reached for the coffee can, dug out that terrified limp member of mine and joyfully relieved myself. The last drip was leaving my body when the sea pounded Broom and sent me staggering, the coffee can went flying and hit the cabin top, turned cartwheels and the contents emptied over me. I remember thinking—at least it's warm. I also remember something else, something I said. Now, I have my doubts about God, but that doesn't stop me from talking to him. And I remember exactly what I said, and when I said it, it was just after I found a tea towel to wipe my brow. "Look God, there has been a few times since I started this trip when you have heard me say, 'boy, I'd sure love to get pissed,' I just thought I'd let you know, that is if you don't mind me saying so, that what has just taken place was not at all what I had in mind." Blown back another thirty mile.

Chapter 20

Years ago the U.S Hydrographic Office made a relationship between the height of the seas in feet and the wind velocity in miles per hour. The relationship being approximately 1 to 2, a wind of 50 m.p.h. being capable of raising a sea of 25 feet high. The ratio for the length from crest to crest being some 20 times the height so that a sea 25 feet high would then measure from crest to crest 500 feet. These figures only applying if the land to windward is 1000 miles or more away. Those are the seas that are known as Greybeards, hence their name.

On Nov. 27 my position. N 40 degrees 25 minutes. W 167 degrees 27 minutes. Eureka, California, N 40 degrees 50 minutes. W 124 degrees 0 minutes. Juan de Fuca Strait, N 48 degrees 15 minutes, W 124 degrees 0 minutes. Yet, I am 100 miles closer to the Juan de Fuca Strait that I am to Eureka, California. We are also [yes, the Broom and I] 2700 miles west of Morioka, Japan. 2000 miles east of Eureka, California, and to our south Midway in the Hawaii Islands, 1100 miles away. The nearest land to us directly north lies Dutch Harbour in the Aleutians Islands, 1000 miles, a direction that I have no intention of heading.

And there we were, we, who had traveled to where the monsoons battle for supremacy of the sea, we, who had journeyed to the birth place of typhoons, and now where are we? Smack dab in the middle of the Greybeard sea, where the raging wind with a thousand miles of open ocean before it flogs the uncertain sea, and the sea hurrying to escape, climbs, higher and higher .... until! And there we were, where the progeny of the wind, those Old Greybearded bastards could come along and let us know that we were not at all welcome on their ocean.

Yet, hold on and let me ease your mind for there were times when all became quite different, and strange as it may be, I felt a sense of affinity with those white maned old Greybeards. Transported, yes that's what I felt, and I willingly reached out, grasped, and absorbed all that surrounded me. Aye, for there was no finer sense of spirit, of the sublime energy that this world has offer than that, that was portrayed before me and which I innocently and naively had found myself so warmly accepting. It flooded through me this feeling, leaving me overwhelmed by an intense sense of belonging, of being part of this natural richness that I was surrounded by, and carried away by my thoughts I found myself altering the scene. For those raging white headed Greybeards that were once bent on sending me down into those cold blue green depths, are now proud and mighty white maned stallions racing joyously, surrounded by their mares and young, and have allowed me to celebrate with them in their life, their zest, their vigour. Yes, they were part of a whole, and how well they blended and accepted me.

Aye, the wind, the master of the sea, recognize its invisibility yet acknowledge its power, and as the ocean reacts to its rage, white streaken it runs, heaping itself over its own kind until steeple top high, it stumbles --. Notice how the sea is stirred as if by a giant mixmaster, see how it swells and the enormity of foam that it creates --. Listen, can you not hear it? The howl of the wind as it rages through the rigging and creates that ear wrenching scream --. Feel the vibration as those outrageous seas crash pummel batter and ravage your vessel, and how it all seems to resound, through you --. And why? You're in an echo chamber and all that there is of you, is your ears, still, there is that other sense --. Tactile, as you secure yourself by grasping onto the nearest object and through the steel hull you feel the vibration—the pounding—the drumming. Aye, and how well they compliment one another.

Aye, that's how it was, but now it was time for me to also recognize ... the vulnerability of my little ship and I, for are we not one? So let us put all else aside for the moment had come. I had no other choice. It was my responsibility to make Broom more secure and ensure that she would suffer no serious damage. A sea anchor could be most beneficial, which I didn't have, but was about to. Of course there are those who will wait till the last minute to manufacture one, such as I, and the expense seems to be of the least concern. Unless, as you may and fairly enough, put a value on floorboards, bunkboards, galley sinks, bags of sails, in other words anything that you may have aboard that you think will stop you from coming too soon, to a watery death. Yes, ingenuity is so commendable, cost was of no consequence. Being a Scot I find that quite admirable. As for what was now happening and continued in December was that Broom and I were pawns in a show of strength. We were a well bruised and beaten ball in a tennis match of the grandest proportions being played between the West and the East. What we gained to the east from a westerly, we lost when the Easterlies blew. Hence my despair. In my flights of fancy I began to feel that I was sentenced to spend eternity out there on those hellish seas. Endlessly struggling, gaining one day only to lose it the next. My own private and personal hell.

When those westerly storms blew and created those horrendous seas they did most thankfully, send me on my way, but when we became becalmed and the easterly storms came it did not sit at all well with me. Aye, it was, whether I liked it or not, time to drag the bunk boards up on deck, they were just over six foot long by two foot wide and made from three quarter inch plywood. They had a series of two inch diametre holes drilled in them, the purpose of the holes being to allow air to enter the foam mattresses. Those holes put in for ventilation served my purpose for the sea anchor. I brought them on deck then with two pieces of wood, one inch by four inch by four foot long and four cee clamps I assembled a sea anchor. Stored in the bilge was a Swedish rock anchor with four folding flukes, those flukes entered the holes in the plywood. Attached to the anchor was a fifty foot length of quarter inch chain and a two hundred foot length of anchor rode. I was quite impressed when I had it all together. It was a prime example of the ingenuity of man. I can assure you if you had seen it you would have thought I knew what I was doing. Shaped like a raft it was, in size just over six foot by just over four foot, the rock anchor sat right in the middle. I ran that anchor rode through my port anchor roller and all the way back to where my sea anchor sat on the bridge deck, and there shackled the chain on to the sea anchor. As the westerly blast eased I started organizing this conglomeration that now littered the deck. I had this gut feeling that we were in for another easterly blow, this time I was prepared. I stood admiring my handiwork when I turned and looked to the east. A heavy low lying black cloud dominated the horizon, yes, we were in for another unwelcome visitor though I seldom paid attention to those ill favoured guests. Was I learning toleration, I doubt it. It was probably more that there was little that I could do about it, that is, except for this time, that is, if I could get this unwieldy contraption off the deck and in to the sea. Unexpectedly, that was an easier chore than what I had anticipated. By the time the easterly was upon us it was over the side. It looked good as it slowly sank and drifted away from Broom. The weight of the anchor and chain taking it down, the plywood sheets lying at a right angle to the anchor rode just as I hoped they would. It was settling and submerging into the sea just as I wished and all I had to do was to keep feeding out the anchor rode. Bloody great I thought, watching it as it slowly drifted and sinking exactly in the manner that I had wished, I was extremely well pleased with what I had just created. Oh, I remember it well. I can see myself standing there with an idiot grin on my smug face.

The eastern wind was now upon us, yet my eyes dwelt only on the sea anchor. Except as I watched I realized there's something not quite right, for it's not where it should be. The last time I tried sea anchoring that five hundred pound brute hung straight down. This time it would not be like that, for the drag would not be straight down, but out there, of the bow, where it will be giving a more efficient leverage to force the bow around to face the wind. Except, it ain't. It's over there, of the beam. Now just in case you are as confused as I am, the line that I have ran to this so called sea anchor is attached to the bow, however that good looking ingenious contraption that I have created is away off to the side. It's not supposed be away off to the side, it's supposed to be away off to the front. In other words the position of Broom hasn't changed, she is still sitting sideways to the wind and seas, and simply dragging this ingenious abortion along. It was all very quick and rather sad but there it was, my future as a sea anchor consultant was over. Sorry Voss.

The next morning I awoke, feeling down, and thought of three scenarios. I make it, I don't, or I abandon Broom, a sound hull. I have criticized people for doing that. At least now I know what they may have felt, and, so as you may clearly understand what I mean by my saying abandon, let me explain. I do not in any way mean jumping in to the dinghy, put that idea out of your head, no, I meant more along the lines of a freighter coming alongside. Although I had not seen any as yet I was bound to see them as I got closer to the Juan de Fuca Strait. Then as I gave some thought to that, forget it. Can you imagine one those huge bloody condominium monstrosities bearing down on me as they came to my rescue. And Broom bouncing up and down like a polo ball, punched this way and that way by those young up and coming Greybearded buggers, and that great bloody freighter sitting stoically, like its embedded in concrete, and the crew no doubt thinking that I was mad, throw a rope ladder over the side. And that's when I make a graceful leap, grasp the ladder with my nimble strong hands and with the utmost agility and ease, clamber up and aboard in to the arms of my rescuers. Oh piss off, fat bloody chance. No, we will forget about that scenario. Just as a matter of interest, I am back where I was a week ago.

Log: Dec. 9. Was quite a surprise for that day for I actually made 50 miles in the right direction, then the barometer fell to a low of 27.08. Lay ahull expecting a horrendous storm from the east, but thank God, yes, I did say thank God, it came from the west and the result of that low barometer reading became apparent. It was another night of the banshees screaming in the rigging, the thunderous roar of an approaching sea on its collision course to Broom, the overwhelming detonation as the sea explodes against the hull, the sound of a Niagara cascading over the gunwale with its thundering wild path sending sea water squirting from everywhere. And I, buried in my damp berth, my Nepal fur hat pulled tightly down over my eyes and ears, my old and well loved car blanket tugged down over my head trying to drown out the terrors of the night. I lying there in utter humility, cowering and praying that hell would go away.

For some reason that night I went in to the head, yes I was shitting myself, but my bowels had nothing to do with it. My bowels were totally on strike and as long as they didn't bother me, I was not about to worry. I have no idea why I went in there, for all thought dramatically disappeared when I casually looked in the mirror. For there looking back at me was not my face at all. The fur hat from Nepal was mine. The long and weak wispy gray hair that hung free were mine. My squaw man's car blanket held together at the neck with a rusty safety pin and draped over my old Mustang floater coat, yes that was mine. That scraggly gray beard that now hung half way down my chest, yes, that was mine—but the face was not mine.

If those were my eyes they lay sunken in a skull overlaid by a thin blue vein streaked skin. In the weak light from the electric lamp the bone of my nose shone glistening, bone white, if it was mine it had grown enormously. Long gray hairs sprouted from my nostrils. My cheeks, were they mine? Hollow and cadaverous, my cheek bones? that I had never noticed before, stood out, defiantly. The eyes, intense, the expression, grave, the aura haunted. Oh, I had no trouble at all knowing that face, those things from long ago that you thought forgotten, a past that lies shrouded in the darkness of your mind becomes unveiled at times like these. Yes, I knew that face, the deep and painful searching severity of those eyes, that stared back at me. I knew. What was I, eight years old? When my older sister took me to see my father, just before he died, his face wracked with pain, his body filled with cancer. The face that I saw in the mirror.

I have recalled little of my father, I had forgotten that time and to see his face in mine left me shocked. My head bowed, my hands tightly grasping the rim of the sink, I stood, saturated with the emotion that flooded through me, as if all the nerve endings in my body were reaching out and absorbing, while my mind struggled to calm itself. Yes, that evening was dramatic enough, aye, if it had only been that evening, yet there was much more. For I had noticed that I was becoming an emotional sponge for strange and bizarre things were happening to me, senses that I never knew, now existed. Like those nights when I raised my head out of the hatch and felt transported, or that day when the thundercloud angered over my shoulder and I steered Broom, except did I? Or the nights when I somehow knew and the sails would be lowered before Danny Boy played and Beveridge reef, I've forgotten Beveridge reef, yes that too. Was there an intuition forming between I and the sea? Could such a thing exist? Does that make sense? There was also this premonition that I had that should I go over the side it would be evil, evil is not a word I use, why would that word ever come into my head? And what on earth do I mean by even thinking that? I am not one of those religious fanatics that run around screaming that the world is coming to an end and that we will all end up in hell if we don't change our ways. Not that presently mine could not be improved upon, and as for ending in hell, well, it would be a damn sight warmer than here. Yet, evil is exactly the word I mean. Also, there was that strange thing that happened that night. I had went over to light my oil lamp and as the barometer hangs close by, had glanced at it. After seeing how quickly it had fallen I realized that I had to go on deck and lower sail. I opened the hatch.

At arms length hung a starless black sky, while a white cap making wind drove icy pellets through cold and darkening air. We were in for another easterly blast and they were things I had to do. I released the main sail halyard, and lowered the sail. With hands rapidly becoming red and raw I let fall the stay sail, by this time the wind had doubled in strength, hail the size of moth balls shot from that cold black cloud and ricocheted of the deck. With eyes barely open, my head bowed, I crossed the deck to the main mast. Previously I had merely zig-zagged my sheets and halyards to their respective cleats, on this voyage, I found that I had to finish them with a half-hitch. I went to release the mainsail halyard, then stopped and looked dumbly at my fingers.

I stood stunned, slow witted, unable to quickly appraise the problem, as if the cold and dampness had also entered my brain cells. My eyes slowly traveled from the halyard to my stiff frozen fingers, unable to grasp what had taken place yet unwillingly realizing that those fingers of mine were incapable of movement. My good and dependable hands were in a frozen cramp, useless. But on deck that night, the hail stones, the cold sleet laden wind, the seas soon to grow wild, the witches ready to scream in the rigging, all had vanished from my mind. For all that dominated my thoughts as I stood there huddled against the mast, was my useless stiff frozen hands, how could

I manage without them? Then quickly, my bladder needed my undivided attention and nature, miraculously, stepped in.

Out of that bitter wind flew the hurried sleet while my right arm snugly wrapped itself around that frigid mast, my left claws frozen talons fiercely dug through my innumerable pairs of pants. Then having found my barely warm limp member I crouched, sheltering it from the stinging hail I closed my eyes and without thought gleefully pissed my warm urine gratefully on my frigid claws. Aye, the welcome and blessed relief that I felt when the heat from my wasted bodily fluid returned life and movement to my fingers. Huddled there, my once frozen claws now beginning to flex, the warmth of my life giving blood slowly flowing through them, and with that thought drowning out all others, I stood as if gone mad, my head thrown back, my eyes tightly closed that billow making wind pounding hail against my face, my mouth opened wide sucking in the salt spirited air, and like a primal creature, I howled. Aye, assuredly it's an animal that I am.

By the time I had tucked my vulnerable, and extremely useful body part away it was pitch black. I released the stay sail halyard and clawed down the sail, then half kneeling, half crawling, struggled desperately to get the sail ties on before my fingers again froze stiff. Stooped, with my right knee on the cabin top my left leg stretched out supporting me, my right arm encircled around the boom, I made my way to its end, shivering from the cold and exhausted from fighting the flogging of the sail, but the elements were not yet willing to let me go. The wind raged and the sea, reacting to it created a Niagara like wave that roared as it headed towards Broom. I heard it coming, turned and saw a white mountain of water heading towards me, it pounded the hull and a cataract of white sea and foam leapt over the gunwale. The boom firmly enclosed in my embrace, I closed my eyes and waited. The boarding sea swept the deck and washed out my leg from under me, and like a piece of long lost driftwood the sea lifted me and sent me slithering along the cabin top, and without thought my legs entwined themselves in a mad and frightening embrace around the boom. Broom responding to the sea listed heavily to port and pressed me against the stay sail boom, then shed the sea and slowly recovering, became erect.

And I, without thought, slowly regained my footing and found myself crouched, half upright, my arms wrapped around the boom, my numb feet enclosed in my sixteen inch high rubber gum boots over flowing with freezing sea water. Frozen to the bone, breathing deeply in an attempt to calm myself, half starved and knowing that what lay before me would be another hellish night with the witches entertaining me with their intolerable screeching, while I like a coward, hid under my damp bedding ... then the unexpected that caused all distractions to flee from my thoughts for that one single ridiculous act removed all ... for there on my left shoulder ... was a grasp of a hand. I hesitated, then quickly turned and bowing my head to the biting spray, I stared with eyes almost unseeing through a glistening haze that lingered on the left shoulder of my yellow jacket, slowly the mist faded and I saw the icy hail as it pelted on my jacket, saw how it gathered in the creases on the rubber sleeve, and as it melted, trickled down my arm.

My eyes tightly closed my head bowed, and with hands once again frozen I stumbled my cold watery way below. Closed the hatch, yet left the cabin doors open, pried my gum boots off and raised them to the doorway and emptied out the sea water, closed the cabin doors. My boots fell on the floor, struggled out of my wet weather jacket and removed my wet weather pants and hung them up. I buried my frozen hands inside the waist of all I was wearing and nestled them between my thighs, my testicles hid. Walked in my bare feet on the wet sodden carpet over to my pausing place, and there, with eyes closed and head bowed, and with the roar of the sea and the howl of the wind for company, I stood in the damp and lonely darkness, my mind empty of thoughts, except for one that I couldn't escape, one concept that dominated all. Could that unseen hand that had pressed so firmly on my shoulder, the hand that had worked far harder than mine and had so little to show for its efforts, the hand that was now giving me strength and comfort,—could that have been—my Father's.

Chapter 21

I lit the stove and placed on it my filled pot, then on either side where the blue flame escaped from the bottom of the pot, I laid my mitts. I reached up, draped on the edge of my rusty colander was a damp gray woolen hat, knitted by my once Kiwi crew. Took it and placed it on the lid of pot so that it too almost touched the blue flame, my mitts now starting to singe I lifted them and with savage delight placed my chilled hands into them. The warmth and comfort they gave me far surpassed the other method that I had used, though this method did come from a more depletable source, the other practice however came from an unquenchable supply. Steam now rising from my woolen hat I lifted it from the pot and placed it upon my bald and freezing skull. Ah, it was almost, but not quite, like having an orgasm, except the pleasure lasted so much longer. No crown could have given me more joy than the delight of that hot woolen hat pulled down tightly over my hairless head and my ice tipped ears.

I bent down and opened the oven door of the cook stove and took out my blanket and like an old Indian squaw man draped its warm comfort over my shoulders. Until now I had never given thanks, everything I had in life was due to my own hard working efforts, but all of that was changing. I had, and quite unconsciously, found that when I struck a match and it lit, and when I took the flame to the oil lamp and it lit, I would give spoken thanks to the match for lighting, and to the lamp for its golden light and its warming heat. When I took the flame over to the gas stove and it lit, I would say, "thanks stove." How wonderfully enriching it was that something so simple as a match that lights, and the darkness is gone, and the stove lights and soon before me lies a hot meal, why would I not give thanks and why did I not do it years ago. Was I really such a bloody fool? When with each tumble on the barometer I went on deck and lowered my already well reduced sail, and when they came down without rips and tears, I again gave thanks. When I awoke in the morning after some of those hellish nights and found that not only that I was alive, but that Broom was also afloat. I can assure you I gave thanks. It had also become my habit at night when I took my boiling pot to bed, to give probably, the deepest thanks of all.

My macaroni now cooked, I added half a can of fish. Wearing my gloves that were rapidly cooling I lifted the pot of the stove and holding it close to my body, carried it, as if it was nectar from the Gods to my berth and there the pot and I buried ourselves in my damp bedding. Snuggled in the bedding, my squaw blanket draped over my head and wrapped around my shoulders and chest, enclosing within it the heat from the pot that I now held warmly embraced between my frigid thighs. My head bowed so that the heat from the pot rose and caressed my face. I now held the warmth of the pot in my bare hands. My meal was still far too hot to eat, and as hungry as I was, I was in no hurry to start. I was quite happy pleasuring myself in the luxury of the heat. When it cooled I would dine, but before that.

My education in the Gorbals, a poor, rough, working class area in Glasgow, was rather limited. Our teachers were a formidable lot and discipline in those days was extremely important. It struck me as I got older that our education was based on the assumption that they, the education system, thought that we, the riffraff of the slums were only good for three careers. A miner, a shipyard worker, or something that always seemed in demand, cannon fodder. I saw little future for myself in the latter. As a wee lad I was quite fond of prose and verse, odd for one such as I. What we received was mainly that of the English writers, such as Tennyson and Wordsworth. There was a smidgen from a Scotsman, Sir Walter Scott, he was known to have Conservative sympathies, a condition that was not at all approved of in the shipyards. There was little from that other Scot, the one that leaned to the left and had a tendency to turn his back to the church. He had little tolerance for organized religions, something I too suffer from. One of his many writings was that simple grace that I did not learn at school, and those words that had flowed from his pen expressed my own feelings so beautifully.

The hailstones were back again. A burst from a machine gun ricocheted of the cabin top and deck, a passing sea lifted us and roared as it broke on our leeward side. There was no way that I was going on deck for under these circumstances I was as warmly ensconced as I was ever going to get. I lifted the lid from my now warm pot, buried my face in its warmth, my nostrils sniffed the foodfilled odours, my mouth salivated. I put the lid aside then placing my spoon in the pot, quoted Burns.

"Some Hae meat an canny eat, and some Hae nane and wantit,
But Ah Hae meat and Ah can eat, so let the Lord be thankit."

Food had never been so cherished. Eaten with such gusto. Tasted so sumptuous as those meals I ate, there, where the weak golden flame from the oil lamp flickered with every blast, and the wild rolling sea sent shadows dancing on the cabin walls, and the witches feeling a need to once again bewitch me, would with their black edged nails pluck the shrouds and do there best to distract me with their funereal jigs. I ignored all and filled my coffee can, crawled under my damp blankets and quickly fell fast asleep.

I awoke with half a smile on my face, what the hell was I smiling about, 65 days, that's that's what it was, 65 days what?—without food—I had read that somewhere. I couldn't help it, I laughed. Is something telling me that I can live 65 days without food, out on those seas are they mad. 65 days he says.! Och Aye Nae Bloody Bother.

Do you realize how it could be, getting up in the middle of those blustering freezing nights. Trying to uncleat halyards with fingers frozen stiff, knowing that I would have to get that sail down or I would lose the bastard. 'Och Aye Nae Bother! big deal.' Digging with my frozen claws through two pairs of wet weather gear, a pair of heavy pants and two pairs of jogging pants, reaching for my poor and urine frightened limp member, which, I only wish was as stiff as my fingers, pissing on my claws and finding once again the blessed relief of fingers that could again move. 'Och Aye Nae Bloody Bother—65 days why that's bugger all.' Fighting the icy hail, lowering those bloody stiff freezing buggers, going below to my cosy and mildewed bunk with the enticing screech of the wind for company. Sticking my fingers in my mouth for whatever good that may have done. Then when the wind at last eases, back on deck hauling those frozen buggers up and after that gratifying task, going below for a refreshing glass of ice cold water, then jumping into my damp and squishy bunk, covering my fatless and bone flourishing body with sodden blankets, where moss has welcomely found a home.

And there I find myself envisioning long before those 65 days are up. Broom has found itself washed ashore, piled high on jagged weed strewn rocks and now abandoned by the ebbing tide, lies, like so much rejected flotsam, firmly aground somewhere on the wild rugged coast of Vancouver Island, vulnerable to the carrion and those who plunder. And the remnants of what was I, gray, gaunt, and ghastly, lying in my mildewed and mossy berth, with at last my constipation troubles over as one long leaden projectile oozes out of my shrunken bony buttocks. Then unexpectedly, a harmless beachcomber with lungs filled with pot and with rings dangling from his body orifices appears, sights the wreck of Broom and feeling that he can give life to the half drowned aboard with mouth to mouth resuscitation, my heroic rescuer, with pounding heart stumbles over the barnacled rocks and climbs aboard. Then with lowered eyes and fingers fiercely grasping his nostrils he hesitates, then quickly flounders below, and on finding me lying there looks down on my obscene remains and quickly changes his mind. Nevertheless, this well meaning romantic idiot most touchingly says. "Poor old bastard he must have loved the sea I'll take what's left of him and dump it out there on the rolling brine"—Oh God.

Perhaps you may have grasped that my chances of surviving 65 days out here in those conditions without food, is highly unlikely. I do hope so for I fear that they are times when I do not get my point across as clearly as I may wish, and the other point I would like to make, and hopefully I may do it with clarity, is the freezing damp cold. Being a bit of a romantic idiot I have in the past given thought to being buried at sea. Those were the days when I was more of a romantic than I am now. That was when I was chained to a job, well fed, perspired freely, and drank copious amounts of cold water. Oh, I shudder at the thought, except for the well fed part. These days all I can think of is that excellent poem from Robert Service that emphasizes what I feel so well.

'The Cremation of Sam M'Gee' and that line, 'It's the cursed cold and it's got right hold till I'm chilled clean through the bone, yet it ain't being dead it's my awful dread of the icy grave that pains'. How well I understood that line, for it wasn't dying that bothered me, it was going over the side into that icy outrageous ocean, that was where the concept of me feeling that it would be evil, came from. So let it be most clearly understood that should it be my misfortune to be found in such unpleasant circumstances, I most emphatically declare that I do not wish that my body or parts thereof be consigned to that cold and angry sea. For myself I will most happily, and need I say warmly settle for --- keeping the door closed.

An ocean below, and up there, an ocean freed from the serfdom of the clouds, pouring down upon me as they celebrate their returning union with the sea, and I, I am once again as well settled as I can get in my humble berth, finishing the last of my well appreciated evening meal. No. I have not by any means eaten my fill, yet I am sufficed. Yes, I know it does sound silly, yet out there on the Greybeard sea I have never felt so much alive.

In those clear moonlit nights when the stars hid and the moon sailed blithely across the heavens its cold splendour radiated below, and its light, reflected from the foam crowned sea blessed all on deck, but in my lowly cabin only faint shimmers of its light could be seen as they timidly ventured through the flagging tattered sail covers. Aye, pitch black it was and my sleep forever broken for I could only manage an hour or two at a time, and I was never too sure that I was asleep or not, for I never knew, was I in this world or another?

I lay with eyes tightly closed, my squaw mans shawl draped over my shoulders and wrapped snugly around my head, striving to drown out the outrageous and angry sound of the sea .. the sound? But, has it changed? It was happening again. No, yes it has. And there was I, the old fool arguing with himself, yet ever wishing only to bury his head into untroubled slumber and snore the night away, yet aware of where he was and, unwilling and unconsciously, listening.

It has, it has, it's far more muffled now, before you could clearly hear the sea, the sea? Yes, no, it was the clatter banging, grinders roaring, and shouting. Shouting? are you mad! Shouting? I haven't heard that for months and roaring, ssh, listen. I don't want to listen. Snuggling ever deeper into my damp bedding, drawing my squaw mans shawl ever tighter around my balding head, closing my eyes ever tighter to separate, yet there I was ... listening. Yes, it is different now.

Slowly, doubtfully. I opened my sleep filled eyes. Cautiously and amazed, I gazed around. I was in an area, five foot square, walled in by the severe harshness of painted steel. Overhead a bare and bright light bulb shone, directly before me lay a slab of steel, almost three foot square, in the centre of it was a three inch hole. On the top of the unpainted steel were scrape marks. By my left hand was a small sledge hammer. My right arm ached and when I looked at it I realized why, I was holding a heavy grinder, my eyes flew to the scrape marks, and instantly I remembered. I was twenty years old, in the bowels of a ship under construction, as low as one could possibly get. I was fitting heavy chocks under the engine mounts. I would pound it in then knock it out and grind the marks until the hole in the chock lined up with hole in the engine mount. I smiled and closed my eyes, yes, I was dreaming, but what was that? I could hear a high pitched wail, no, it wasn't the screech of the wind. Hesitantly my eyes again opened, then there was voices and a rushing scrambling sound, then an utter death like ... silence. The light bulb began to flicker, then went out. The steel chamber was pitch-dark, I turned, a dim light came through the oval opening that I had entered. I thrust my head out, all was buried in a dark and ominous silence, I raised my head and looked upwards. Overhead hung a dense cloud that was slowly descending, panicking, I crawled out the opening and ran to where the ladder was. Before I reached it I was enveloped in it and ran blindly into the engines turning gear. I fell, and whether it was my collision or my breathing of the gaseous fumes that made me unconscious, I know not.

I awoke gasping, sucking God's clean air into my fouled lungs. I opened my eyes and looked around in amazement, I could see for miles, then realized, I couldn't move. I was securely strapped on a stretcher, I strained my neck and far below I could see the ship, over it and slowly dissipating from it was a gray fog. Directly above my head was the hook of the crane that I dangled from. I closed my eyes and quickly fell asleep.

Log: Dec. 18. Slowly that morning the dream came back to me, so startlingly clear, so exact, but it wasn't a dream, but a memory. And that dream, that memory, was the start of others that would fill my nights for in this final stage of my voyage it was the nights that held me in their grasp, for they were longer than the days. The oil lamp never gave sufficient light for me to read, even if it had, I had no interest in reading. My mind was far too busy digging through the scrabble that lay buried in it. In any case I had less than two litres of kerosene left and I had no wish to lose the comforting golden glow from my lamp, or the warm drying effect of its flame. Yet the fact was, I was slowly becoming resigned to my surroundings. The depths of despair that I had suffered were easing. I felt that deep inside me a kind of intuitive reasoning was happening, a balance of sorts was taking place, that intellectually, I had nothing to do with. However, that morning pleased me when I realized that we were 61 miles closer to home.

I have been lying ahull for three days and three nights. On the first night the witches had changed their repertoire, they played "Farewell to Nova Scotia." Which I thought was quite considerate of them, thankfully, they only knew the first bar. The seas thoughtlessly, never changed their repertoire for they continued with their incessant pounding. I may not have liked the strength of the wind or the buffeting of the sea, but at least they were sending us east. As it began to ease I hauled up my little spitfire jib and stay sail. Two days later a tear appeared, my afternoon chore for the day apparent, I cut a patch and threaded a needle, and with patch in hand, the needle pinned to my lapel, I went on deck and freed the stay sail halyard, then after inspecting the tear realized as always, it was worse than I had hoped for. To the west the dying rays of a warmless sun was reaching that cold black horizon, to the east, in what was quickly becoming unending darkness lay home, while overhead a brilliant heaven with Polaris becoming ever brighter in that early darkening sky, pointing my way. From the skylight the oil lamp shone its comforting golden glow and with that welcome though bitter breeze cutting through me, I stood by the mast, sewing. After numerous trips below to bring life to my chilled and stiffened fingers, and before all light had gone, I had the sail repaired. With hands once again going into that frozen cramp like state I hoisted sail, exhausted, hungry, chilled, empty, I stood with my body firmly pressed against the mast, coiling the remaining line. All the while clenching and unclenching my fingers, hoping that some vestige of blood would keep flowing through them. I stood looking into that dark and wind whipped night, and asked myself the eternal question, why? I mean, what's it's all about?

And there I was the old fool, acting as if I was drunk, aye, how I would love to have been, remembering, yet forgetting where I was, just remembering the words, what's it all about ... Alfie? Then the music came to me. "What's it all about Alfie, is it just for the moment we live." How the words of the song raged through me. How well I knew what they meant. To be there in that bitter cold and challenging night, alone on that vast black eternal ocean, with a panorama of ever changing brilliancy overhead, and to ask myself, 'is it just for the moment I live?' Bloody right it is, and it was then, that it happened—again.

I don't understand any of it. No, I have to rephrase that, that's not quite true, that would have been true a few months ago, but not now. I feel that I understand, but simply can't put it into words, not yet. I was facing forward and by my left side, the same place as before, I felt a presence. There was no hand clasp, no, yet there was that same sense, that same feeling that came over me, that same overwhelming impression that I wasn't alone. Was it my imagination? of course it must have been, yet, there was an intensity about it, as if I was being told something, but I didn't understand what it was. Had my mind created it—but that very reason in itself only made it all the more interesting. For if it was all in my mind, why did my mind create it, what was its purpose?

That night while I lay in my berth, the sea lashing the hull, the howling scream of the wind, I thought. If it was all in my mind and I was fooling myself, why? Or if it was not in my imagination and there really was a visiting spirit, again, why? What my mind was struggling with was not what had taken place. No, what my mind was focusing on, was the purpose, the reason, that's what mattered. For whatever it was, it was the reason for the experience, all else relating to it just made it confusing. You will recall that I had sensed so strongly that should I go overboard that it would be an act of evilness. If you were to add that to my two, what I now thought of as, reassuring, visiting spirits, what in heavens name was I supposed to make of it. No pun intended. The thing was that I was slowly making sense of it. There was in some strange way, a logic, a balance, a meaning that was slowly becoming clear.

I went below with my fingers back into that frozen claw like state. I made my sloth like way over to my pausing place, there I lifted my useless unfeeling hands to the enticing warmth rising from the oil lamp. If you think that as I stood there that my head was filled with deep thoughts and that I could not escape this demanding mystery that I had to solve, you are wrong. My mind was completely blank. It was as if all those preconceived concepts, all long held assumptions had been cleansed from my murky gray cells. I felt in a strange way, innocent. My hands lifted like that, my palms facing each other, yet held apart by the golden glass as if in a prayerful worship to the flame. Then slowly, as if my unworded and unthought of prayer had been answered, life and blood returned to my hands. I ate, blew out the oil lamp, slept and a dream of a time a millennium ago entered.

I was kneeling and facing east, waiting for the warmth of the life giving sun to rise above those blue far distant hills. Between those hills and I lay a lake. As I looked down I realized there was a patch of new dug earth directly in front of my knees.

I raised my eyes to the sun, slowly it rose above the distant hills, I looked down at my hands, they faced me with closed palms upwards. I opened them and saw that each held a handful of dried peas. I took my gaze back to the sun and waited. When the lower arc of the sun kissed the horizon. I planted the peas.

Chapter 22

As I lay there on my damp and cold berth in those long dark nights there was no lack of time or opportunity for me to think and meditate on the word evil, or the reason for my visitors, but there was another question that intrigued me, and that was prayer and its meaning. I had taken everything for granted in the past and had never felt any requirement to give a simple thanks for having a hot meal before me. Now, I had found to my surprise that when I said that little Burn's grace before my meal, in some strange and unexpected fashion, it gave me peace. Is it not then comprehensible that my thoughts would take me in that direction.

But those nights my thoughts, though hesitant, first led me to times long gone. I had never known that going back to where I had spent my younger days would affect me so, as it did that first time when I went back to the Gorbals, after been gone for 26 years, perhaps that alone said something, I was 47. How little we know of ourselves until it faces us. I had never given it the slightest thought that it would bother me in any fashion. Yet as we got off the tram car, near where I had spent my childhood, my shirt was already stuck to my back with rivers of sweat, I can assure it was not from the heat. How innocent I was to be so disturbed, the question was, what was it that upset me so. The tenement building that I had spent my childhood in, and where I had lived until I was approaching my 21st birthday had been demolished, but the left over rubble of the building still lay scattered. If only my mind could have been scattered, instead it seemed focused in sensing, in absorbing, in going back to that long ignored and better forgotten time. I had never felt trauma like that before, why, it was as if my brain was no longer under my control, part of it trying desperately to stop the flood of all those best unremembered memories, and yet the other part so tuned into receiving, so willing to accept this deluge, this overpowering clamour of words and emotions that came from my distant past. My mind was an unwilling, and yet somehow a receptive traveler to being mentally transported back to those days. Aye, I know what triggered it, although I had already warned myself that something may occur, hadn't I, when I had got off the tram car with my shirt sticking to my back. I know what aroused those thoughts, and I know what pulled me out of it.

Though the tenements were long gone there was that, that had remained, and it lay there, so blatantly, so brazenly, as if it had sat there all those years just waiting for my return. Was it I, and I alone that could read those signs, those hieroglyphics that lay so clearly and demandingly before me, and how could they have so easily awakened my far and long gone past, and so quickly have sent me back, to where I had no wish to go. What a fool I was to be affected so, and not to know. The concrete sidewalks that had suffered the tread of all those working class people lay as it had when I was young, with the same age old cracks. I looked at those cracks, and I—- remembered them, I remembered them, and there I was, back again—- innocent and ignorant—- with my satchel on my back, hopping over those cracks like a young goat on my way to Abbotsford Street School. I was the second in the family to get up every morning for it was my chore to run down those three flights of stairs to the dairy. The top two flights were white washed, the third red washed, did she think she was better than us—a pint of milk, a square loaf and a half dozen porter rolls. I skipped over the cracks to the dairy. The dairy was just to the right of that crack that looks like a crooked W. It was those cracks on the sidewalk that transported me, as I in a state of shock stared amazingly at those cracks that had painted that scene of my distant past so dramatically before my eyes. And it was those cracks that brought me back, for as I stood there looking down I noticed tiny splashes of water appearing between my feet, like drips falling on to that old and well used sidewalk. I raised my hand and realized that the sweat that had gathered so freely on my brow, had found a sympathetic channel along the ridge of my nose. I was relieved when we left, I thought I had forgotten it—I thought I had.

But those black nights when the wind screamed in the rigging and the angry sea pounded the hull, and I lay cowering in my damp bedding my brain was condemned to go back, and back. My mind seemed immersed in the long ago and as I lay there and hesitantly opened my eyes, the middens appeared, they sat on the barren ground at the back of those once clean sandstone tenements, that had so quickly become soot covered squalid hovels. The middens where the housewives dumped their garbage, in overflowing long dented garbage cans, where garbage lay spilled and scattered on the coal ash strewn floor. In the area between the tenements and the middens lay 15 feet of dead soil, where hung an eternity of clothes lines. I lay there and my mind, as if I had no control over it kept slowly creeping back. I couldn't stop it. Alongside the middens they had built bomb shelters, where, when the sirens howled we hustled down to, except for my older brother who refused to get out off bed. Soon the bomb shelters became playhouses and stunk of urine. Oh, how I hated having to practice wearing those hideous gas masks, they drew it down tightly over my head and that nauseating odour of rubber filled my nostrils, my head enveloped in that rubber mask, my eyes tightly shut, the eyeglass already steamed over by my breath—I had to breathe harder to get air into my lungs—I gasped.

I opened my eyes and my mind switched channels, the scene had again changed. I was running up the stairs of the tenement building with my first friend, a wee Jewish lass as old as I was, Jeanette Chitterer, we were not yet five year old and too young for school, so and up and down the stairwell and in and out of the bomb shelters we happily played. Until another young family moved into the tenement building, they had a son the same age as myself, and I forgot about my first friend and played with—Campbell. It's a name that seems to follow me. I must have ignored Wee Jeanette. I never realized what I had done, she was not very happy, and her father no doubt noticing, asked her what was wrong, and she in her innocence, mentioned me. That was all that was required, for he who had never exchanged a word with my father, or he to him, spoke to my father and he with his leather shaving strop grasped firmly in his sinewed hand beat the hell out of me—for what?—I didn't know then why. Though I think I do now.

The wind may have stopped screaming, the tap—tap—tap of the torn sail cover long silenced, the rain no longer lashing the deck, all may have gone. It mattered little to me for my mind and soul was in that hole in the wall where my bed was, in the top storey of the tenement building in Mc Kinlay Street, and my bare behind stinging from the blows from the belt that my father honed his razor on. I hold no grudges against my father, or grudges against Jeanette, whose family soon moved away. Then one day she came back.

Again my memory unfettered flew and I who had always thought it cluttered, found it exact and clear. I was sixteen years old and crossing Turiff Street, a girl had crossed diagonally from me though I never noticed her till she quietly said, "Ronnie?" I turned, and looking into those big brown eyes, I knew, it was Jeanette. I never answered, but instead turned and walked away with my nose held high in the air. I laid there that night—wishing so badly that I had spoken to her. Suddenly, I was eight, it was raining, my head was bowed, I was staring at brown disturbed earth at my feet, then someone handed me a thick white rope and quietly said, 'when we lower, you lower'. I was burying my father.—I tightly closed my eyes.—I was a child walking hand in hand with my father, he was buying me a new pair of shoes, the shoes were called the young duke, somehow it pleased him.—I was walking again with him, he was carrying a glass cased motor cycle battery, he was taking it to get it charged.—I was on my father's shoulder he had lit a match and was lighting the gas light.—I was a toddler, I was standing in front of a brown painted door, someone had knocked, then someone came and opened it. Two men dressed in white entered, one carried a long object made of canvas and wood. They went in to the kitchen where my mother and father slept, minutes later they returned. The long object they had carried was now opened, they were at either end carrying it, something was lying on it covered by a white sheet. As they passed me an arm fell out. I saw my mother's hand. I reached up and touched it, it was cold. I never saw my mother again.

Oh God, I buried my head in my hands. I had deliberately wiped so much from my mind, and here it was, a thousand fold clearer, a thousand fold more exact than if I had allowed myself to remember it through those long years. My young and innocent [for it was once] mind dazed, my quickly aging mind overwhelmed by those feelings that flooded through me. Oh Dear God.

Cloistered in my steel bound floating hermitage, engulfed by the clamorous screech of the winters wind, the constant relentless barrage of the seas against the hull, and now a riveters hammer pounding the deck with bullet like hail. I lay in the coal black endless dark, only able to sleep one hour at a time, my mind half asleep and half awake ever wandering, separated itself from my surroundings and found itself dwelling on anything that entered it.

A line from a book by Iris Murdoch popped into it. Marian says, 'Yours is a melancholy sort of religion Denis, I'm afraid I don't believe in God,' Denis answers, 'Ah you do, but you don't know his name.' That line appealed to me for I didn't know his name either, and yet more interesting, I didn't want to know his name. They gave me his name in my childhood, that big fierce looking man sitting on that huge stone chair, glaring at me, intimidating me into being good, when I was far too timid to do otherwise. No thank you.

Later I thought how frightening it would be if this life that I was now living should continue, for I had found that I, with my eyes tightly closed, with the wind and witches screaming in the rigging, the barraging sea for company, I could transport myself back to past times. Then my eyes would open wide and I would be there, and see the place of my childhood, recall scenes, and my ears would hear the sounds and words from what I thought was, a forgotten past. Then suddenly, as if to reinforce what I had just thought I was back in my childhood Sunday school and there before me was God. A big powerfully built man with a thick gray curly beard and a fine head of thick wavy hair, with muscular arms and powerful legs, he sat on this great marble chair that was floating on a cloud, he stared fiercely into my eyes as he pointed at the words etched in to this bloody great marble slab that rested on his brawny thighs. The Ten Commandments. There was no need to scare the hell out of me when I was a wee lad, again no pun intended, I was timorous enough.

And with that memory, I began to remember the Lord's prayer. 'Our father which art in heaven hallowed be thy name.' I was doing pretty good until, how did it go? 'as it is done in heaven let it be done on earth.' Well, I said it a few times and struggled with myself saying it, but there it was. If I can't believe in angels. I can't believe in heaven, or hell. We humans are quite capable of creating either heaven or hell, and as far as hell is concerned, Satan can learn a few tips from us—who are created in God's image—? You staunch and fearless atheists, you won't hold the fact that I said the Lord's prayer a few times against me? And you Bible clad God fearing devout Christians, will you also hold it against me, for when I say those words, I get the same feeling of discomfort, the same feeling that I felt those many long years ago. If so, console yourself for I was a young fool, ignorant and not too bright. Yes, not too different than I am today. Except, that was so long ago, we change but not very much. Then—Good God, I've just remembered, another line from the Lord's prayer, 'deliver us from evil'.

I must stop and let me try again, and be clear, for I may have lost you, but I have not lost me. Me, in that cavity in my skull I have a functioning brain that has now found itself swimming through a sea of thoughts and memories. Stroke after stroke, with arms stretching out through a calm and warm sea, one hand then the other reaching to grasp that which is just out of reach. Ahead of me and through the dark sea mist, land appears, slowly I drag myself on to a golden shore and there, emerging through the lightening mist the sun rises; and I find the reason for my visitors, and even more intriguing, the reason for—Evil?

But I must slow down, for first I must give thought to prayer. I wanted to pray. The question was to who? And why? And what for? The what for was far the easiest question to answer. Saying Burn's grace had went down so well with me, almost as well as the meal, also Burns words, as simple as they were came from my own cultural heritage, that meant a great deal to me. In foreign lands I had seen, and envied, those who willingly accepted that bond that linked them to their forebears that was so incredibly important to their well-being. For the feeling that I had ever carried though well buried in the depths of my young and naive mind, was of a solitary sense, as if I was an orphan in a world of strangers. I had simply accepted that as being part of my character. Yet that night when overhead the firmament radiated that glorious light and below me the ocean gleamed with living phosphorescence, that feeling had faded, and out there in the middle of the Greybeard sea, there on this expansive and raging ocean, when that hand had pressed on my shoulder, and later, that presence. I was overwhelmed with a sense of belonging. Had I casually stepped into a continuity, an affinity with my peers, had I found a comforting lineal link that had been there all that time and only now reached out through time and space, and touched me.

Yet, it was also so much more than that that had taken place, for it was also the spiritual aspect that had embraced me. That time when I had reached up and my finger tips had vapourized into the chilling fog, and for the first time I thought what soul may mean, from then, and that simple feeling—and now—and my visitors. I buried my head in my hands. I had never told anyone about my childhood, but it's there—and that night I recalled a photograph of a little boy that stands shyly grasping on to a wall, hoping that it won't fall and all the time wishing to be alone, and—wondering why?

Sequestered snugly in my damp bedding, my Nepal fur hat pulled down over my ears, my squaw blanket wrapped around my shoulders and covering my face. I lay half asleep, half dreaming, whiling away those long nights, pondering, reasoning. Trying to simplify and simplify, first I shall have to ignore the image that I have of that angry and vengeful God of my childhood, that was absolute nonsense. Then there was God, why is he portrayed as masculine? Next, if there is a God out there, he, she, is also in me. That thought sat very comfortably with me I had no problem with that. There was also the thought that God and man went if not hand in hand, at least they went together. That, however, brings up the little niggly question, can you have one without the other, by that I mean, if man had not appeared on earth, could there still have been a God? I doubt it, but I most willingly will lay it aside. Then there is the aspect of loving God; I have just realized that I have used the word loving, whoa, just a minute. I should have used the word, worshipping, yes, there is a difference. Perhaps that's what bothered me about the God of my childhood, if you didn't worship him you went to hell, that never sounded to me like a very loving God. Was that the reason that I saw him as vengeful.

Aye, it's amazing the thoughts that trickle into your head when you're alone out there on that wild extent of cold ocean, and how they came so easily, tripping over each other in there enthusiam when they realized that there was a willing ear, waiting. Yet, I wonder, were these thought always there, like seeds lying on a dry and arid land waiting for the clouds to weep, to nurture them so they would take root and grow. Had the seas and those squall laden clouds nourished mine, and those roots of mine, those branches, if they grew and came to fruition, what would hang from the boughs? Yet, here in the luxury of the freedom that existed around me my mind was ever given to wander, yet I stopped and returned to my earlier thought.

If God is out there and in me, then by loving God am I not also loving myself, and if I am making peace with God, am I not also making peace with myself. Doesn't it also follow that if I am praying to God, I'm also praying to myself. It seems that I may have gone around a circle, except, I can't pray to God to save me. I'm well aware that they are worthier souls than mine that need looking to. Yet, I'm still praying, in reality what I was doing, was conjuring out of myself, invoking from those deep hidden recesses that lie unused within all of us, strength, courage, endurance, and most of all spirit. Spirit.

What a grand word spirit is, it travels all the way from the supernatural, to a liquid in a bottle. Would it surprise you if I said that I was far closer to the supernatural, than I was to the liquid in the bottle. I felt I had began to understand the reason behind the visits from my supernatural, or hallucinatory guests, for I felt that their purpose was to give me what I so badly needed, spirit, and if that was so, I was not as alone as I had always thought I was. The last visitor, was he also one who had faced those same trials as I was now facing, were they also by my side. Did that mean that I was part of an ancient lineage, that stretched back in time, whether family or seafarers. I who had always felt—alone.

Then there was the word. Evil. Why was that word—EVIL—yes, in capital letters, impressed in to my head, and isn't it interesting that the words 'deliver us from evil' are also in the Lords Prayer. The overwhelming impression I had, was, if I went over the side and into the sea it would be evil. If I had died aboard it wouldn't have been evil. Just wait a minute, what was it that I had though earlier. Could there be an intuition forming between me and the sea? Was that why it had came into my head? Could it simply be that I was being warned, that if I did not ease off in my almost pathetic struggles on deck, that I would surely go over the side, and if I did, it would be because of my own reckless stupidity? Could it be as simple as that, was I being ... forewarned? Is there such a thing as fate? Could destiny had decreed that I should not die in that manner. Was that when I embraced—all. Was that when I realized—what soul was. Was that when my—fear—had left?

By noon on Christmas eve the steady Southerlies had ceased, by midnight we were back to gale force winds and another hellish night. I had promised myself a good meal for my Christmas supper. This was my last can of ham, though I don't mind saying that if I could have traded that can of ham for flour, pasta, rice or oats, I would have most gladly have done so. I opened that small can and cut the ham in to six pieces, there was no need to concern myself about refrigeration. I opened my second from last can of peas and poured a third of them in my rice, added my one small piece of the ham, and my grand Christmas feast was ready. But I was in no hurry to dine, though my saliva gland was putting in overtime as my nostrils savoured the cooking odours. My hands hovering over the lid of the pot were losing that stiffness and chill that had made them unpliable claws. My well singed mitts lay on either side of the gas flame, close enough that steam rose from the moist leather. My Nepal fur cap that I had placed on the pot lid until steam had began to issue from under the lid, I rapturously pulled down over my chilled bald pate and laid it snugly around my ears, and there I was, dressed for my Christmas dinner in every piece of clothing that I had left Madang wearing, and had merely added layer after layer to. Meanwhile, wrapped around my shoulders like an old squaw man and now sewn together [for the safety pin had long rusted out] was my car blanket. The pot simmering on the hot stove, the oil lamp casting its shimmering golden glow, my hands firmly interred in my well singed mitts. I took the lid of the boiling pot, stuck my face in it, and sang out as loudly as I could. "Merry Christmas Ron."

And there was I about to take my hot pot to bed with me when I thought I would try picking up something on my little short wave radio. Surprise, at last the sound of a human voice, naturally, it was all about religion, well, it was Christmas. The talk consisted of two speakers, one male and one female, they each spoke for a half an hour, they were both Roman Catholics. My hot pot was now on hold, though my body was in dire need of that hot food, there was obviously another part of me that required a different kind of sustenance. I turned the stove down to simmer, placed my night cap on top of the pot lid and listened to the first human voices that I had heard in months.

She gave her half hour talk on feminism and its place in the Church, however, the seats were all taken and there wasn't even standing room for feminists. He was then introduced and his talk was going to be on the history and meaning of the Holy Trinity. I can assure my ears picked up when I heard that, you may have gathered by this time that perhaps I can accept the supernatural. The great mystery that lies out there that poses us unanswerable questions. I don't have any problem with that. The problem I have, is when man in his attempt to solve this great mystery makes it even more confusing. I had a hard enough time trying to believe in the Virgin Mary, but the Holy Trinity! I could never get that through my thick skull. Body, soul and spirit, aye, that I can understand, but the Father, Son and the Holy ghost, that was a way too much for my limited mind to grasp. With the barometer steady, no one to bother me, why I'd never get a better opportunity than now to listen and understand. I jammed myself snugly in my pausing place and was all ears.

Just off my shoulder the oil lamp shed its warm shivering golden glow, the rush of the sea could be heard as it swept over the cabin top, water gathered around a portlight no longer as well sealed as it once was, and as I watched water collected then dribbled down the cabin wall and pooled onto the empty book shelf. The sail cover tapped an indecipherable message on the portlight, meanwhile my little Radio Shack short wave radio mounted on the wall just above the bookshelf, waited for my aged ears to tune themselves to the voice of the speaker. While I with a voracious appetite hungrily devoured every word that issued from Father What'sis name's mouth, after all, it was Christmas. There couldn't have been a better time, or place, or situation for me to listen and pay attention to Father What'sis name's lecture. Yes, I sure did listen, but the understanding, that was quite different, and as I said I ate it up, but the swallowing and digesting, well, that was another thing entirely. One thing I did learn was that you can't be a Christian unless you believe in the Holy Trinity. I never knew that, and so on that Christmas Day there was one thing I knew, and that was—I wasn't a Christian.

Becalmed overnight and when that sad and unhappy dawn broke it brought with it a light Northerly. It was our wedding anniversary and this was another one that I had missed, in any case there was no point on going on deck until the weather decided on what it was going to do. Which was just as well, for within two hours it was blowing 40 knots. I had acquired in my travels a drawer filled with dried herbs and spices, they had been brought aboard by my crew, most of them having no knowledge of cooking, they, however, thought that herbs and spices solved that problem. The containers were nameless for with the dampness their labels had fallen off, and as coffee and tea was now a forgotten memory, I had taken to flavoring my mug of hot water with some of those unnamable flavours. I was now down to two small meals a day. A half a cup of flour for breakfast, and a half a cup of rice for supper. My breakfast, which consisted of one skinny pancake, I would put off making as long as I could, at least until daybreak, and that many times was not so easy to tell.

Two nights later, in the middle of that witch screaming roller pounded night I awoke, and slowly the insane shrieks from the rigging and the pummels of the sea faded from my hearing. I quickly sat up and my hand flew to my opened gasping mouth, my eyes agape saw not the blackness that enfolded me, for I was listening intently to quiet words that came out of the darkness and somehow entered my ears; 'I—think—I—do—now'. With my head buried in my squaw blanket I bowed to hear better, it got louder, 'I think I do now' until it was shouting, 'I think I do now'. Yes, it was me that had said that—and slowly I—understood.

And there was I, this Old bloody fool, with this blinding light blazing through my empty skull reminding me that for all those years that my father had beat me because I had been too friendly with a little Jewish girl—at five years old? and at this very instant realizing that that couldn't have been the reason, that couldn't have been the reason at all, but what was it? or was it that he needed a reason, and found it. I sat, my hands tightly grasping my squaw blanket, pulling it chokingly around my neck, my God, if Jeanette wasn't the reason, what was it? I closed my eyes no, I did not wish to remember—- but I did..

Aye, I was remembering, remembering, when we walked in hand and he calling me the young Duke, and again walking to get the motor cycle battery charged, and when I was on his shoulder as he lit the gas light. He was a kind and loving father then—but that was—yes, that was before my mother died.

Afterwards things changed, aye, he had became cold with me, and I in my childlike unconsciousness had quickly learned to stay away from him, but it is only now, after all those years have past, that I find myself unwillingly—facing it.

When the news of his death came the whole family were together, my three older sisters, my older bother and my two young step brothers and my stepmother. My older sister Bessie, who had taken care of me after my Mother's death and who was always arguing with him, was heart broken, but that didn't stop her from being furious with me when she found me standing there, with dry eyes.

Aye, its all true, yet why was that? was it that I in my innocence, felt that he too had died, when my mother had, or had he became cold to me because he felt that I was somehow too blame? Had he? And had that, made me react in the same manner to him—cold? Yet, the child, as I was once, innocent and naive with little ability to comprehend wanders through their family and sees with one pair of wide open eyes all, yes all, all the acts, all the plays that takes place. Though never do they or can they put the pen to words, or can they speak off it, yet it can lie forever in their thoughts, as it did in mine. Yet it is only now that that childlike mind awakes, and I unwillingly and hesitantly see that which I'd rather not, for it appears so blatantly before me that what I had once held so tightly sealed, had now became free. I bowed my head, my eyes tightly closed, my finger tips almost burying themselves into my skull and that long gone past, unwished for yet still slowly—emerges.

Dear God, I shall for ever and ever and over and over be asking myself, why would he beat me so hard, because I stopped playing with a little girl, or could it really be because she was Jewish, or could it be—because of the death of my—Mother?

Chapter 23

Log. Dec. 29. That day I did the dirty task of cleaning out the oil heater. A sea had swept down the smoke flue and in the bottom of the heater lay a black gooey mess. A task not willingly done and had it not been in the back of my head the thought, that in one of those cold and windless nights when the planets ruled the heavens and the chill of winter froze my joints, I would light it, and watch how the blue gaseous flame licked the little glass window and I would again, become entranced by its dancing presence, and the dry and welcomed heat would freely enter my cold and frigid body. Later that day when the winters sun was seeking morn's elsewhere and the wind died and the cold made its discomforting presence felt. I lit the oil lamp and gloried in its golden glow, then without giving it much thought, I splurged, and lit the oil heater. "God bless it" I cried—"and Broom and all of the ship's crew," and that dry warm heat flooded the cabin and as I joyously admired those little spirited blue flames licking the glass shield, I sang happily.

Have I mentioned that one of the problems of spending too much time alone is, that it is so easy for your mind to get carried away with your thoughts, or a simple word, such as sang, for one of the things that had I noticed that had changed, was my voice. I've been told that I have a fine strong bass voice, mind you as it was my wife that said that you will have to take that under consideration. Nevertheless, my strong bass voice has gone, now I find that my voice is a sort of rather gentle high tenor. I can now reach notes that I never could before. It is as if a particular external body part and I, have parted company. So there was I in my fine new tenor voice, finding myself singing that touching piece from the musical Cats, 'Memories', and the words, 'when the wind begins to moan' or 'a new day has begun' seemed to hold such meaning to me. Aye, and whatever it was that saturated that evenings air it soothed my soul and the despondency that I had felt so filled with, left, and the warmth from the little oil stove penetrated my body, and the weak little blue flame gave enough light to make shadows dance on the cabin wall .. and I was happy.

Log: Dec. 30. I awoke, and found myself crying, "Happy New Year Ron." Aye, it was Hogmanay and we Scots are ever ready to celebrate in advance, but was that the reason for my exuberance. Aye, it was strange and that morning, why, I spent it in bed, doing something that I had never done before— writing verse and poetry. I can't possibly explain that. Was that why those words, 'a new day has begun' touched me. No, I wasn't about to do fifty pushups, nor, was I about to shed my well soiled garments and wash my cold and naked body. No, it wasn't like that, it was more like, that I had been reprieved, that I had been tried and tested and let go, set free. Yes, Scot-free.

But that morning there was something else on my mind, it was something that I had once read, about time, Chronus, was that it? The Greek word for linear time, the time that we all live in, but they had another word for time another concept. Kairo? Kairos? That was it. When time converges and becomes condensed and intense, the sort of time that you would experience had you been told that you only had a short time to live. When all the unresolved dreams, half thought plans, religious ideas, political views, family problems, love, when that incredible and unclear jumble of ill comprehended emotions and reflections that you have ever carried, and never really had taken time to think of, suddenly face you, and you only have a short time to sort them out and make sense of them. But you can't, why? You lack that necessity, that requirement, but what is it? Was it the reason that a long haired Guru sits atop a wind battered mountain top. Solitude. That, you will never get, and I had, out on that outrageous sea ... aplenty.

Was it that, that I was doing? Was that what had happened to me, when all those vague concepts and imaginings that had long brewed and lingered in my head all those years, had coalesced, and like grain well thrashed, had came tumbling out. Could that be it? That as I lay there in those black and storm ravaged nights, battered by the maddening sea, brutalized by the insane shriek of the incensed wind, while I, the old fool dug up my petty past and splayed it out before my eyes, as if it was of worth. Weighing the pros and cons of my paltry existence. Was I making peace with God? Or, was it just that I was making sense out of my life? My reason for being? Could it be the same thing, does it matter. Is that what I had always been seeking? That cleansing time? And had found it. Is that why I felt so free and happy? Had I? Did I? Could that be the reason that I felt this great sense of relief ? Could I have journeyed through, and more importantly, reaped ... Kairos time?

'Have you swept the visioned valley with the green stream streaking through it. Searched the vastness for something you have lost: Have you strung your soul to silence? Then for God's sake go and do it; Hear the challenge learn the lesson pay the cost.' Robert Service.

I rose from my berth and heated a mug of water, added spice, and took it back to bed with me and with no concern of the weather whatsoever, reached over and picked up my log book, scraps of damp paper and a pen and spent rest of the morning in bed. Amusing myself. I went through that New Year's day as if I didn't have a care in the world. Yes, it is true what I had said, my fear had left. Forgive me, suffer my poetry.

A Wee Bit Flour

Once I was fit and healthy, well perhaps a little fat.
But now I'm lean and hungry, and I'm not very fond of that.
My appetite is excellent my appetite is good,
The problem simply is, I haven't any food.
A wee bit flour for breakfast, a wee bit rice for lunch.
And all I have for supper is, my finger nails to munch.

But if I ever get to land well all of that will change.
For the pots will all be boiling, upon my kitchen range.
I'll have lamb chops for my breakfast, steak pie will do for lunch.
And served up for my supper, a chicken leg to crunch.

Rice and oh, plum puddings, will be my daily fare.
And if I should get peckish, a chocolate eclair.
Coffee coffee by the pot, I'm very fond of too.
Then if I should get thirsty, a glass of rum will do.

I'll raise a brood of feathered food.
And I'll feed them well, you'll see.
And when they're big and healthy,
I'll stuff them inside me.

And if someone should ask me, why I eat this way.
This is what I'll tell them, this is what I'll say.
A wee bit flour for breakfast, a wee bit rice for lunch.
And all I had for supper was, my finger nails to munch.

1996. Sunny with a cold breeze, then went back once more to being becalmed. I didn't care, we had but 148 miles to go. I could already feel my body soaking in a tub filled to over flowing with hot water, and the frozen marrow that had congested in my old bones, thaw. I could taste the flavour of the hot coffee, with lots of cream, as it trickled down my throat, and that glass of rum that sat teasingly on the edge of the bath tub, without the need of ice, that I, when ever my fancy took would reach over with my warm and flexible fingers, raise and have a good swig. Then there was food.

I would be moored right downtown in Victoria. It could be possible that my wife would be at work at St. Mary's Hospital and that I would not be able to get a hold of her. Nae Bother. Just up the block from where I'll be moored is that fine Scottish fast food chain, Mac something. Aye, that's what I needed, fast food. I gave it some serious thought, then I created another scenario. Not too far from there is the bus stop. I could board a bus that would take me to Esquimalt, I'd get off at the shopping mall where Mr. Grocer lives. There they have big fat juicy barbecued chickens, the fact that those chickens may never have seen sunlight never bothered me at all. They also have big crispy buns and great big dobs of butter, and fat filled potato mayonnaise salad and slabs of Canadian cheddar cheese. Perhaps I would be totally outrageous and buy a bottle of barbecue sauce, well, just a small bottle. If I leave from the door beside the roasted chickens, even the words made me drool, there is a seat, and there I would collapse and gorge. What were the words that Goofy sung? And the tune, wasn't it from Gilbert and Sullivan, I remember. "I'll, eat'n eat'n eat'n eat'n eat'n until ah die."

Log: Jan. 10. By noon the westerly had changed to south west. In the afternoon the sun shone, the seas calmed, and I raised the floor boards and brought them up out of the bilge and lined the deck with them. I complimented them on the extra ballast that they had given me, for though it may have slowed me down in those conditions that we had gone through they had made Broom far more stable, then I grew—silent.

Concepts, ideas, thoughts, questions, were tumbling head over heels in this head of mine, a stew of images danced. Had the course I followed already been written for a man such as I? This journey of mine, was it not just happenstance? Is there really such a thing as destiny? I had known far earlier that I should have been alone. I really didn't know what to think, then ridiculous and outrageous as it was, it blatantly faced me. Could that bloody old rusted hulk have sat on that beach waiting for an old fool like I, to come along and take that million dollar cargo, and use it, for what—ballast. Christ it was nonsensical, of course it was, but that didn't stop me from opening my hands and burying my head in them. I grimaced, smiled, laughed, and damn near choked myself, me, me, this unworthy old baldy headed bastard—me, this nobody, this poorly educated idiot, this dreg of the slums.

As the day died I sat with my feet upon the binnacle, admiring the sun as it sank into the clear blessed western horizon. I opened the nearest box and removed a bag, lifted my scissors and cut the bag open, tipped it and noticed how the breeze carried the white powder up, then slowly it fell and settled upon the dark cold sea. Dropped the empty box into the sea, glug—glug—glug, and my eyes settled on it while it slowly submerged. By the time the sun had gone and the horizon had turned into that black medium, it lay, trailing astern, a white path shedding its dying light on to that cold dark sea.

At dawn on the Jan 11, the sky was filled with dull sombre clouds giving an air of despair and dread, but there was no despondency aboard Broom. That south westerly had stayed all night, but more than that, the seas had been calmer and the faithful Broom had taken advantage of those kindlier seas. I reckoned that by noon we would have ran eighty miles, the best days run we had done for quite a while. By 9:30 a.m., my willing ears could hear the welcome sound of the raucous squabbling cry of the glaucous gull. At 11:00 a.m. the cragged black rocks of Cape Flattery emerged hesitantly out of the drizzling mist. The sea around us has changed once more, for we have now found ourselves in a rip-tide, the flow constantly eddying and swirling, then bursting into a series of tiny water spouts. The wind being entrapped by the land has picked up strength, yet has made little difference to our progress in those seas. There was no way that I could make a reasonable passage in those waters, there was naught that I could do but motor sail out into the middle of the Juan de Fuca Strait.

It is probably hard to believe but they are times, when I do, everything right. I had petted my little Sabb diesel. I had nursed my engine starting battery. I had ensured that I would have sufficient fuel for the long run down the Strait, for I could not possibly believe that the weather would be fair so that I could sail to Victoria. I placed the engine starting key in the ignition, crossed my legs and turned the key, and the starter spun and bless it, the engine started. I motor sailed out of that simmering stew and unwillingly turned the wheel and headed north out into the Strait. Had the tide turned? Was it ebb, or flood? If the tide was ebbing, why that meant that I would be bucking both the wind and tide. What could I do? By noon we had cleared Cape Flattery and we were in the middle of Juan de Fuca Strait. The cold drizzle had stopped, the sky began to clear, and I had given up hope of reaching Victoria.

Mind you, I had other scenarios, for I had hordes of time and my imagination was ever a worthwhile companion. I had considered if I should meet a south east gale when I was halfway down the Juan de Fuca Strait, I could enter Port San Juan, but would be stuck there until the gale blew itself out. Would I be fit enough to anchor, and forget about unloading the dinghy from atop the cabin. I could run back to Port Bamfield, though I wasn't too keen about that either. I was about to say next and last Ucluelet, but, Neah Bay lay just around the corner there I would also be anchoring, and should go through U.S. customs. No, I never gave much thought to that. Oh, and there was another consideration that helped me make up my mind. Neah Bay definitely was, and I felt quite sure that Port Renfrew was, and Bamfield, I wasn't too sure. Dry.

So it was Ucluelet, I had been in there a few times and had cleared customs easily. By noon we had cleared Cape Flattery and the tide rips. I stood there debating on how long it would take me to get to Ucluelet, for I was not at all enthusiastic of navigating that winding channel at night, especially as I was without navigation lights. I tacked, then somehow all those scripts that I had played in my damp and foolish mind were thrown away. Why, it was as if some giant and obviously caring hand had turned off the wind switch. There was now no sign of a head wind. There are times when it would be so easy to believe in a supreme being, that acknowledges your presence and in some strange fashion, cares. To believe that there was someone listening when I poured my heart out in those despair ridden hellish nights, out there, on the Greybeard Sea, that Kairos of my life, or, was it just that my timing was right. Could it be just that simple? For when I headed into the Strait there was not a cloud in the sky, and the sun had proclaimed the heavens for itself and as it made its all too short winters crossing, blessed my day.

The sun voyaged across that clear blue sky and I knew that the weather would hold. Which meant that I could indulge myself and eat up my meagre supply of food. I cooked a cup of rice and added my last can of peas, my last can of fish and mixed them, then with great delight stuffed as much as I could into my willing mouth. Or, as the Kiwis and Ozzies say. I wrapped my body lovingly around that well deserved nourishing meal. It was not too long before I was filled. Ah, it was grand, it had been a long time since I had last ate my fill, mind you, I had no doubt that my stomach was a great deal smaller than it had been. Which was all the better for it meant that when ever the thought of food entered my head, why I'd pop below and stuff another spoonful in my mouth.

Chapter 24

I crossed the Strait to the Canadian side, my G.P.S was on the blink again but I didn't care, I knew where I was going. The sun had gone and taken what little heat that it had offered with it and it had grown bitterly cold, but my inners were glowing. Singing a few snatches of this and that, the stars coming out one by one, and I dashing down below for another spoonful, why I was as happy as a pig in something. Then the fog came. I shan't let that bother me, why I'll just stay close to shore and follow the coastline. It is all remarkably easy for as I motor along the shore is on my left, the open Strait on my right, and the way to Victoria straight ahead. Then slowly emerging through the descending fog objects appeared ... could that be land that lay directly ahead? I glanced to the right and there too I saw what could be land, then I look behind, and to the left, land. Do you think that just, perhaps, that I have Broom and I stuck in the middle of a little bay? In heavy fog, somewhere between the entrance to Sooke Harbour and Race Rocks. Any light that managed to filter through the fog was rapidly disappearing, there was naught that I could do but turn the engine off. I went below.

With the oil lamp lit, I gave thought to lighting the oil stove, that is, if there was enough fuel to take me the rest of the way into Victoria. Entered the engine room and slid the clear plastic hose over the pipe nipple, opened the valve and watched the diesel fuel as it sneaked up the hose. On the side of the tank I had marked 5 Gallon, it registered just under that mark. I had more than enough. I lit the oil stove and turned it up high. It would have been far quicker to cook my supper upon my faithful propane stove but I was in no hurry, why should I be? I placed on the heater my pot with two cups of water, my last cup of rice to which I added my last handful of raisins, then just before the water had all but gone I added my piece de resistance. I had been keeping it for a moment such as this, just out of eyesight lest in my weakness I should be tempted. The Kiwis not only produce fine healthy strapping women, they also produce a fine healthy strapping cream powder, which I now mixed with water. Note, that I said 'Cream' not that watery, wimpy, skim milk powder that North America proudly produces. The rice almost ready I put into it my powdered mixture of 'Kiwi Cream.'

Had I ever sat so comfortably, had I ever felt so happy, so free, so secure in mind and in spirit, and as old as I was so divinely innocent. As if all the wrong that I had ever done—I had in some fashion atoned for, my slate had been washed completely clean. I felt that I had unloaded unwelcome baggage and had been given an opportunity for a new start, perhaps not so much a start, but more that I had came to the end of one way, one journey, and with courage another venture would unfold for me.

I shall always relish the memory of that evening, unquestionably the most poignant evening of my life, but it wasn't just that evening, no, it was far more than just that evening. For in all fairness that evening was the climax to this voyage that had awaited me, for regardless of the hardships and trials that I had suffered I would not have missed those ordeals that I had endured for all the wealth that there is in this vain and mundane world that we humans have created. Could I possibly hope that I would have enough spirit to face another grand adventure like that, I doubt it. That evening I sat in front of the oil stove, letting its warm soothing heat soak into my chilled bones and the cheer of its little dancing blue flame enchanted me, for here in this fog ridden silent bay wicked witches would never dare to enter, here where there was not a sound from my musical shrouds, shrouds? Even the word conceives death, I mused, meditated and thought.

God, if there is one and soon I should die, could I do it in this little Bay, for it is ideal for me. For here I could quite happily pass from this confusing mortal life, for here all is so enriching, and could I carry that radiance away with me, and have my arms tightly wrapped around those warm memories I have of the vitality of life that I have somehow newly found, and please, let me peacefully die in its loving and wondrous embrace. And so I sat, pondered and mused and smiled as I spooned that most delicious dessert into my bony body, and my body glowed with warmth. I dozed that wonderful quiet night away, there in front of the dry glowing heat from the oil stove. Though occasionally I would open my eyes and admire the little blue gaseous flames as they licked warmly on the small glass window of the stove, and when the need came upon me, reach out with my most flexible fingers and enjoy another spoon filled with my creamy rice pudding, and I warm in heart and in body, blessed the Kiwis. Some time before dawn I aroused myself from my happy dozing state and thought I would once again attempt to fix the G.P.S.. I went back into the cold damp aft cabin and sat at the chart table and fiddled with the wires. Then abruptly the G.P.S lit up, and I too, for the numbers as they flashed on the screen removed me from my semi-slumber state, for they not only gave me a position they also told me that I was moving, there is not the slightest zephyr of a breeze and yet we are moving, at 1.9 knots, towards amazingly, Victoria. I stopped, buried my head in my hands and closed my eyes. This incredible voyage, this quest that I had found myself on, those nights while I lay there dragging up the interred remains of hidden memories while I scrabbled through them looking for? That inner spark O nature's fire? Was I searching the vastness for something that I had lost? Nonsense, yet, was it? And this gentle bay, this sanctuary, this peaceful haven that I have so joyously blundered into, blundered? Or was it, could it have been, led into? This perfect place to spend my last night at sea, where I could peacefully wonder at all that had happened. This refuge. This retreat, where I had been given me time to ponder, to weigh, to balance, to prepare myself before once again meeting ... the maddening ... horde.

The next morning when the dawn slowly broke, I, with a mug of hot zing in my hand saw the rocky outcrops appear through the slow rising fog; then surprisingly—the bay quickly became alive with birds. If Marlene had been there she would have told me all their names, as she has done numerous times before, and like numerous times before I would have paid little attention, and forgot. Yet, I am not too sure about this time for they all were so joyously alive. Those birds looked as if they didn't have a care in the world, the diving ducks, diving, the dabblers, dabbling, while the glaucous gulls did their usual squabbling acts, they all looked so enraptured and filled with life. Then a family of sea otters appeared, seeming so much in play and gamboling happily on the weed strewn rocks, even the rocks seemed to me so full and alive. The light from the sun filtered its way through the fog and as it lightly caressed their rugged forms it created fresh water tears that collected here and there on their rough hewn craggy shapes, the weeping drops pooled, then they dribbled slowly down and mixed freely with the salted sea. Why did it all seem so richly colourful, when I knew that it was all in shades of black and gray, it wasn't as if I had not seen all of this before. Had I always been this blind.

The fog now feeling the warmth of that early morning winter's sun hung just above my finger tips and I recalled that time when I had raised my fingertips to its cold ghostlike form. The thick cold gray blanket slowly rose and lightened, then sparkled like diamonds as the suns morning rays reflected of that dew soaken cloud. Again, there was that feeling that though

I was alone, I was not. And that same intense impression that I had before, that somehow I had been accepted. By—? Could all that have been caused by my experience? Was it really Kairos? Was it both?

I had left my little tea pot boiling merrily on the oil heater and went below and prepared myself another cup of hot zing. I stood there in my pausing place looking out of the portlight. I could now see the trees that had taken root on that rocky shore, their branches leisurely emerging out of the slow rising damp fog, then I heard the "Chug—Chug—Chug" of a diesel engine. On deck with mug in hand I looked in the direction that the sound was coming from, slowly the bow of a small tug came into view pushing its way through the heavy fog. I turned and gazed around at my surroundings, on my portside was the steep forested shore of the small Bay, to starboard lay a rock bound cragged island, in the fog they had appeared as if connected. The way that I came so came the small tug, following it, as if it too was having a hard time pushing the fog aside, was a log boom.

It would have been utterly impossible for me to have planned, inconceivable of me to have chosen for my last night at sea, a more perfect spot. In essence it was the absolute opposite, the antithesis of the Greybeard Sea, and yet, somehow it was all part of the total package. There was a balance that was being made that was beyond my imaginings. A statement beyond my intelligence to grasp. A meaning that held such beauty that it exceeded my comprehension. I had left Papau New Guinea and had willingly stepped into a voyage of personal discovery that had calmly waited for me. I had reached that particular moment in life when destiny had decided that it was my time. I was a plum ripe for the picking and a greater hand than mine had plucked. Aye, I was aged and only too willing for this personal trial that had unconsciously lurked in the depths of my mind, and whether I was capable of this journey or not, mattered little. It was time. It had naught at all to do whether

I was qualified enough that I could handle it. It was far more that I was mature enough to reap from my sufferings a deeper sense of the intangible, those things that one can sense, but are quite unable to put their finger on, for I could not believe had I been so much younger that I would have been so receptive to all those ideas and impressions that had flowed through me. There was also the joyfulness that I now felt, it was far more than being so close to home, for, I was home. I had reached my land, but there was also something else, and that was, if hell had been sent to me out there on the Greybeard Sea, heaven had been sent to me here, in this little Bay.

As the tug neared Broom I could see that the crew in the wheel house were observing me quite intently, no doubt wondering what this bedraggled vessel was doing hanging around in this foggy Bay. I raised my hand and waved, they all waved in return, then one left the comfort of the wheel house and climbed atop the cabin, no doubt to get a better look then gave another wave. As they passed me I turned the engine key and that little Sabb once more rattled, and as the tug and its log boom pulled ahead, I followed them out of my nights refuge. Though fate had brought me safely into the sanctuary of the Bay, it seemed only realistic that the tail of the log boom would show me the way out. The log boom and I soon parted company as Broom and I headed home.

The concept of the bays, one being the beginning and the other the end of a journey, I found interesting, but perhaps that's only true of this particular journey of my life. I have said that I would happily have left this mortal world that night, but it wasn't quite true. For it was in the morning as the fog lifted, when trees appeared like ghosts out of that dewy mist and the rocks streamed with tears, and the birds and ducks and otters, it was then, when my eyes feasted on that happy scene it was really then I could have happily left this world. I doubt that in my future years that I, and any spirit that I may ever possess could be so prime and willing. I have this impression that I should end it just like that, for was not this part of my voyage,—like it had all started; a passage into one Bay and the time spent there and a demanding and soul searching passage into another. Yet it was much more than that, for it had all began long before. Had it not started when I had watched the oil streaken River Clyde take all before it out to the cleansing sea, and as I watched with my head filled with nothing, then thought, could it take me, and if it did, would I come back with this empty head of mine—filled. Was that when it all really started—when I was seventeen years old?

I passed Ogden Point and entered Victoria Harbour. On my way to the Customs clearance wharf I passed the end of the Public wharf. That was when I heard a voice crying, "Ron—Ron." I looked over, and there was Marlene, waving, her bicycle lying at her feet. I gazed at her in shock, then my eyes flew to my tattered log book. I raised my hand and pointed to the frost wire fenced Customs wharf, she grasped my meaning and started running down the finger and round to the wharf. I motored towards the wharf my head thinking of another poem that I had written on that incredible morn. Home. By the time we were alongside [again forgive me I have a hard time not thinking of Broom and I as not we] she was standing there gazing at me with her fingers enmeshed in the locked frost wire gate. I waved to her and threw my bow and stern mooring lines on to the jetty. I neither leapt nor did I jump, nor could I possibly have, for when I put my foot out to step on to the wharf, somehow it wasn't there. I came off Broom like a drunken half starved creature, part man, part something dragged out of the sea. My knees bent, my knuckles scraping the wooden timbers, staggering, totally unable to get my balance, my hand unconsciously seeking a handhold and finding none. I weaved a half stumbling, half crawling path to the bow line and cleated it, then took my inept staggering way aft to the stern line.

The stern of Broom now being caught in the incoming tide was wandering away from the wharf. I barely managed to haul her in. I cleated the line, Broom now secure my attention was on Marlene. I stumbled over to the wire fence, the look on her face changed as she got a better look at me then quickly she reached into her pocket and took out her glasses and put them on. Then on her face appeared a look of shock and astonishment, her eyes opened wide flooded with tears. I put my fingers through the same openings in the wire mesh and held her hands. We both, stood ... crying.

My knees bent, my knuckles scraping the wooden timbers, staggering, my hand unconsciously seeking a handhold and finding none. I weaved a half stumbling, half crawling path to the bow line and cleated it, then took my inept staggering way aft to the stern line.

Epilogue

Aye, how wonderful it was to clear customs so easily, could it have been, my odour? of course not, then Marlene came aboard and we untied my lines from the customs dock and moved to the public wharf where helping hands appeared from everywhere, some being those that were there when I had left. In her early mornings Marlene had been in the habit of going down to Fleming Beach and with binoculars grasped in her hand, searched the waters around Race Rocks hoping to sight Brooms arrival. That morning she had been roused by the lonesome call of the foghorn and hadn't bothered. Later she received a phone call from her brother and his wife, who from their high rise balcony over looking the harbour had seen the rust streaken and bedraggled Broom entering. It was the eye that her brother recognized, the eye that I had painted on the bow of Broom to keep evil spirits away, it had worked extremely well I thought, except for Martinique Rum.

My ability to walk on an unmoving surface was slowly returning, yet still I felt sure that at any moment I would have to reach out and grab something. Undoubtedly pleased, though awkward, I climbed into our car and Marlene drove me home. We entered our house that sat so stable, comfortable and secure, and I with my head at last free from the total responsibility for myself and Broom. Without the semblance of a thought in my moss green mind I stood, not quite believing that I was home, meanwhile, I could hear sounds as Marlene bustled and filled the bathtub with hot soapy water.

*My mind at last responded and I saw thread by thread break
free from the cloth of the sail and watched them, as they did
that same rigid fluttering act and like a movie filmed in slow
motion the clew on my sail of many colours slowly began to
come apart, piece by piece. I left the wheel and was halfway up
the deck when it literally exploded and pieces of the sail flew off
and joined the white scurrying foam. And I was quite incapable
of removing it.*

With that wonderful odour of coffee brewing filling the air she led me into the bathroom and took my clothes off. I can assure you that sex was the last thing on my mind. My skin salivated as my body slowly slid under the warm enfolding, all encompassing sleep making slumber drooling tender loving warmth of the bath. She threw my clothes down the basement stairs to the laundry room, then quickly returned, or so I may have thought for my mind and body was in no hurry, whatsoever. She appeared by my side, in one hand she held a mug of creamy coffee which she placed on the port side of the bathtub, while on her other hand was a glass of rum, need I say without ice cubes, that she placed on the starboard side, then she bustled about doing something else. I can assure you I haven't the slightest idea what she was up to, it had been a while since I had last bustled.

She returned and scrubbed me down with? A piece of sandstone from Glasgow Cathedral? Or some such object what did I care, then after thoroughly scrubbing me down, though I have never been sure whether that stone was layered with Ajax or was it oven cleaner, she suggested that I should have a shower. I was not at all in the mood to argue, she managed to remove my mug of coffee and the glass of rum from my hands then closed the shower doors and turned the hot soothing spray of the shower on. I struggled to my feet and indulged myself in what was a wonderful warm fresh summer's rain, but it was only when she reached in and turned the shower off and slid open the shower door and I saw myself in the full length mirror that faced the bathtub, that I was shocked. And it wasn't my fathers blue veined brow or my wild scraggly hair and beard that startled me, it was what had happened to what was once my muscular body. Or so I had thought, for what I was now seeing was a body of an inmate of Belsen, my ribs brandished themselves as if they were proud to be seen as bones, my sunken gut appeared as if enamoured by my spine, then as I turned I realized why it was that when I had tried to sleep on my back it had bothered me so. My gluteus maximus were gone, those once muscular buttocks who had served me well all those years had disappeared, and the bottom of my fat free bony spine now without its well curved and comforting presence had suffered the painful consequences. My once fine shapely thighs had disappeared, but my predominant Scottish knobby knees had never suffered they shone as proudly as my ribs, calves or whatever I may have had were gone, but my feet which I had never given much thought to, for, if they don't bother me, I won't bother them, were big and fat. Is that why I had never felt them cold? I avoided looking at my face, you do understand why. I flexed my biceps and saw a boiled egg, though balanced well atop a scrawny white branch. I stepped on to the bathroom scales and found that I had lost over fifty pounds, my mind easily triggered by that wondered, why were my feet so fat?

That night I slept on a warm dry bed in a nonmoving and silent room, covered in dry warm blankets and wearing socks, two pairs of jogging pants, tee shirt and sweater, and a dry fresh woolen hat pulled down around my ears. And just before I fell asleep I remembered the poem that I had written that incredible Christmas morning and where the idea had came from, Hemingway's, the 'Snows of Kilimanjaro.'

Home.

Should I die tomorrow, alone out here at sea,
My mind not filled with sorrow, of the things that couldn't be.
I have a dream embedded, a dream that fills my head,
A dream that I will rejoice in, even though I may be dead.

I'm entering Victoria Harbour, on the early morning tide,
For there in Victoria Harbour, my love and I reside.
The battle now is over, my harbour now is won,
My spirit is jubilant in the early mornings sun.

My vessel enters proudly, though her hull is streaked red,
And her ragged sails flutter gallantly, as we pass yachts in their bed.
I hear a voice a calling "Ron—Ron," a calling out to me,
And there a figure waving, from a high rise balcony.

I motor gently to the wharf, there to moor alongside,
And there she stands a crying, with her arms stretched open wide.
I hold her warmly to my breast, her tears enmeshed in mine
And --

Yes, I did write that, on that remarkable Christmas morning and it's also true that I was dry and comfortable on that very special day, January 12, yet, still I wondered, would I ever really feel warm again. The following morning Marlene drove me to the Esquimalt clinic where Doctor Hepburn checked me out, he told me my blood pressure at 120/80 was first-rate, well, that was a bit of a shock for I have always had high blood pressure, and although it was excellent, he was not about to recommend my particular method of lowering my blood pressure to his other patients. He said my fat feet were caused by edema, my bodily fluids collecting at the lowest extremity of my body. He was very pleasant with me and so I didn't care to mention to him how cold his office was.

I had been moored in Victoria for two days before I went down and removed my tattered jib that hung so despairingly from my bowsprit and my sad and bedraggled sail covers, that was when I recognized how fortunate I had been. The sail cover on my port side though no longer of any use, still resembled what it once was. The sail cover on the starboard side was far the ruined of the two, and when I took it off I realized why. The trunk cabin though built of one eighth steel and at its widest point fourteen inches had been bent in almost three quarters of an inch by the force of those seas. Now I knew why the portlights leaked. My ravaged jib and my sail covers I placed in the dumpster. Afterwards, when I realized what I had done it didn't sit well with me, saying not a word about that sail as I deposited it with the garbage. It gave what it could and for no fault of its own, gone, did it not also deserve credit, or was it I, who found everything so personal and so filled with meaning out there on that raging sea, and now on land, quickly becoming smug and secure how could I so easily have forgotten. Yes, that troubled me.

In early April I cleared a small piece of land, on the following day before the morning sun had risen I kneeled in front of that area. My eyes were on Mount Baker. I lowered them and looked down at my hands, they faced me with closed palms upwards. I opened them and saw that each held a handful of dried peas. I took my gaze back to the sun and waited. When the lower arc of the sun kissed the horizon. I planted the peas.